THE ILLUSTRATED EDITION
LIFE AND TIMES OF
FREDERICK DOUGLASS

THE ILLUSTRATED EDITION
LIFE AND TIMES OF
FREDERICK DOUGLASS

Frederick Douglass

INTRODUCTION BY HENRY LOUIS GATES JR.

ZENITH
PRESS

CONTENTS

An abridged edition of *Life and Times of Frederick Douglass, Written by Himself*, published in 1892 by De Wolfe & Fiske Co., Boston.

FIRST PART

SECOND PART

THIRD PART

INTRODUCTION
THE LITERARY BRILLIANCE OF FREDERICK DOUGLASS

FROM *CLASSIC SLAVE NARRATIVES* BY HENRY LOUIS GATES JR.

Alone among all literary traditions, the canon of African American literature rests on the framework built, by fits and starts, by first-person narratives of persons who were once legally defined as property—

The most famous of them all is Frederick Douglass's 1845 *Narrative*. Classic and elegant in its simplicity and its gripping readability, Douglass's compelling lucidity belies his narrative's literary complexity, a complexity that masks or disguises itself precisely because Douglass was a master rhetorician, expert in both spoken and written English. Douglass tells such a good tale that his text opens itself to all classes of readers, from those who love a good adventure story to those who wish to have rendered for them in startling detail the facts of human bondage—what it meant to discover that one was a slave and what one proceeded to do about it while someone else simultaneously was doing all manner of horrendous things to keep that slave from imagining himself or herself otherwise. Douglass's rhetorical power convinces us that he is "the" black slave, that he embodies the structures and thoughts and feelings of all black slaves, that he is the resplendent, articulate part that stands for the whole, for the collective slave community. His superb command of several rhetorical figures—metaphor, irony, synecdoche, apostrophe, and especially chiasmus—enables him to chart with fine precision in only a few pages not only "how a man was made a slave," but also "how a slave was made a man." And that chiasmus most succinctly summarizes the political intention of the genre of the slave narratives.

Douglass's narrative demonstrates not only how the deprivation of the hallmarks of identity can affect the slave but also how the slaveowner's world negates and even perverts its own values.

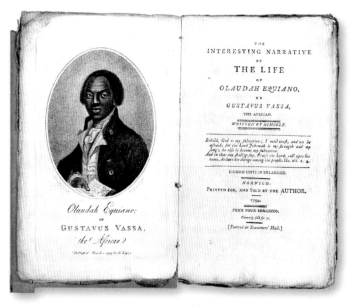

The frontispiece and title page from The Interesting Narrative of the Life of Olaudah Equiano, *published in 1794.*

Deprivation of a birth date, a name, a family structure, and of legal rights makes of the deprived a brute, a subhuman, says Douglass, until he comes to a consciousness of these relations: through that consciousness, he comes to see that it is the human depriver who is inhumane, the actual barbarian within the plantation system. With painstaking verisimilitude, Douglass reproduces a system of signs that we have come to call plantation culture, an ordering of the world based on a profoundly relational type of thinking. In this world, a strict barrier of difference forms the basis of a class rather than, as

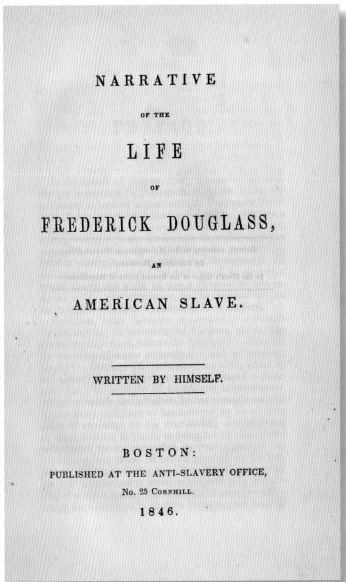

The frontispiece and title page from an original edition of Narrative of
the Life of Frederick Douglass, an American Slave.

in other classification schemes, an ordering based on resemblances or the identity of two or more elements. Douglass's narrative strategy seems to be this: he brings together two terms in special relationships suggested by some quality that they share; then, by opposing two seemingly unrelated elements, such as the sheep, cattle, or horses on the plantation and the specimen of life known as a slave, Douglass's language is made to signify the presence and absence of some quality. In this case, humanity itself. Douglass uses this device to explicate the slave's understanding of himself and of his relation to the world. Not only does his *Narrative* depict two diametrically opposed notions of genesis, origins, and meaning, but its structure actually turns on an opposition between nature and culture as well.

What great slave narrative informed Douglass's? Although it is obvious that Douglass read widely, and avidly devoured those narratives published by other ex-slaves between 1831 and 1845, was he revising another classic slave narrative, one whose form and themes he could appropriate and "rewrite" in that profound art of grounding that creates a literary tradition? I am not the only scholar who believes that Douglass was, and that the 1789 slave narrative of Olaudah Equiano was his "silent second text."

This photograph shows an enslaved African American family (or perhaps families) in front of a cabin on a plantation in Hanover County, Virginia.

FIRST PART

CHAPTER I

AUTHOR'S BIRTH

AUTHOR'S PLACE OF BIRTH—DESCRIPTION OF COUNTRY—ITS INHABITANTS—GENEALOGICAL TREES—METHOD OF COUNTING TIME IN SLAVE DISTRICTS—DATE OF AUTHOR'S BIRTH—NAMES OF GRANDPARENTS—THEIR CABIN—HOME WITH THEM—SLAVE PRACTICE OF SEPARATING MOTHERS FROM THEIR CHILDREN—AUTHOR'S RECOLLECTIONS OF HIS MOTHER—WHO WAS HIS FATHER?

In Talbot County, Eastern Shore, State of Maryland, near Easton, the county town, there is a small district of country, thinly populated, and remarkable for nothing that I know of more than for the worn-out, sandy, desert-like appearance of its soil, the general dilapidation of its farms and fences, the indigent and spiritless character of its inhabitants, and the prevalence of ague and fever. It was in this dull, flat, and unthrifty district or neighborhood, bordered by the Choptank river, surrounded by a white population of the lowest order, indolent and drunken to a proverb, and among slaves who, in point of ignorance and indolence, were fully in accord with their surroundings, that I, without any fault of my own, was born, and spent the first years of my childhood.

The reader must not expect me to say much of my family. Genealogical trees did not flourish among slaves. I never met with a slave in that part of the country who could tell me with any certainty how old he was. Few at that time knew anything of the months of the year or of the days of the month. They measured the ages of their children by spring-time, winter-time, harvest-time, planting-time,

and the like. Masters allowed no questions concerning their ages to be put to them by slaves. From certain events, however, the dates of which I have since learned, I suppose myself to have been born in February, 1817.

My first experience of life, as I now remember it, and I remember it but hazily, began in the family of my grandmother and grandfather, Betsey and Isaac Bailey. They were considered old settlers in the neighborhood, and from certain circumstances I infer that my grandmother, especially, was held in high esteem. She was a good nurse, and a capital hand at making nets used for catching shad and herring. In planting-time Grandmother Betsey was sent for in all directions, simply to place the seedling potatoes in the hills or drills; for superstition had it that her touch was needed to make them grow.

Whether because she was too old for field service, or because she had so faithfully discharged the duties of her station in early life, I know not, but she enjoyed the high privilege of living in a cabin separate from the quarters, having imposed upon her only the charge of the young children and the burden of her own support. The practice of separating mothers from their

A rare photo showing enslaved children (taken in Tennessee, circa 1860).

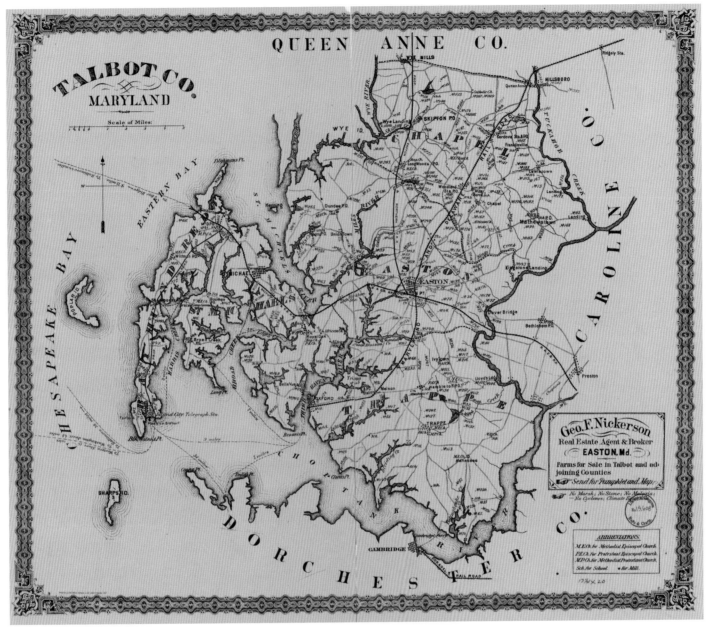

A circa 1875 map of Talbot County, Maryland.

children and hiring them out at distances too great to admit of their meeting, save at long intervals, was a marked feature of the cruelty and barbarity of the slave system; but it was in harmony with the grand aim of that system, which always and everywhere sought to reduce man to a level with the brute.

My grandmother's five daughters were hired out in this way, and my only recollections of my own mother are of a few hasty visits made in the night on foot, after the daily tasks were over. These little glimpses of my mother, obtained under such circumstances and against such odds, meager as they were, are ineffaceably stamped upon my memory. She was tall and finely proportioned, of dark, glossy complexion, with regular features, and amongst the slaves was remarkably sedate and dignified. There is, in "Prichard's Natural History of Man," the head of a figure, the features of which so resemble my mother that I often recur to it with something of the feelings which I suppose others experience when looking upon the likenesses of their own dear departed ones.

Of my father I know nothing. Slavery had no recognition of fathers, as none of families. That the mother was a slave was enough for its deadly purpose. By its law the child followed the condition of its mother. The father might be a freeman and the child a slave. The father might be a white man and the child ranked with the blackest slaves. Father he might be, and not be husband, and could sell his own child without incurring reproach, if in its veins coursed one drop of African blood.

CHAPTER II

REMOVAL FROM GRANDMOTHER'S

AUTHOR'S EARLY HOME—ITS CHARMS—AUTHOR'S IGNORANCE OF "OLD MASTER"—HIS GRADUAL PERCEPTION OF THE TRUTH CONCERNING HIM—HIS RELATIONS TO COL. EDWARD LLOYD—AUTHOR'S REMOVAL TO "OLD MASTER'S" HOME—HIS JOURNEY THENCE—HIS SEPARATION FROM HIS GRANDMOTHER—HIS GRIEF.

Living thus with my grandmother, whose kindness and love stood in place of my mother's, it was some time before I knew myself to be a slave. I knew many other things before I knew that. Her little cabin had to me the attractions of a palace. Its fence-railed floor—which was equally floor and bedstead—up stairs, and its clay floor down stairs, its dirt and straw chimney, and windowless sides, and that most curious piece of workmanship, the ladder stairway, and the hole so strangely dug in front of the fire-place, beneath which grandmamma placed her sweet potatoes, to keep them from frost in winter, were full of interest to my childish observation. Nor were these all the attractions of the place. At a little distance stood Mr. Lee's mill, where the people came in large numbers to get their corn ground. The mill-pond, too, had its charms; and with my pin-hook and thread-line, I could get amusing nibbles if I could catch no fish.

It was not long, however, before I began to learn the sad fact that this house of my childhood belonged not to my dear old grandmother, but to some one I had never seen, and who lived a great distance off. I learned, too, the sadder fact, that not only the home and lot, but that grandmother herself and all the little children around her belonged to a mysterious personage, called by grandmother, with every mark of reverence, "Old Master."

I learned that this old master, whose name seemed ever to be mentioned with fear and shuddering, only allowed the little children to live with grandmother for a limited time, and that as soon as they were big enough they were promptly taken away to live with the said old master. These were distressing revelations, indeed. This mysterious old master was really a man of some consequence. He owned several farms in Tuckahoe, was the chief clerk and butler on the home plantation of Colonel Lloyd, had overseers as well as slaves on his own farms, and gave directions to the overseers on the farms owned by Colonel Lloyd. Captain Aaron Anthony, for such is the name and title of my old master, lived on Colonel Lloyd's plantation, which was situated on the Wye river, and which was one of the largest, most fertile, and best appointed in the State.

Above: The Way They Live, *painted in 1879 by Thomas Anshutz (1851–1912).*
Opposite: A lone black woman stands in front of a "slave pen" in Alexandria, Virginia, in the 1860s.

This 1884 lithograph depicts an idealized cotton plantation on the Mississippi River.

DOUGLASS'S EARLY CHILDHOOD AND HIS GRANDMAMMA BETSY

From *Frederick Douglass* by William S. McFeely

Throughout his life, Frederick Douglass was obsessed with an eagerness to know about his origins—to know who he was. Dickson Preston, a meticulous and sympathetic historian, has brought together an astonishingly rich cluster of facts confirming Douglass's account of his early life, firmly establishing the family lineage, and determining from an inventory of his master's slaves the time of Frederick's birth—February 1818 (a year later than the date that Douglass himself calculated). But Preston's diligent scholarship has not revealed the fact Douglass most wanted to know—who his father was.

"My father was a white man. He was admitted to be such by all I ever heard speak of my parentage," he wrote in *Narrative of the Life of Frederick Douglass*. Doubtless he remembered such talk from Betsy's cabin, as people accounted for his difference in color from his brothers and sisters. This talk would have led to his first consciousness of what is termed racial difference; he would have looked at his body and learned that he was "yellow"—had a muted, dull complexion lighter than that of his "quite dark" grandparents and, he would observe later, that of his still "darker" mother. He also heard talk of a legendary and perfectly plausible Indian ancestor; something in the bone structure and the set of the eyes suggested this, not only in Frederick but in his mother and grandmother. He was probably still too young, in Betsy's cabin, to articulate any queries about his paternity although it is more than likely that he had already heard it "whispered," even if he had not understood what he heard, "that my master was my father."

Douglass wrote later of his boyhood in Betsy's cabin as "spirited, joyous, uproarious, and happy," but drew a picture of the surrounding area that does not just reflect what he saw as a child. His description of the "worn-out, sandy, desert-like appearance of its soil," the "general dilapidation of its farms," and the "ague and fever" that rose from the Tuckahoe is more a metaphor for the barrenness of slavery than the recollection of a six-year-old. It does, however, return attention from the idyllic to the realities of carving out a living in this remote country. As a free Black woodcutter in a rural area of a slave state, Isaac Bailey was on the margin of the economy; he and

Five generations of an enslaved family are gathered in this photograph taken at a plantation in Beaufort, South Carolina.

Betsy and the family in their charge probably lived in extreme poverty. His security was even more precarious than that of his kin who were slaves; he had no master to fall back on when he was injured, as a worker with saws and axes was apt to be, fell ill, or simply got old. Betsy, living for so long as the wife of a free man, may have been in similar danger. There are conflicting stories about whether her master felt any obligation to care for her when she was old and widowed. She did stay on in her cabin.

If the small house was indeed in the woods, as Douglass remembered it, the problem of providing food was immediate; you cannot grow vegetables under trees. The Baileys were allowed the use of some arable land—perhaps they had cleared it themselves—but even so, their future as an independent black family was not assured. Contrary to myth, country people do not have some intuitive knowledge of how to make the earth bloom; even with a good plot of ground, families may fail to produce a crop adequate for survival.

In this realm Betsy became legendary. Intelligent and physically powerful, she had made herself an expert in fishing and farming. The nets she wove were in "great demand" in the nearby towns of Hillsboro and Denton, and she also put them to good use herself. Douglass remembered her being "in the water half the day" gathering in the abundant shad and herring. When spring came, she not only planted her own sweet potatoes but was called on to help others in the neighborhood get theirs into the ground properly. At harvest time, her fork went into the ground so deftly that none of the crop was pierced and lost, and she had the foresight to put aside sound seed potatoes for planting the next season. As Douglass noted, her "good luck" was, in fact, her "exceeding care" in every step in the achievement of sufficient and nutritious food.

Douglass's stress on the impressive competence of his grandmother in what might have been thought of as masculine functions, his ascription both to her and to his mother of a bearing that would have fit men of dignity and accomplishment, is significant. There is no similar description of his grandfather or of any other man he knew while a slave. For the rest of his life Douglass looked to women as confidants, companions, and sources of strength. They rather than men could be comprehended and counted on to be able.

They could also be the source of immense anguish. If Betsy was allowed extraordinary liberty to run her own life and to make her own living, she paid a great price for this freedom. She apparently was required to care for all of the infants in the Bailey family, so that their mothers—her daughters—could work. They labored on the Tuckahoe farms in which her master, Aaron Anthony, had invested, or were hired out by him to work in the fields of others.

Anthony was an absentee master; he lived a dozen miles away at Wye House, the estate just in from the Chesapeake Bay that he managed for the Lloyd family. What provision, if any, he made for the care of the children he owned is unknown; perhaps Betsy bought her independence by agreeing to rear her grandchildren without any assistance, such as rations of corn. Their care must have been taxing, and before they were old enough to help her with a hoe or the nets, they were summoned to Wye House by Anthony. There they lived in "Captain Anthony's" house or in quarters adjacent to it. Frederick's older brother and sisters, Perry, Sarah, and Eliza, and his cousin Tom had already made this move.

On a summer day in August 1824, when Frederick was six, he and his grandmother left the cabin, walked up to the crossroads, and turned southwest. The walk was long, much longer he soon learned than the one in the other direction, to Hillsboro, probably the only town he had been to. For much of the trip his powerful grandmother must have had to carry the tall, heavy child. It may well be a mark of the austerity

The chimneys of countless slave quarters at Cumberland Island, Georgia.

of Anthony's Tuckahoe farms, that there was no horse the resourceful Betsy could commandeer for the day. Turning at one crossroads town, they walked between great fields, blanketed in heat, to reach another, and soaked in perspiration kept resolutely on through the Lloyds' "Long Woods." Finally, having walked twelve miles, they came to Wye House. A generous lawn's-width short of the long, straight drive leading under great trees to the main house was a parallel road that led to the slave quarters. They took it; through the trees between the narrow roads, Frederick could catch sight of the great house, and as the two of them came past, they reached their master's small, neat cottage and the quarters where their relatives lived. Looking off the other way across Long Green, they saw the broad stretch of the Wye River.

Suddenly, the long, hot trek was over. Curious children came out to look over the newcomer, and followed him and their grandmother into the kitchen, where the two got desperately needed drinks of water. Cautiously, Frederick agreed to go back into the yard with them, but he did not join in as they ran "laughing and yelling around me." Their exuberance would have been more intimidating if he had not known that his grandmother was back in the house. But soon she was not. Taking what she saw as the least tormenting way to accomplish the parting she was resigned to, Betsy quietly left to walk the long miles back to Tuckahoe. When one of the children, with "roguish glee" shrieked at him, "Fed, Fed! grandmammy gone!" he fled back to the kitchen to find her.

But she was gone. He rushed out to the road; she was not in sight, and he could not run down its emptiness alone. He threw himself on the ground, and crying, pummeled the dry dust. When his older brother, Perry, tried to console him with a peach, he threw it away. He was carried in to bed and cried himself to sleep. And he never fully trusted anyone again.

A slave cabin, St. Mary's County, Maryland.

About this plantation and this old master I was most eager to know everything which could be known; and, unhappily for me, all the information I could get concerning him increased my dread of being separated from my grandmother and grandfather. But the time came when I must go, and my grandmother, knowing my fears, and in pity for them, kindly kept me ignorant of the dreaded moment up to the morning (a beautiful summer morning) when we were to start; and, indeed, during the whole journey, which, child as I was, I remember as well as if it were yesterday, she kept the unwelcome truth hidden from me. The distance from Tuckahoe to Colonel Lloyd's, where my old master lived, was full twelve miles, and the walk was quite a severe test of the endurance of my young legs. The journey would have proved too severe for me, but that my dear old grandmother (blessings on her memory) afforded occasional relief by "toteing" me on her shoulder.

As the day advanced the heat increased, and it was not until the afternoon that we reached the much-dreaded end of the journey. Here I found myself in the midst of a group of children of all sizes and of many colors— black, brown, copper-colored, and nearly white. I had not before seen so many children. Affectionately patting me on the head, [my grandmother] told me to be a good boy and go out to play with the children. They are "kin to you," she said, "go and play with them." She pointed out to me

my brother Perry, and my sisters, Sarah and Eliza. I had never seen them before, and though I had sometimes heard of them and felt a curious interest in them, I really did not understand what they were to me or I to them. Brothers and sisters we were by blood, but slavery had made us strangers. They were already initiated into the mysteries of old master's domicile, and they seemed to look upon me with a certain degree of compassion. Entreated by my dear grandmother, I went to the back part of the house to play with them and the other children. Play, however, I did not, but stood with my back against the wall witnessing the playing of the others. At last, while standing there, one of the children, who had been in the kitchen, ran up to me in a sort of roguish glee, exclaiming, "Fed, Fed, grandmamma gone!" I could not believe it. Yet, fearing the worst, I ran into the kitchen to see for myself, and lo! she was indeed gone, and was now far away, and "clean" out of sight. Almost heart-broken at the discovery, I fell upon the ground and wept a boy's bitter tears, refusing to be comforted. I had never been deceived before and something of resentment mingled with my grief at parting with my grandmother.

It was now late in the afternoon. The day had been an exciting and wearisome one, and I know not where, but I suppose I sobbed myself to sleep; and its balm was never more welcome to any wounded soul than to mine.

CHAPTER III

TROUBLES OF CHILDHOOD

Col. Lloyd's plantation—Aunt Katy—Her cruelty and ill-nature—Capt. Anthony's partiality to Aunt Katy—Allowance of food—Author's hunger—Unexpected rescue by his mother—The reproof of Aunt Katy—Sleep—A slave-mother's love—Author's inheritance—His mother's acquirements—Her death.

***

Once established on the home plantation of Col. Lloyd—I was with the children there, left to the tender mercies of Aunt Katy, a slave woman, who was to my master what he was to Col. Lloyd. Disposing of us in classes or sizes, he left to Aunt Katy all the minor details concerning our management. Ambitious of old master's favor, ill-tempered and cruel by nature, she found in her present position an ample field for the exercise of her ill-omened qualities. She had a strong hold upon old master, for she was a first-rate cook, and very industrious. She was therefore greatly favored by him—and as one mark of his favor she was the only mother who was permitted to retain her children around her, and even to these, her own children, she was often fiendish in her brutality. Want of food was my chief trouble during my first summer here. Captain Anthony, instead of allowing a given quantity of food to each slave, committed the allowance for all to Aunt Katy, to be divided by her, after cooking, amongst us. The allowance consisted of coarse corn-meal, not very abundant, and which, by passing through Aunt Katy's hands, became more slender still for some of us. I have often been so pinched with hunger as to dispute with old "Nep," the dog, for the crumbs which fell from the kitchen table. Many times have I followed, with eager step, the waiting-girl when she shook the table-cloth, to get the crumbs and small bones flung out for the dogs and cats. With this description of the domestic arrangements of my new home, I may here recount a circumstance which is deeply impressed on my memory, as affording a bright gleam of a slave-mother's love, and the earnestness of a mother's care. I had offended Aunt Katy. I do not remember in what way, for my offences were numerous in that quarter, greatly depending upon her moods as to their heinousness, and she had adopted her usual mode of punishing me: namely, making me go all day without food. Sundown came, but no bread; and in its stead came the threat from Aunt Katy, with a scowl well-suited to its terrible import,

A young, enslaved boy clothed in rags, circa 1863 (shown with digital color).

Left: An illustration appearing in the 1892 edition of Life and Times of Frederick Douglass.
Right: A portrait of Colonel Edward Lloyd, painted by Maryland artist Florence MacKubin (1857–1918).

that she would starve the life out of me. Brandishing her knife, she chopped off the heavy slices of bread for the other children, and put the loaf away. I went out behind the kitchen wall and cried like a fine fellow. When wearied with this, I returned to the kitchen, sat by the fire and brooded over my hard lot. I was too hungry to sleep. While I sat in the corner, I caught sight of an ear of Indian corn upon an upper shelf. I watched my chance and got it; and shelling off a few grains, I put it back again. These grains I quickly put into the hot ashes to roast. My corn was not long in roasting, and I eagerly pulled it from the ashes, and placed it upon a stool in a clever little pile. I began to help myself, when who but my own dear mother should come in. The scene which followed is beyond my power to describe. The friendless and hungry boy found himself in the strong, protecting arms of his mother. I have before spoken of my mother's dignified and impressive manner. I shall never forget the indescribable expression of her countenance when I told her that Aunt Katy had said she would starve the

life out of me. There was deep and tender pity in her glance at me, and, at the same moment, a fiery indignation at Aunt Katy, and while she took the corn from me, and gave in its stead a large ginger-cake, she read Aunt Katy a lecture which was never forgotten.

My mother had walked twelve miles to see me, and had the same distance to travel over again before the morning sunrise. I do not remember ever seeing her again. Her death soon ended the little communication that had existed between us, and with it, I believe, a life full of weariness and heartfelt sorrow. I have since learned that she was the only one of all the colored people of Tuckahoe who could read. How she acquired this knowledge I know not. I can therefore fondly and proudly ascribe to her an earnest love of knowledge. In view of this fact, I am happy to attribute any love of letters I may have, not to my presumed Anglo-Saxon paternity, but to the native genius of my sable, unprotected, and uncultivated mother—a woman who belonged to a race whose mental endowments are still disparaged and despised.

CHAPTER IV

A GENERAL SURVEY OF THE SLAVE PLANTATION

Home plantation of Colonel Lloyd—Its isolation—Its industries—The slave rule—Power of overseers—Author finds some enjoyment—Natural scenery—Sloop *Sally Lloyd*—Windmill—Slave quarter—"Old Master's" house—Stables, store houses, etc., etc.—The great house—Its surroundings—Lloyd—Burial-place—Superstition of slaves—Colonel Lloyd's wealth—Negro politeness—Doctor Copper—Captain Anthony—His family—Master Daniel Lloyd—His brothers—Social etiquette.

I t was generally supposed that slavery in the State of Maryland existed in its mildest form, and that it was totally divested of those harsh and terrible peculiarities which characterized the slave system in the Southern and South-Western States of the American Union. The children and grandchildren of Col. Lloyd were taught in the house by a private tutor (a Mr. Page from Greenfield, Massachusetts, a tall, gaunt sapling of a man, remarkably dignified, thoughtful, and reticent, and who did not speak a dozen words to a slave in a whole year). The overseer's children went off somewhere in the State to school, and therefore could bring no foreign or dangerous influence from abroad to embarrass the natural operation of the slave system of the place. Here, not even the commonest mechanics, from whom there might have been an occasional outburst of honest and telling indignation at cruelty and wrong on other plantations, were white men. Its whole public was made up of and divided into three classes, slaveholders, slaves, and overseers. Its blacksmiths, wheelwrights, shoemakers, weavers, and coopers were slaves. Whether with a view of guarding against the escape of its secrets, I know not, but it is a fact, that every leaf and grain of the products of this plantation and those of the neighboring farms belonging to Col. Lloyd were transported to Baltimore in his own vessels, every man and boy on board of which, except the captain, were owned by him as his property. In return, everything brought to the plantation came through the same channel. To make this isolation more apparent, it may be stated that the estates adjoining Col. Lloyd's were owned and occupied by friends of his, who were as deeply interested as himself in maintaining the slave system in all its rigor. These were the Tilgmans, the Goldboroughs, the Lockermans, the Pacas, the Skinners, Gibsons, and others of lesser affluence and standing.

George Washington's plantation, Mount Vernon, in Virginia. The Founding Father practiced slave ownership throughout his life, but did posthumously free the people he enslaved.

The conservatory of the Wye house.

Though civilization was, in many respects, shut out, nature could not be.

There were, of course, no conflicting rights of property, for all the people were the property of one man, and they could themselves own no property. Religion and politics were largely excluded. One class of the population was too high to be reached by the common preacher, and the other class was too low in condition and ignorance to be much cared for by religious teachers, and yet some religious ideas did enter this dark corner.

This, however, is not the only view which the place presented. Though civilization was, in many respects, shut out, nature could not be. Though separated from the rest of the world, though public opinion, as I have said, could seldom penetrate its dark domain, though the whole place was stamped with its own peculiar iron-like individuality, and though crimes, high-handed and atrocious, could be committed there with strange and shocking impunity, it was, to outward seeming, a most strikingly interesting place, full of life, activity, and spirit, and presented a very favorable contrast to the indolent monotony and languor of Tuckahoe. Here, for the first time, I saw a large windmill, with its wide-sweeping white wings, a commanding object to a child's eye. This was situated on what was called Long Point—a tract of land dividing Miles river from the Wye. In the river, or what was called the "Swash," at a short distance from the shore, quietly lying at anchor, with her small row boat dancing at her stern, was a large sloop, the *Sally Lloyd*, called by that name in honor of the favorite daughter of the Colonel. These two objects, the sloop and mill, awakened as I remember, thoughts, ideas, and wondering. There was the little red house up the road, occupied by Mr. Sevier, the overseer. A little nearer to my old master's stood a long, low, rough building literally alive with slaves of all ages, sexes, conditions, sizes, and colors. This was called the long quarter. Besides these, there were numerous other slave houses and huts scattered around in the neighborhood, every nook and corner of which were completely occupied.

Old master's house, a long brick building, plain but substantial, was centrally located, and was an independent establishment. Besides these houses there were barns, stables, store-houses, tobacco-houses, blacksmith shops, wheelwright shops, cooper shops; but above all there stood the grandest building my young eyes had ever beheld, called by every one on the plantation the great house. This was occupied by Col. Lloyd and his family. It was surrounded by numerous and variously-shaped out-buildings. The great house itself was a large white wooden building with wings on three sides of it. In front, extending the entire length of

The back of the Wye house.

the building and supported by a long range of columns, was a broad portico, which gave to the Colonel's home an air of great dignity and grandeur.

The carriage entrance to the house was by a large gate, more than a quarter of a mile distant. The intermediate space was a beautiful lawn, very neatly kept and tended. Outside this select enclosure were parks, as about the residences of the English nobility, where rabbits, deer, and other wild game might be seen peering and playing about, with "none to molest them or make them afraid." The tops of the stately poplars were often covered with red-winged blackbirds, making all nature vocal with the joyous life and beauty of their wild, warbling notes. Not far from the great house were the stately mansions of the dead Lloyds—a place of somber aspect. Vast tombs, embowered beneath the weeping willow and the fir tree, told of the generations of the family, as well as of their wealth. Superstition was rife among the slaves about this family burying-ground. Strange sights had been seen there by some of the older slaves, and I was often compelled to hear stories of shrouded ghosts, riding on great black horses, and of balls of fire which had been seen to fly there at midnight, and of startling and dreadful sounds that had been repeatedly heard.

At Lloyd's, was transacted the business of twenty or thirty different farms, which, with the slaves upon them, numbering, in all, not less than a thousand, all belonged to Col. Lloyd. Each farm was under the management of an overseer, whose word was law. His slaves alone, numbering as I have said not less than a thousand, were an immense fortune, and though scarcely a month passed without the sale to the Georgia traders, of one or more lots, there was no apparent diminution in the number of his human stock.

The reader has already been informed of the handicrafts carried on here by the slaves. "Uncle" Toney was the blacksmith, "Uncle" Harry the cartwright, and "Uncle" Abel was the shoemaker, and these had assistants in their several departments. These mechanics were called "Uncles" by all the younger slaves, not because they really sustained that relationship to any, but according to plantation etiquette, as a mark of respect, due from the younger to the older slaves.

Among other slave notabilities, I found here one called by everybody, white and colored, "Uncle" Isaac Copper. When the "Uncle" was dropped, he was called Doctor Copper. He was both our Doctor of Medicine and our Doctor of Divinity. Where he took his degree I am unable to say, but he was too well established in his profession to permit question as to his native skill or attainments. One qualification he certainly had. He was a confirmed cripple, wholly unable to work, and was worth nothing for sale in the market. His remedial prescriptions embraced four articles. For diseases of the body, epsom salts and castor oil; for those of the soul, the "Lord's prayer," and a few stout hickory switches.

Everybody in the South seemed to want the privilege of whipping somebody else. Uncle Isaac, though a good old man, shared the common passion of his time and country. I was not long in my new home before I found that the dread I had conceived of Captain Anthony was in a measure groundless. Instead of leaping out from some hiding-place and destroying me, he hardly seemed to notice my presence. He was the chief agent of his employer. The overseers of all the farms composing the Lloyd estate were in some sort under him. The Colonel himself seldom addressed an overseer, or allowed himself to be addressed by one. To Captain Anthony, therefore, was committed the headship of all the farms. He carried the keys of all the store-houses, weighed and measured the allowances of each slave, at the end of each month; superintended the storing of all goods brought to the store-house; dealt out the raw material to the different handicraftsmen; shipped the grain, tobacco, and all other saleable produce of the numerous farms to Baltimore, and had a general oversight of all the workshops of the place.

The family of Captain Anthony consisted of two sons—Andrew and Richard, and his daughter Lucretia and her newly-married husband, Captain Thomas Auld. In the kitchen were Aunt Katy, Aunt Esther, and ten or a dozen children, most of them older than myself. Captain Anthony was not considered a rich slave-holder, though he was pretty well off in the world. He owned about thirty slaves and three farms in the Tuckahoe district. The more valuable part of his property was in slaves, of whom he sold one every year, which brought him in seven or eight hundred dollars, besides his yearly salary and other revenue from his lands. I have been often asked, during the earlier part of my free life at the North, how I happened to have so little of the slave accent in my speech. The mystery is in some measure explained by my association with Daniel Lloyd, the youngest son of Col. Edward Lloyd. While this lad could not associate with ignorance without sharing its shade, he could not give his black playmates his company without giving them his superior intelligence as well. Without knowing this, or caring about it at the time, I, for some cause or other, was attracted to him, and was much his companion.

I had little to do with the older brothers of Daniel—Edward and Murray. They were grown up and were fine-looking men. Edward was especially esteemed by the slave children, and by me among the rest—not that he ever said anything to us or for us which could be called particularly kind. It was enough for us that he never looked or acted scornfully toward us. The idea of rank and station was rigidly maintained on this estate. The family of Captain Anthony never visited the great house, and the Lloyds never came to our house. Equal non-intercourse was observed between Captain Anthony's family and the family of Mr. Sevier, the overseer.

The graveyard of the Lloyd family, located behind their stately mansion.

CHAPTER V

A SLAVEHOLDER'S CHARACTER

INCREASING ACQUAINTANCE WITH OLD MASTER—EVILS OF UNRESISTED PASSION—APPARENT TENDERNESS—A MAN OF TROUBLE—CUSTOM OF MUTTERING TO HIMSELF—BRUTAL OUTRAGE—A DRUNKEN OVERSEER— SLAVEHOLDER'S IMPATIENCE—WISDOM OF APPEAL—A BASE AND SELFISH ATTEMPT TO BREAK UP A COURTSHIP.

Although my old master, Captain Anthony, gave me, at the first of my coming to him from my grandmother's, very little attention, and although that little was of a remarkably mild and gentle description, a few months only were sufficient to convince me that mildness and gentleness were not the prevailing or governing traits of his character. These excellent qualities were displayed only occasionally. He could, when it suited him, appear to be literally insensible to the claims of humanity. He could not only be deaf to the appeals of the helpless against the aggressor, but he could himself commit outrages deep, dark, and nameless. Yet he was not by nature worse than other men. A man's character always takes its hue, more or less, from the form and color of things about him. The slaveholder, as well as the slave, was the victim of the slave system. Under the whole heavens there could be no relation more unfavorable to the development of honorable character than that sustained by the slaveholder to the slave. Reason is imprisoned here, and passions run wild. Could the reader have seen Captain Anthony gently leading me by the hand, as he sometimes

did, patting me on the head, speaking to me in soft, caressing tones, and calling me his little Indian boy, he would have deemed him a kind-hearted old man, and really almost fatherly to the slave boy. But the pleasant moods of a slaveholder are transient and fitful. Even to my child's eye he wore a troubled and at times a haggard aspect. He seldom walked alone without muttering to himself, and he occasionally stormed about as if defying an army of invisible foes. But when his gestures were most violent, ending with a threatening shake of the head and a sharp snap of his middle finger and thumb, I deemed it wise to keep at a safe distance from him.

One of the first circumstances that opened my eyes to the cruelties and wickedness of slavery and its hardening influences upon my old master, was his refusal to interpose his authority to protect and shield a young woman, a cousin of mine, who had been most cruelly abused and beaten by his overseer in Tuckahoe. This overseer, a Mr. Plummer, was, like most of his class, little less than a human brute. In one of his moments of drunken madness he committed the outrage which brought the young woman in question down to my old master's for

Above: This lithograph card shows an enslaved African American being whipped. Opposite: This page of an account book from the merchants Austin & Laurens of Charleston, South Carolina, shows accounts relating to the sale of enslaved people. The smallest columns indicate if the person was a man, woman, boy, or girl.

Acco.t of Sale [N.o 235] Charges & Net Proceed of 118. new Negroe Slaves. Received by the Schooner Polly Edward Lloyd Commander from the Windward Coast of Africa. on Acc.t of Mess.rs Will.m Davenport & C.o Owners of said Schooner Merchants in Liverpoole

Purchasers.	Men	Women	Boys	Girls	Terms of Payment	Amount
1758						
July. 4. Robert Raper	4			1	paid	1275
George Cooper			1	1	£131.12½ paid. Rem.r next January	450
Stephen Townsend			1		next January	200
Elizabeth Charles			1		ditto	220
Edward Weyman	1				paid	260
John Armstrong &						
Rich. Coldiron	3		2		next January	360
Samuel Perroneau	1		1		paid	510
Paul Douxsaint			1	1	next September	120
Samuel Screven			1	1	next January	380
Sam. Wainwright	2				next December	510
Elizabeth Dean				1	paid	160
Charles Lewis	6				next January	1500
Rob.t Rothmahler	6				ditto	1500
Estate of Royal Spry	4				paid	1000
Paul Stroyer			2		next January	350
Jonathan Wittir			1		paid	230
Benjamin Seabrook	1				next November	200
Richard Dowse	1	1			paid	500
John Wragfall	3				next January	750
Capt. Gibson			1		paid	250
John Jenkins	2				½ next September. ½ next January	500
Thomas Hargrave	1				in 20 3 months	200
Abraham Spitler			1		paid	195
Samuel Screven	3				next January	795
William Woodroff				1	next January	160
William Walker		2			next January	430
Daniel Horry			9	3	in 12 Months	2700
7. William Vanvelzen &						
Will.m Matthews	2				next January	450
Ancrum Lance & Loocock	1				next September	225
David Adams	3	2			next January	950
Will.m Bampfield &						
George Appleby	15	19			next January	5725
John Milner				2	very small & sick. next January	160
Men 56.	56	20	21	11		£23575
Women 20.						
Boys 21.						
Girls 11. 118 Slaves.					Carried forward	

They wielded the lash without any sense of responsibility.

protection. The poor girl, on her arrival at our house, presented a most pitiable appearance. Her neck and shoulders were covered with scars, newly made; and, not content with marring her neck and shoulders with the cowhide, the cowardly wretch had dealt her a blow on the head with a hickory club, which cut a horrible gash, and left her face literally covered with blood. In this condition the poor young woman came down to implore protection at the hands of my old master. I expected to see him boil over with rage at the revolting deed, and to hear him fill the air with curses upon the brutal Plummer; but I was disappointed. He sternly told her in an angry tone, "She deserved every bit of it, and if she did not go home instantly he would himself take the remaining skin from her neck and back."

I did not at that time understand the philosophy of this treatment of my cousin. I think I now understand it. This treatment was a part of the system, rather than a part of the man. To have encouraged appeals of this kind would have occasioned much loss of time and would have left the overseer powerless to enforce obedience. Nevertheless, when a slave had nerve enough to go straight to his master with a well-founded complaint against an overseer, though he might be repelled and have even that of which he at the time complained repeated, and though he might be beaten by his master, as well as by the overseer, for his temerity, the policy of complaining was, in the end, generally vindicated by the relaxed rigor of the overseer's treatment.

The overseer very naturally disliked to have the ear of the master disturbed by complaints; and, either for this reason or because of advice privately given him by his employer, he generally modified the rigor of his rule after complaints of this kind had been made against him. For some cause or other, the slaves, no matter how often they were repulsed by their masters, were ever disposed to regard them with less abhorrence than the overseer. And yet these masters would often go beyond their overseers in wanton cruelty. They wielded the lash without any sense of responsibility. They could cripple or kill without fear of consequences.

The circumstances which I am about to narrate and which gave rise to this fearful tempest of passion, were not singular, but very common in our slave-holding community.

The reader will have noticed that, among the names of slaves, that of Esther is mentioned. She was tall, light-colored, well formed, and made a fine appearance. Esther was courted by "Ned Roberts," the son of a favorite slave of Col. Lloyd, and who was as fine-looking

a young man as Esther was a woman. Some slave holders would have been glad to have promoted the marriage of two such persons, but for some reason Captain Anthony disapproved of their courtship. He strictly ordered her to quit the society of young Roberts, telling her that he would punish her severely if he ever found her again in his company. But it was impossible to keep this couple apart. Meet they would and meet they did.

Abhorred and circumvented as he was, Captain Anthony, having the power, was determined on revenge. I happened to see its shocking execution, and shall never forget the scene. It was early in the morning, when all was still, and before any of the family in the house or kitchen had risen. I was, in fact, awakened by the heart-rending shrieks and piteous cries of poor Esther. My sleeping-place was on the dirt floor of a little rough closet which opened into the kitchen, and through the cracks in its unplaned boards I could distinctly see and hear what was

This lithograph card shows a man being sold into slavery.

going on, without being seen. Esther's wrists were firmly tied, and the twisted rope was fastened to a strong iron staple in a heavy wooden beam above, near the fire-place. Here she stood on a bench, her arms tightly drawn above her head. Her back and shoulders were perfectly bare. Behind her stood old master, cowhide in hand, pursuing his barbarous work with all manner of harsh, coarse, and tantalizing epithets. Again and again he drew the hateful scourge through his hand, adjusting it with a view of dealing the most pain-giving blow his strength and skill could inflict. After laying on I dare not say how many stripes, old master untied his suffering victim. When let down she could scarcely stand. From my heart I pitied her, and child as I was, and new to such scenes, the shock was tremendous. I was terrified, hushed, stunned and bewildered. The scene here described was often repeated, for Edward and Esther continued to meet.

CHAPTER VI

A CHILD'S REASONING

THE AUTHOR'S EARLY REFLECTIONS ON SLAVERY—AUNT JENNIE AND UNCLE NOAH—PRESENTMENT OF ONE DAY BECOMING A FREEMAN—CONFLICT BETWEEN AN OVERSEER AND A SLAVE WOMAN—ADVANTAGE OF RESISTANCE—DEATH OF AN OVERSEER—COL. LLOYD'S PLANTATION HOME—MONTHLY DISTRIBUTION OF FOOD—SINGING OF SLAVES—AN EXPLANATION—THE SLAVES' FOOD AND CLOTHING—NAKED CHILDREN—LIFE IN THE QUARTER—SLEEPING PLACES, NOT BEDS—DEPRIVATION OF SLEEP—CARE OF NURSING BABIES—ASH CAKE—CONTRAST.

The incidents related in the foregoing chapter led me thus early to inquire into the origin and nature of slavery. Why am I a slave? Why are some people slaves and others masters? These were perplexing questions and very troublesome to my childhood. I was very early told by some one that "God up in the sky" had made all things, and had made black people to be slaves and white people to be masters. I was told too that God was good, and that He knew what was best for everybody. This was, however, less satisfactory than the first statement. It came point blank against all my notions of good-ness. Besides, I could not tell how anybody could know that God made black people to be slaves. Then I found, too, that there were puzzling exceptions to this theory of slavery, in the fact that all black people were not slaves, and all white people were not masters.

An incident occurred about this time that made a deep impression on my mind. My Aunt Jennie and one of the men slaves of Captain Anthony ran away. A great noise was made about it. Old master was furious. He said he would follow them and catch them and bring them back, but he never did, and somebody told me that Uncle Noah and Aunt Jennie had gone to the free states and were free.

The success of Aunt Jennie and Uncle Noah in getting away from slavery was, I think, the first fact that made me seriously think of escape for myself. I could not have been more than seven or eight years old at the time of this occurrence, but young as I was I was already, in spirit and purpose, a fugitive from slavery. Up to the time of the bru-tal treatment of my Aunt Esther, already narrated, and the shocking plight in which I had seen my cousin from Tuckahoe, my attention had not been especially directed to the grosser and more revolting features of slavery. But after the case of my Aunt Esther I saw others of the same disgusting and shocking nature. The one of these which agitated and distressed

A young, enslaved "Samboe" woman (a term once used to describe someone of predominantly black ancestry but with some Caucasian aspect) bound and flagellated, much like the woman Douglass saw whipped. This 1793 engraving is by William Blake (1757–1827) after John Gabriel Stedman (1744–1797).

An Overseer Doing His Duty, *by Benjamin Henry Latrobe (1764–1820).*

me most was the whipping of a woman, not belonging to my old master, but to Col. Lloyd. The charge against her was very common and very indefinite, namely, "impudence." This crime could be committed by a slave in a hundred different ways, and depended much upon the temper and caprice of the overseer as to whether it was committed at all. The offender was nearly white, to begin with; she was the wife of a favorite hand on board of Mr. Lloyd's sloop, and was besides, the mother of five sprightly children. Vigorous and spirited woman that she was, a wife and a mother, with a predominating share of the blood of the master running in her veins, Nellie (for that was her name) had all the qualities essential to impudence to a slave overseer. My attention was called to the scene of the castigation by the loud screams and curses that proceeded from the direction of it. When I came near the parties engaged in the struggle the overseer had hold of Nellie, endeavoring with his whole strength to drag her to a tree against her resistance. Both his and her faces were bleeding, for the woman was doing her best. Amid the screams of the children, "Let my mammy go! Let my mammy go!" the hoarse voice of the maddened overseer was heard in terrible oaths that he would teach her how to give a white man "impudence." There were times when she seemed likely to get the better of the brute, but he finally overpowered her and succeeded in getting her arms firmly tied to the tree towards which he had been dragging her. The victim was now at the mercy of his merciless lash. What followed I need not here describe. When the poor woman was untied her back was covered with blood.

She was whipped, terribly whipped, but she was not subdued, and continued to denounce the overseer and to pour upon him every vile epithet of which she could think. Such floggings are seldom repeated on the same persons by overseers. They prefer to whip those who are the most easily whipped. That slave who had the courage to stand up for himself against the overseer, although he might have many hard stripes at first, became while legally a slave virtually a freeman. I do not know that Mr. Sevier ever attempted to whip Nellie again. He probably never did, for he was taken sick not long after and died. It was commonly said that his death-bed was a wretched one, and that, the ruling passion being strong in death, he died flourishing the slave whip and with horrid oaths upon his lips.

In Mr. James Hopkins, the succeeding overseer, we had a different and a better man; as good perhaps as any man could be in the position of a slave overseer. Though he sometimes wielded the lash, it was evident that he took no pleasure in it and did it with much reluctance. He stayed but a short time here, and his removal from the position was much regretted by the slaves generally.

For the present we will attend to a further description of the business-like aspect of Col. Lloyd's "Great House" farm. There was always much bustle and noise here on the two days at the end of each month, for then the slaves belonging to the different branches of this great estate assembled here by their representatives, to obtain their monthly allowances of corn-meal and pork. These were gala days for the slaves of the outlying farms, and there was much rivalry among them as to who should be elected to go up to the Great House farm for the "Allowances," and indeed to attend to any other business at this great place, to them the capital of a little nation. The chief motive among the competitors for the office was the opportunity it afforded to shake off the monotony of the field and to get beyond the overseer's eye and lash. Once on the road with an ox-team, and seated on the tongue of the cart, with no overseer to look after him, one felt comparatively free.

Slaves were expected to sing as well as to work. A silent slave was not liked, either by masters or overseers. "Make a noise there! Make a noise there!" and "bear a hand," were words usually addressed to slaves when they were silent. This, and the natural disposition of the negro to make a noise in the world, may account for the almost constant singing among them when at their work. There was generally more or less singing among the teamsters, at all times. It was a means of telling the overseer, in the distance, where they were and what they were about. But on the allowance days those commissioned to the Great House farm were peculiarly vocal. While on the way they would make the grand old woods for miles around reverberate with their wild and plaintive notes. They were indeed both merry and sad.

The Hunted Slaves *by Richard Ansdell (1815–1885) was painted in 1861 at the start of the Civil War.*

The remark in the olden time was not unfrequently made, that slaves were the most contented and happy laborers in the world, and their dancing and singing were referred to in proof of this alleged fact; but it was a great mistake to suppose them happy because they sometimes made those joyful noises. The songs of the slaves represented their sorrows, rather than their joys. Like tears, they were a relief to aching hearts. Sorrow and desolation have their songs, as well as joy and peace.

The men and the women slaves on Col. Lloyd's farm received as their monthly allowance of food, eight pounds of pickled pork, or its equivalent in fish. The pork was often tainted, and the fish were of the poorest quality. With their pork or fish, they had given them one bushel

Slaves were expected to sing as well as to work.

of Indian meal, unbolted, of which quite fifteen per cent. was more fit for pigs than for men. With this one pint of salt was given, and this was the entire monthly allowance of a full-grown slave, working constantly in the open field from morning till night every day in the month except Sunday. The yearly allowance of clothing was not more ample than the supply of food. It consisted of two tow-linen shirts, one pair of trowsers of the same coarse material, for summer, and a woolen pair of trowsers and a woolen jacket for winter, with one pair of yarn stockings and a pair of shoes of the coarsest description. Children under ten years old had neither shoes, stockings, jackets, nor trowsers. They had two coarse tow-linen shirts per year, and when these were worn out they went naked till the next allowance day—and this was the condition of the little girls as well as of the boys. As to beds, they had none. One coarse blanket was given them, and this only to the men and women. The children stuck themselves in holes and corners about the quarters, often in the corners of huge chimneys, with their feet in the ashes to keep them warm. Time to sleep was of far greater importance. For when the day's work was done most of these had their washing, mending, and cooking to do, and having few or no facilities for doing such things, very many of their needed sleeping hours were consumed in necessary preparations for the labors of the coming day. The night, however, was shortened at both ends. The slaves worked often as long as they could see, and were late in cooking and mending for the coming day, and at the first gray streak of the morning they were summoned to the field by the overseer's horn. They were whipped for over-sleeping more than for any other fault. Young mothers who worked in the field were allowed an hour about ten o'clock in the morning to go home to nurse their children. This was when they were not required to take them to the field with them, and leave them upon "turning row," or in the corner of the fences.

As a general rule the slaves did not come to their quarters to take their meals, but took their ash-cake (called thus because baked in the ashes) and piece of pork, or their salt herrings, where they were at work.

But let us now leave the rough usage of the field, where vulgar coarseness and brutal cruelty flourished as rank as weeds in the tropics and where a vile wretch, in the shape of a man, rides, walks and struts about, with whip in hand, dealing heavy blows and leaving deep gashes on the flesh of men and women, and turn our attention to the less repulsive slave life as it existed in the home of my childhood. Some idea of the splendor of that place sixty years ago has already been given. The contrast between the condition of the slaves and that of their masters was marvelously sharp and striking. There were pride, pomp, and luxury on the one hand, servility, dejection, and misery on the other.

CHAPTER VII

LUXURIES AT THE GREAT HOUSE

CONTRASTS—GREAT HOUSE LUXURIES—ITS HOSPITALITY—ENTERTAINMENTS—FAULT-FINDING—SHAMEFUL HUMILIATION OF AN OLD AND FAITHFUL COACHMAN—WILLIAM WILKS—CURIOUS INCIDENT—EXPRESSED SATISFACTION NOT ALWAYS GENUINE—REASONS FOR SUPPRESSING THE TRUTH.

The close-fisted stinginess that fed the poor slave on coarse corn-meal and tainted meat, wholly vanished on approaching the sacred precincts of the "Great House" itself. There the scriptural phrase descriptive of the wealthy found exact illustration. The highly-favored inmates of this mansion were literally arrayed in "purple and fine linen, and fared sumptuously every day." The table of this house groaned under the blood-bought luxuries gathered with pains-taking care at home and abroad. Fields, forests, rivers, and seas were made tributary. Immense wealth and its lavish expenditures filled the Great House with all that could please the eye or tempt the taste. Fish, flesh, and fowl were here in profusion. Chickens; ducks, Guinea fowls, turkeys, geese and pea-fowls; all were fat and fattening for the destined vortex. Beef, veal, mutton, and venison, of the most select kinds and quality. The teeming riches of the Chesapeake Bay, its rock perch, drums, crocus, trout, oysters, crabs, and terrapin were drawn hither to adorn the glittering table. The dairy, too, poured its rich donations of fragrant cheese, golden butter, and delicious cream to heighten the attractions of the

gorgeous, unending round of feasting. The fertile garden, many acres in size, was not behind, either in the abundance or in the delicacy of its contributions. The tender asparagus, the crispy celery, and the delicate cauliflower, cantelopes, melons of all kinds; and the fruits of all climes and of every description, from the hardy apples to the lemon and orange culminated at this point. Here were gathered figs, raisins, almonds, and grapes from Spain, wines and brandies from France, teas of various flavor from China, and rich, aromatic coffee from Java, all conspiring to swell the tide of high life, where pride and indolence lounged in magnificence and satiety.

Behind the tall-backed and elaborately wrought chairs stood the servants, fifteen in number, carefully selected. Not only with a view to their capacity and adeptness, but with especial regard to their personal appearance, their graceful agility, and pleasing address. These servants constituted a sort of black aristocracy. They resembled the field hands in nothing except their color, and in this they held the advantage of a velvet-like glossiness, rich and beautiful. The hair, too, showed the same advantage.

The Wye house.

The "crib house" at the Wye plantation was an open-air structure where corn was husked.

The smokehouse on the Wye plantation.

In the stables and carriage-houses were to be found the same evidences of pride and luxurious extravagance. Here were three splendid coaches, gigs, phaetons, barouches, sulkeys, and sleighs. Here were saddles and harnesses, beautifully wrought and richly mounted. Not less than thirty-five horses of the best approved blood, both for speed and beauty, were kept only for pleasure. The care of these horses constituted the entire occupation of two men, one or the other of them being always in the stable to answer any call which might be made from the Great House. Over the way from the stable was a house built expressly for the hounds, a pack of twenty-five or thirty, the fare for which would have made glad the hearts of a dozen slaves. The hospitality practiced at the Lloyds' would have astonished and charmed many a health-seeking divine or merchant from the north. Viewed from his table, and not from the field, Colonel Lloyd was, indeed, a model of generous hospitality. His house was literally a hotel for weeks, during the summer months. In master Daniel I had a friend at court, who would sometimes give me a cake, and who kept me well informed as to their guests and their entertainments. Viewed from Col. Lloyds' table, who could have said that his slaves were not well clad and well cared for? Who would have said they did not glory in being the slaves of such a master? Who but a fanatic could have seen any cause for sympathy for either master or slave? Alas, this immense wealth, this gilded splendor, this profusion of luxury, this exemption from toil, this life of ease, this sea of plenty were not the pearly gates they seemed to a world of happiness and sweet content to be. Lurking beneath the rich and tempting viands were invisible spirits of evil, which filled the self-deluded gormandizer with aches and pains, passions uncontrollable, fierce tempers, dyspepsia, rheumatism, lumbago, and gout, and of these the Lloyds had a full share.

I had many opportunities of witnessing the restless discontent and capricious irritation of the Lloyds. My fondness for horses attracted me to the stable much of the time. The two men in charge of this establishment were old and young Barney—father and son. Old Barney was a fine-looking, portly old man of a brownish complexion, and a respectful and dignified bearing. He was much devoted to his profession, and held his office as an honorable one. He was a farrier as well as an ostler, and could bleed horses, remove lampers from their mouths and administer medicine to them. In nothing was Col. Lloyd more unreasonable and exacting than in respect to the management of his horses. Any supposed inattention to these animals was sure to be visited with degrading punishment. No excuse could shield old Barney if the Colonel only suspected something wrong about his horses, and consequently he was often punished when faultless. It was painful to hear the unreasonable and fretful scoldings administered by Col. Lloyd, his son Murray, and his sons-in-law, to this poor man. Something was always wrong. However groundless the complaint, Barney must stand, hat in hand, lips sealed, never answering a word in explanation or excuse. One of the most heart-saddening and humiliating scenes I ever witnessed was the whipping of old Barney by Col. Lloyd. These two men were both advanced in years; there were the silver locks of the master, and the bald and toil-worn brow of the slave—superior and inferior here, powerful and weak here, but equals before God. "Uncover your head," said the imperious master; he was obeyed. "Take off your jacket, you old rascal!" and off came Barney's jacket. "Down on your knees!" Down knelt the old man, his shoulders bare, his bald head glistening in the sunshine, and his aged knees on the cold, damp ground. In this humble and debasing attitude, that master, to whom he had devoted the best years and the best strength of his life, came forward and laid on thirty lashes with his horsewhip. I do not think that the physical suffering from this infliction was severe, but the spectacle of an aged man humbly kneeling before his fellow-man, shocked me at the time; and since I have grown older, few of the features of slavery have impressed me with a deeper sense of its injustice and barbarity than did this existing scene. I owe it to the truth, however, to say that this was the first and last time I ever saw a slave compelled to kneel to receive a whipping.

Another incident, illustrating a phase of slavery to which I have referred in another connection, I may here mention. Besides two other coachmen, Col. Lloyd owned one named William Wilks, and his was one of the exceptionable cases where a slave possessed a surname, and was recognized by it, by both colored and white people. Wilks was a very fine-looking man. He was about as white as any one on the plantation, and in form and feature bore a very striking resemblance to Murray Lloyd. It was whispered and generally believed that William Wilks was a son of Col. Lloyd, by a highly favored slave woman, who was still on the plantation. It was notorious too that William had a deadly enemy in Murray Lloyd, whom he so much resembled, and that the latter greatly worried his father with importunities to sell William. Indeed, he gave his father no rest, until he did sell him to Austin Woldfolk, the great slave-trader at that time. Before selling him, however, he tried to make things smooth by giving William a whipping, but it proved a failure. It was a compromise, and like most such, defeated itself—for Col. Lloyd soon after atoned to William for the abuse by giving him a gold watch and chain. Another fact somewhat curious was, that though sold to the

remorseless Woldfolk, William outbid all his purchasers, paid for himself, and afterwards resided in Baltimore.

The real feelings and opinions of the slaves were not much known or respected by their masters. The distance between the two was too great to admit of such knowledge, and in this respect Col. Lloyd was no exception to the rule. His slaves were so numerous that he did not know them when he saw them. Nor, indeed, did all his slaves know him. It is reported of him, that, riding along the road one day, he met a colored man, and addressed him in what was the usual way of speaking to colored people on the public highways of the South: "Well, boy, who do you belong to?" "To Col. Lloyd," replied the slave. "Well, does the Colonel treat you well?" "No, sir," was the ready reply. The Colonel rode on; the slave also went on about his business, not dreaming that he had been conversing with his master. He thought and said nothing of the matter, until, two or three weeks afterwards, he was informed by his overseer that, for having found fault with his master, he was now to be sold to a Georgia trader. He was immediately chained and handcuffed; and thus, without a moment's warning, he was snatched away, and forever sundered from his family and friends by a hand as unrelenting as that of death. It was partly in consequence of such facts, that slaves, when inquired of as to their condition and the character of their masters, would almost invariably say that they were contented and their masters kind. Slaveholders are known to have sent spies among their slaves to ascertain, if possible, their views and feelings in regard to their condition; hence the maxim established among them, that "a still tongue makes a wise head." They would suppress the truth rather than take the consequences of telling it, and in so doing they prove themselves a part of the human family. I was frequently asked if I had a kind master, and I do not remember ever to have given a negative reply. I did not consider myself as uttering that which was strictly untrue, for I always measured the kindness of my master by the standard of kindness set up by the slaveholders around us.

Above: William Wilks, the presumed son of Colonel Lloyd, was given a gold pocket watch after a futile beating, which he used to buy his own freedom at auction. This 1820s pocket watch is of the same era.

CHAPTER VIII

CHARACTERISTICS OF OVERSEERS

AUSTIN GORE—SKETCH OF HIS CHARACTER—OVERSEERS AS A CLASS—THEIR PECULIAR CHARACTERISTICS—THE MARKED INDIVIDUALITY OF AUSTIN GORE—HIS SENSE OF DUTY—MURDER OF POOR DENBY—SENSATION—HOW GORE MADE HIS PEACE WITH COL. LLOYD—NO LAWS FOR THE PROTECTION OF SLAVES POSSIBLE OF BEING ENFORCED.

The comparatively moderate rule of Mr. Hopkins as overseer on Col. Lloyd's plantation was succeeded by that of another, whose name was Austin Gore. I hardly know how to bring this man fitly before the reader; for under him there was more suffering from violence and bloodshed than had, according to the older slaves, ever been experienced before at this place. I speak of overseers as a class, for they were such. They were arranged and classified by that great law of attraction which determines the sphere and affinities of men and which ordains that men whose malign and brutal propensities preponderate over their moral and intellectual endowments shall naturally fall into the employments which promise the largest gratification to their predominating instincts or propensities. Mr. Gore was one of those to whom a general characterization would do no manner of justice. He was an overseer, but he was something more. With the malign and tyrannical qualities of an overseer he combined something of the lawful master. He was one of those overseers who could

torture the slightest word or look into impudence, and he had the nerve not only to resent, but to punish promptly and severely. There could be no answering back. Guilty or not guilty, to be accused was to be sure of a flogging. Other overseers, how brutal soever they might be, would sometimes seek to gain favor with the slaves by indulging in a little pleasantry; but Gore never said a funny thing or perpetrated a joke. He was always cold, distant, and unapproachable and needed no higher pleasure than the performance of the duties of his office. Among many other deeds of shocking cruelty committed by him was the murder of a young colored man named Bill Denby. He was a powerful fellow, full of animal spirits, and one of the most valuable of Col. Lloyd's slaves. In some way, I know not what, he offended this Mr. Austin Gore, and, in accordance with the usual custom, the latter undertook to flog him. He had given him but a few stripes when Denby broke away from him, plunged into the creek, and, standing there with the water up to his neck, refused to come out; whereupon, for this refusal, Gore shot him dead! It was said that Gore gave Denby

Wesley Harris, a fugitive from slavery, is shown here in a gun fight with slave catchers in a Maryland barn.

Death of Capt. Ferrer, the Captain of the Amistad, July, 1839.

The Amistad *mutiny took place on a trip that was supposed to sail from Havana to Puerto Príncipe, Cuba. Fifty-three enslaved passengers, recently taken from Africa, rose up to commandeer the Spanish schooner they were imprisoned on. They spared the life of the navigator, who tricked them by sailing to America instead of Sierra Leone as instructed. They were jailed in Connecticut, where slavery was still legal. The trial had important repercussions in the abolition movement, as it ruled that though slavery was legal in Cuba, taking people from Africa was not, thus the rebels were legally allowed to fight for their freedom by any means necessary.*

three calls to come out, telling him that if he did not obey the last call he should shoot him. When the last call was given Denby still stood his ground, and Gore, without further parley or making any further effort to induce obedience, raised his gun deliberately to his face, took deadly aim at his standing victim, and with one click of the gun the mangled body sank out of sight, and only his warm red blood marked the place where he had stood.

This fiendish murder produced, as it could not help doing, a tremendous sensation. The slaves were panic-stricken, and howled with alarm. The atrocity roused my old master, and he spoke out in reprobation of it. Both he and Col. Lloyd arraigned Gore for his cruelty; but the latter, calm and collected as though nothing unusual had happened, declared that Denby had become unmanageable; that he set a dangerous example to the other slaves, and that unless some such prompt measure was resorted to there would be an end of all rule and order on the plantation. That convenient covert for all manner of villainy and outrage; that cowardly alarm-cry that the slaves would "take the place," was pleaded, just as it had before been in thousands of similar cases. Gore's defense was evidently considered satisfactory, for he was continued in his office without being subjected to a judicial investigation.

I speak advisedly when I say that in Talbot Co., Maryland, killing a slave, or any colored person, was not treated as a crime, either by the courts or the community. One of the commonest sayings to which my ears early became accustomed, was, that it was "worth but a half a cent to kill a nigger, and half a cent to bury one." While I heard of numerous murders committed by slaveholders on the eastern shore of Maryland, I never knew a solitary instance where a slaveholder was either hung or imprisoned for having murdered a slave. The usual pretext for such

crimes was that the slave had offered resistance. Should a slave, when assaulted, but raise his hand in self-defense, the white assaulting party was fully justified by southern law and southern public opinion in shooting the slave down, and for this there was no redress.

An illustration appearing in the 1892 edition of
Life and Times of Frederick Douglass.

CHAPTER IX

CHANGE OF LOCATION

Miss Lucretia—Her kindness—How it was manifested—"Ike"—A battle with him—Miss Lucretia's balsam—Bread—How it was obtained—Gleams of sunlight amidst the general darkness—Suffering from cold—How we took our meal mush—Preparations for going to Baltimore—Delight at the change—Cousin Tom's opinion of Baltimore—Arrival there—Kind reception—Mr. and Mrs. Hugh Auld—Their son Tommy—My relations to them—My duties—A turning point in my life.

I have nothing cruel or shocking to relate of my own personal experience while I remained on Col. Lloyd's plantation, at the home of my old master. An occasional cuff from Aunt Katy, and a regular whipping from old master, such as any heedless and mischievous boy might get from his father, is all that I have to say of this sort. I was not old enough to work in the field, and there being little else than field-work to perform, I had much leisure. The most I had to do was to drive up the cows in the evening, to keep the front yard clean, and to perform small errands for my young mistress, Lucretia Auld. Miss Lucretia—as we all continued to call her long after her marriage—had bestowed on me such looks and words as taught me that she pitied me, if she did not love me. She sometimes gave me a piece of bread and butter, an article not set down in our bill of fare, but an extra ration aside from both Aunt Katy and old master, and given as I believed solely out of the tender regard she had for me. Then, too, I one day got into the wars with Uncle Abel's son "Ike," and got sadly worsted; the little rascal struck me directly in the forehead with a sharp piece of cinder, fused with iron, from the old blacksmith's forge, which made a cross in my forehead very plainly to be seen even now. The gash bled very freely, and I roared and betook myself home. Miss Lucretia in this state of the case came forward, and called me into the parlor (an extra privilege of itself), and without using toward me any of the hard and reproachful epithets of Aunt Katy, quietly acted the good Samaritan. With her own soft hand she washed the blood from my head and face, brought her own bottle of balsam, and with the balsam wetted a nice piece of white linen and bound up my head.

This woodcut image of an enslaved man in chains appeared on the 1837 broadside publication of John Greenleaf Whittier's antislavery poem, "Our Countrymen in Chains."

Miss Lucretia was after this yet more my friend. I felt her to be such and I have no doubt that the simple act of binding up my head did much to awaken in her heart an interest in my welfare. When very severely pinched with hunger, I had the habit of singing, which the good lady very soon came to understand, and when she heard me singing under her window I was very apt to be paid for my music.

Thus I had two friends, both at important points—Mas'r Daniel at the great house, and Miss Lucretia at home. From Mas'r Daniel I got protection from the bigger boys, and from Miss Lucretia I got bread by singing when I was hungry, and sympathy when I was abused by the termagant in the kitchen.

As before intimated, I received no severe treatment from the hands of my master, but the insufficiency of both food and clothing was a serious trial to me, especially the lack of clothing. In hottest summer and coldest winter I was kept almost in a state of nudity. My only clothing—a little coarse sack-cloth or tow-linen sort of shirt, scarcely reaching to my knees, was worn night and day and changed once a week. The great difficulty was to keep warm during the night. I slept generally in a little closet, without even a blanket to cover me. In very cold weather I sometimes got down the bag in which corn was carried to the mill, and crawled into that. Sleeping there with my head in and my feet out, I was partly protected, though never comfortable. My feet have been so cracked with the frost that the pen with which I am writing might be laid in the gashes. Our corn meal mush, which was our only regular if not all-sufficing diet, was, when sufficiently cooled from the cooking, placed in a large tray or trough. This was set down either on the floor of the kitchen, or out of doors on the ground, and the children were called like so many pigs, and like so many pigs would come, some with oyster-shells, some with pieces of shingles, but none with spoons, and literally devour the mush. I was the most unlucky of all, for Aunt

MARYLAND STATE HOUSE

BUILT 1772-1779

CAPITOL OF THE UNITED STATES
NOVEMBER 26, 1783 - AUGUST 13, 1784

IN THIS STATE HOUSE, OLDEST IN THE NATION STILL
IN LEGISLATIVE USE, GENERAL GEORGE WASHINGTON
RESIGNED HIS COMMISSION BEFORE THE CONTINENTAL
CONGRESS DECEMBER 23, 1783. HERE, JANUARY 14, 1784,
CONGRESS RATIFIED THE TREATY OF PARIS TO END THE
REVOLUTIONARY WAR AND, MAY 7, 1784, APPOINTED
THOMAS JEFFERSON MINISTER PLENIPOTENTIARY. FROM
HERE, SEPTEMBER 14, 1786, THE ANNAPOLIS CONVENTION
ISSUED THE CALL TO THE STATES THAT LED TO THE
CONSTITUTIONAL CONVENTION.

A REGISTERED NATIONAL HISTORIC LANDMARK
MARYLAND HISTORICAL SOCIETY

Katy had no good feeling for me, and if I pushed the children, or if they told her anything unfavorable of me, she always believed the worst and was sure to whip me.

As I grew older and more thoughtful, I became more and more filled with a sense of my wretchedness. The unkindness of Aunt Katy, the hunger and cold I suffered, and the terrible reports of wrongs and outrages which came to my ear, together with what I almost daily witnessed, led me to wish I had never been born.

The ties that ordinarily bind children to their homes had no existence in my case, and in thinking of a home elsewhere, I was confident of finding none that I should relish less than the one I was leaving.

I was in this unhappy state when I received from Miss Lucretia the joyful intelligence that my old master had determined to let me go to Baltimore to live with Mr. Hugh Auld, a brother to Mr. Thomas Auld, Miss Lucretia's husband. I shall never forget the ecstacy with which I received this information, three days before the time set for my departure. They were the three happiest days I had ever known. I spent the largest part of them in the creek, washing off the plantation scurf, and thus preparing for my new home. Miss Lucretia took a lively interest in getting me ready. She told me I must get all the dead skin off my feet and knees, for the people in Baltimore were very cleanly, and would laugh at me if I looked dirty; and besides she was intending to give me a pair of trowsers, but which I could not put on unless I got off all the dirt.

The ties that ordinarily bind children to their homes had no existence in my case, and in thinking of a home elsewhere, I was confident of finding none that I should relish less than the one I was leaving. I had the strongest desire to see Baltimore. My cousin Tom, a boy two or three years older than I, had been there, and, though not fluent in speech (he stuttered immoderately), he had inspired me with that desire by his eloquent descriptions of the place. Tom was sometimes cabin-boy on board the sloop *Sally Lloyd* (which Capt. Thomas Auld

Maryland State House, Annapolis.

A young boy in tattered rags, who was enslaved until being taken as "contraband" during the Civil War.

commanded), and when he came home from Baltimore he was always a sort of hero amongst us, at least till his trip to Baltimore was forgotten. He said a great deal about the Market house; of the ringing of the bells, and of many other things which roused my curiosity very much, and indeed brightened my hopes of happiness in my new home.

We sailed out of Miles River for Baltimore early on a Saturday morning. I remember only the day of the week, for at that time I had no knowledge of the days of the month, nor indeed of the months of the year. On setting sail I walked aft and gave to Col. Lloyd's plantation what I hoped would be the last look I should give to it, or to any place like it. After taking this last view, I quitted the quarter-deck, made my way to the bow of the boat, and spent the remainder of the day in looking ahead; interesting myself in what was in the distance, rather than in what was near by, or behind.

Late in the afternoon we reached Annapolis, but not stopping there long enough to admit of going ashore. It was the first large town I had ever seen, and though it was inferior to many a factory village in New England, my feelings on seeing it were excited to a pitch very little below that reached by travelers at the first view of Rome. The dome of the State house was especially imposing, and surpassed in grandeur the appearance of the "great house" I had left behind.

We arrived in Baltimore on Sunday morning, and landed at Smith's wharf, not far from Bowly's wharf. We had on board a large flock of sheep for the Baltimore market; and after assisting in driving them to the slaughter house of Mr. Curtiss, on Loudon Slater's hill, I was conducted by Rich—one of the hands belonging to the sloop— to my new home on Alliciana street, near Gardiner's ship yard, on Fell's point. Mr. and Mrs. Hugh Auld, my new master and mistress, were both at home, and met me at the door, together with their rosy-cheeked little son Thomas, to take care of whom was to constitute my future occupation. In fact it was to "little Tommy," rather than to his parents, that old master made a present of me, and, though there was no legal form or arrangement entered into, I have no doubt that Mr. and Mrs. Auld felt that in due time I should be the legal property of their bright-eyed and beloved boy Tommy. I was especially struck with the appearance of my new mistress. Her face was lighted with the kindliest emotions; and the reflex influence of her countenance, as well as the tenderness with which she seemed to regard me, while asking me sundry little questions, greatly delighted me, and lit up, to my fancy, the pathway of my future. Little Thomas was affectionately told by his mother, that "there was his Freddy," and that "Freddy would take care of him"; and I was told to "be kind to little Tommy," an injunction I scarcely needed, for I had already fallen in love with the dear boy. With these little ceremonies I was initiated into my new home, and entered upon my peculiar duties, then unconscious of a cloud to dim its broad horizon.

CHAPTER X

LEARNING TO READ

Established in my new home in Baltimore, I was not very long in perceiving that in picturing to myself what was to be my life there, my imagination had painted only the bright side; and that the reality had its dark shades as well as its light ones. The open country which had been so much to me was all shut out. Walled in on every side by towering brick buildings, the heat of the summer was intolerable to me, and the hard brick pavements almost blistered my feet. My new mistress happily proved to be all she had seemed, and in her presence I easily forgot all outside annoyances. Mrs. Sophia was naturally of an excellent disposition—kind, gentle, and cheerful.

She had never been a slaveholder—a thing then quite unusual at the South—but had depended almost entirely upon her own industry for a living. Mrs. Auld was not only kindhearted, but remarkably pious; frequent in her attendance at public worship and much given to reading the Bible and to chanting hymns of praise when alone. Mr. Hugh was altogether a different character. He cared very little about religion; knew more of the world and was more a part of the world, than his wife.

Though I must in truth characterize Master Hugh as a sour man of forbidding appearance, it is due to him to acknowledge that he was never cruel to me, according to the notion of cruelty in Maryland. During the first year or two, he left me almost exclusively to the management of his wife. I had good bread and mush occasionally; for my old tow-linen shirt, I had good clean clothes. I was really well off. My employment was to run of errands, and to take care of Tommy; to prevent his getting in the way of carriages, and to keep him out of harm's way generally.

So for a time everything went well. I say for a time, because the fatal poison of irresponsible power, and the natural influence of slave customs, were not very long in making their impression on the gentle and loving disposition of my excellent mistress. She at first regarded me as a child, like any other. This was the natural and spontaneous thought; afterwards, when she came to consider me as property, our relations to each other were changed, but a nature so noble as hers could not instantly become perverted, and it took several years before the sweetness of her temper was wholly lost.

An illustration appearing in the 1892 edition of Life and Times of Frederick Douglass.

I instinctively assented to the proposition, and from that moment I understood the direct pathway from slavery to freedom.

The frequent hearing of my mistress reading the Bible aloud, for she often read aloud when her husband was absent, awakened my curiosity in respect to this mystery of reading, and roused in me the desire to learn. Up to this time I had known nothing whatever of this wonderful art, and my ignorance and inexperience of what it could do for me, as well as my confidence in my mistress, emboldened me to ask her to teach me to read. With an unconsciousness and inexperience equal to my own, she readily consented, and in an incredibly short time, by her kind assistance, I had mastered the alphabet and could spell words of three or four letters. My mistress seemed almost as proud of my progress as if I had been her own child, and supposing that her husband would be as well pleased, she made no secret of what she was doing for me. Indeed, she exultingly told him of the aptness of her pupil and of her intention to persevere, as she felt it her duty to do, in teaching me, at least, to read the Bible. And here arose the first dark cloud over my Baltimore prospects, the precursor of chilling blasts and drenching storms. Master Hugh was astounded beyond measure and, probably for the first time, proceeded to unfold to his wife the true philosophy of the slave system, and the peculiar rules necessary in the nature of the case to be observed in the management of human chattels. Of course he forbade her to give me any further instruction, telling her in the first place that to do so was unlawful, as it was also unsafe; "for," said he, "if you give a nigger an inch he will take an ell. Learning will spoil the best nigger in the world. If he learns to read the Bible it will forever unfit him to be a

This frontispiece and title page are from an American bible printed in 1825, the year before Douglass was sent to Baltimore.

slave. He should know nothing but the will of his master, and learn to obey it. As to himself, learning will do him no good, but a great deal of harm, making him disconsolate and unhappy. If you teach him how to read, he'll want to know how to write, and this accomplished, he'll be running away with himself."

This was a new and special revelation, dispelling a painful mystery against which my youthful understanding had struggled, and struggled in vain, to wit, the white man's power to perpetuate the enslavement of the black man. "Very well," thought I. "Knowledge unfits a child to be a slave." I instinctively assented to the proposition, and from that moment I understood the direct pathway from slavery to freedom.

CHAPTER XI

GROWING IN KNOWLEDGE

My mistress—Her slaveholding duties—Their effects on her originally noble nature—The conflict in her mind—She opposes my learning to read—Too late—She had given me the "inch," I was resolved to take the "ell"—How I pursued my study to read—My tutors—What progress I made—Slavery—What I heard said about it—Thirteen years old—Columbian orator—Dialogue—Knowledge increasing—Liberty—Sadness—unhappiness of Mrs. Sophia—My hatred of slavery.

I lived in the family of Mr. Auld, at Baltimore, seven years, during which time, as the almanac makers say of the weather, my condition was variable. The most interesting feature of my history here was my learning, under somewhat marked disadvantages, to read and write. My mistress, checked in her benevolent designs toward me, not only ceased instructing me herself, but set her face as a flint against my learning to read by any means. It is due to her to say, however, that she did not adopt this course in all its stringency at first.

Mrs. Auld was singularly deficient in the qualities of a slaveholder. It was no easy matter for her to think or to feel that the curly-headed boy, who stood by her side, and even leaned on her lap, who was loved by little Tommy, and who loved little Tommy in turn, sustained to her only the relation of a chattel. I was more than that; she felt me to be more than that. I was human, and she, dear lady, knew and felt me to be so. How could she then treat me as a brute, without a mighty struggle with all the noblest powers of her soul? That struggle came, and the will and power of the husband were victorious. Her noble soul was overcome, and he who wrought the wrong was injured in the fall no less than the rest of the household. When I went into that household, it was the abode of happiness and contentment. The wife and mistress there was a model of affection and tenderness. She had bread for the hungry, clothes for the naked, and comfort for every mourner who came within her reach.

But slavery soon proved its ability to divest her of these excellent qualities, and her home of its early happiness. As my condition in the family waxed bad, that of the family waxed no better. In ceasing to instruct me, my mistress had to seek to justify herself to herself, and once consenting to take sides in such a debate, she was

Douglass learned to write mostly using chalk on fences and pavement.

J. M. W. Turner's (1775–1851) painting The Slave Ship *(1841) depicts people on their way to being sold into slavery being thrown overboard and drowning as a typhoon comes upon the ship.*

compelled to hold her position. She finally became even more violent in her opposition to my learning to read than was Mr. Auld himself. Nothing now appeared to make her more angry than seeing me, seated in some nook or corner, quietly reading a book or newspaper. She would rush at me with the utmost fury, and snatch the book or paper from my hand, with something of the wrath and consternation which a traitor might be supposed to feel on being discovered in a plot by some dangerous spy. I was most narrowly watched in all my movements. If I remained in a separate room from the family for any considerable length of time, I was sure to be suspected of having a book, and was at once called to give an account of myself. But this was too late: the first and never-to-be-retraced step had been taken. Teaching me the alphabet had been the "inch" given, I was now waiting only for the opportunity to "take the ell."

Filled with the determination to learn to read at any cost, I hit upon many expedients to accomplish that much desired end. The plan which I mainly adopted, and the one which was the most successful, was that of using as teachers my young white playmates, with whom I met on the streets. I used almost constantly to carry a copy of Webster's spelling-book in my pocket, and when sent of errands, or when playtime was allowed me, I would step aside with my young friends and take a lesson in spelling.

Although slavery was a delicate subject and, in Maryland, very cautiously talked about among grown up people, I frequently talked with the white boys about it, and that very freely. I would sometimes say to them, while seated on a curbstone or a cellar door, "I wish I could be free, as you will be when you get to be men." "You will be free, you know, as soon as you are twenty-one, and can go where you like, but I am a slave for life. Have I not as good a right to be free as you have?" Words like these, I observed, always troubled them; and I had no small satisfaction in drawing out from them, as I occasionally did, that fresh and bitter condemnation of slavery which ever springs from natures unseared and unperverted.

When I was about thirteen years old, and had succeeded in learning to read, every increase of knowledge, especially anything respecting the free states, was an additional weight to the almost intolerable burden of my thought—"I am a slave for life." To my bondage I could see no end. It was a terrible reality, and I shall never be able to tell how sadly that thought chafed my young spirit. Fortunately or unfortunately, I had, by blacking boots for some gentlemen, earned a little money with which I purchased of Mr. Knight, on Thames street, what was then a very popular school book, viz., "The Columbian Orator," for which I paid fifty cents. Among much other interesting matter, that which I read again and again with unflagging satisfaction was a short dialogue between a master and his slave. The slave is represented as having been recaptured in a second attempt to run away; and the master opens the dialogue with an upbraiding speech, charging the slave with ingratitude, and demanding to know what he has to say in his own defense. The slave rejoins that he knows how little anything that he can say will avail, seeing that he is completely in the hands of his owner; and with noble resolution, calmly says, "I submit to my fate." Touched by the slave's answer, the master insists upon his further speaking, and recapitulates the many acts of kindness which he has performed toward the slave, and tells him he is permitted to speak for himself. Thus invited, the quondam slave made a spirited defense of himself, and thereafter the whole argument for and against slavery is brought out. The master was vanquished at every turn in the argument, and, appreciating the fact, he generously and meekly emancipates the slave, with his best wishes for his prosperity. I could not help feeling that the day might yet come when the well-directed answers made by the slave to the master, in this instance, would find a counterpart in my own experience. The mighty power and heart-searching directness of truth penetrating the heart of a slave-holder and compelling him to yield up his earthly interests to the claims of eternal justice, were finely illustrated in the dialogue, and from the speeches of Sheridan I got a bold and powerful denunciation of oppression and a most brilliant vindication of the rights of man.

Here was indeed a noble acquisition. If I had ever wavered under the consideration that the Almighty, in some way, had ordained slavery

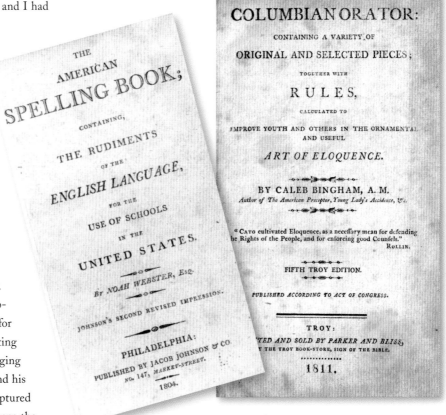

Left: The title page of Webster's American Spelling Book.
Right: The title page of the 1811 edition of The Columbian Orator.

and willed my enslavement for His own glory, I wavered no longer. I had now penetrated to the secret of all slavery and of all oppression, and had ascertained their true foundation to be in the pride, the power and the avarice of man. I have no doubt that my state of mind had something to do with the change in treatment which my mistress adopted towards me. I can easily believe that my leaden, downcast, and disconsolate look was very offensive to her. Poor lady! She did not understand my trouble, and I could not tell her. My feelings were not the result of any marked cruelty in the treatment I received; they sprung from the consideration of my being a slave at all. It was slavery, not its mere incidents that I hated. I had been cheated. I saw through the attempt to keep me in ignorance. I saw that slaveholders would have gladly made me believe that, in making a slave of me and in making slaves of others, they were merely acting under the authority of God, and I felt to them as to robbers and deceivers. The feeding and clothing me well could not atone for taking my liberty from me. The smiles of my mistress could not remove the deep sorrow that dwelt in my young bosom. She had changed, and the reader will see that I too, had changed. We were both victims to the same overshadowing evil, she as mistress, I as slave. I will not censure her harshly.

CHAPTER XII

RELIGIOUS NATURE AWAKENED

Abolitionists spoken of—Eagerness to know the meaning of word—Consults the dictionary—Incendiary information—The enigma solved—"Nat Turner" insurrection—Cholera—Religion—Methodist minister—Religious impressions—Father Lawson—His character and occupation—His influence over me—Our mutual attachment—New hopes and aspirations—Heavenly light—Two Irishmen on wharf—Conversation with them—Learning to write—My aims.

In the unhappy state of mind described in the foregoing chapter, regretting my very existence because doomed to a life of bondage, and so goaded and wretched as to be even tempted at times to take my own life, I was most keenly sensitive to know any and everything possible that had any relation to the subject of slavery. Very often I would overhear Master Hugh, or some of his company, speak with much warmth of the "abolitionists." Who or what the abolitionists were, I was totally ignorant. I found, however, that whoever or whatever they might be, they were most cordially hated and abused by slaveholders of every grade. I therefore set about finding out, if possible, who and what the abolitionists were, and why they were so obnoxious to the slaveholders. The dictionary offered me very little help. It taught me that abolition was "the act of abolishing"; but it left me in ignorance at the very point where I most wanted information, and that was,

A black preacher.

as to the thing to be abolished. A city newspaper—the "Baltimore *American*"—gave me the incendiary information denied me by the dictionary. In its columns I found that on a certain day a vast number of petitions and memorials had been presented to Congress, praying for the abolition of slavery in the District of Columbia, and for the abolition of the slave trade between the States of the Union. There was HOPE in those words. I saw that there was fear as well as rage in the manner of speaking of the abolitionists, and from this I inferred that they must have some power in the country, and I felt that they might perhaps succeed in their designs. The insurrection of Nat. Turner had been quelled, but the alarm and terror which it occasioned had not subsided. The cholera was then on its way to this country, and I remember thinking that God was angry with the white people because of their slaveholding wickedness, and therefore

Nat Turner discovered after leading a rebellion that resulted in many deaths of both black and white people.

his judgments were abroad in the land. Of course it was impossible for me not to hope much for the abolition movement when I saw it supported by the Almighty, and armed with DEATH.

Previously to my contemplation of the anti-slavery movement and its probable results, my mind had been seriously awakened to the subject of religion. I was not more than thirteen years old, when, in my loneliness and destitution, I longed for some one to whom I could go, as to a father and protector. The preaching of a white Methodist minister, named Hanson, was the means of causing me to feel that in God I had such a friend. I consulted a good colored man named Charles Lawson, and in tones of holy affection he told me to pray, and to "cast all my care upon God." This I sought to do; and though for weeks I was a poor, broken-hearted mourner, traveling through doubts and fears, I finally found my burden lightened, and my heart relieved. I loved all mankind, slaveholders not excepted, though I abhorred slavery more than ever. I saw the world in a new light, and my great concern was

to have everybody converted. Uncle Lawson lived near Master Hugh's house, and becoming deeply attached to him, I went often with him to prayer-meeting and spent much of my leisure time on Sunday with him. These meetings went on for a long time without the knowledge either of Master Hugh or my mistress. Both knew, however, that I had become religious, and seemed to respect my conscientious piety. My mistress was still a professor of religion, and belonged to class. Her leader was no less a person than Rev. Beverly Waugh, the presiding elder, and afterwards one of the bishops of the Methodist Episcopal church.

But my chief instructor in religious matters was Uncle Lawson. He was my spiritual father and I loved him intensely, and was at his house every chance I could get. This pleasure, however, was not long unquestioned. Master Hugh became averse to our intimacy, and threatened to whip me if I ever went there again. I now felt myself persecuted by a wicked man, and I would go. The good old man had told me that the "Lord had great work for me to do," and I must prepare to do it; that he

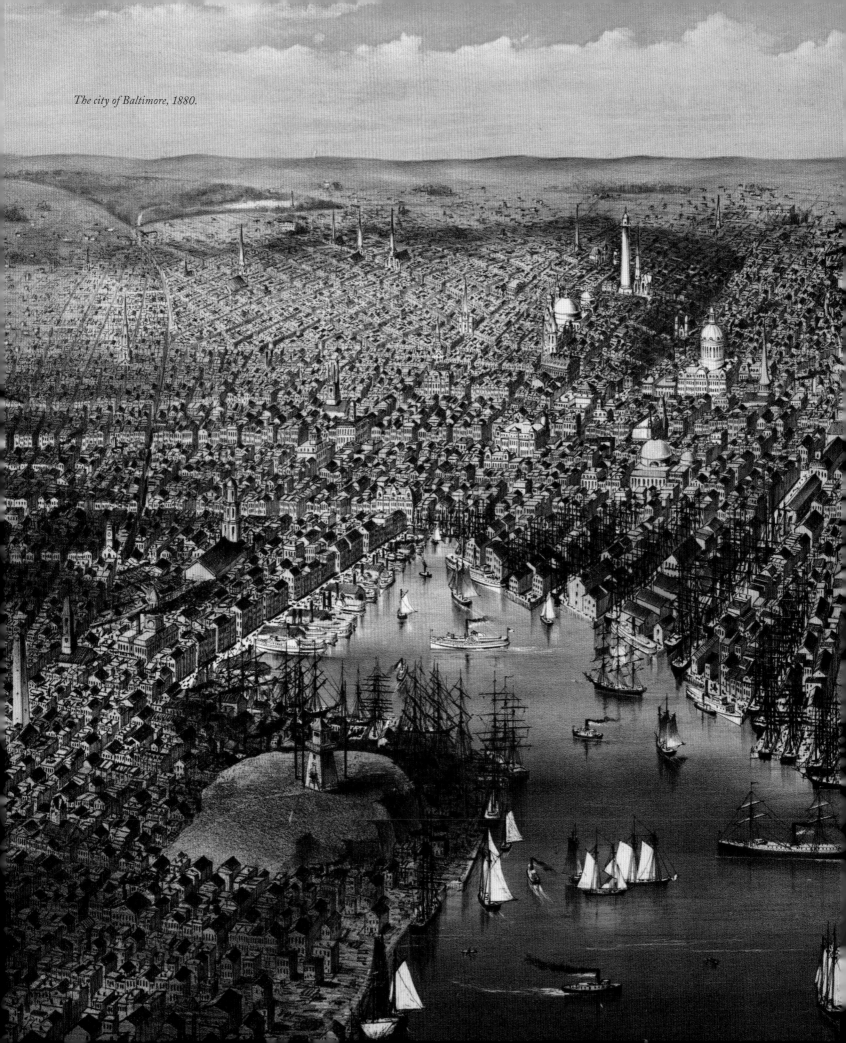

The city of Baltimore, 1880.

A Methodist preacher traveling by horseback in the rain.

the matter, and expressed the deepest sympathy with me, and the most decided hatred of slavery. They went so far as to tell me that I ought to run away and go to the north; that I should find friends there, and that I should then be as free as anybody. I pretended not to be interested in what they said, for I feared they might be treacherous. White men were not unfrequently known to encourage slaves to escape, and then, to get the reward, they would kidnap them and return them to their masters. I nevertheless remembered their words and their advice, and looked forward to an escape to the north as a possible means of gaining the liberty for which my heart panted. I now not only had the hope of freedom, but a foreshadowing of the means by which I might some day gain that inestimable boon. Meanwhile I resolved to add to my educational attainments the art of writing.

After this manner I began to learn to write. I was much in the ship-yard—Master Hugh's, and that of Durgan & Bailey, and I observed that the carpenters, after hewing and getting ready a piece of timber to use, wrote on it the initials of the name of that part of the ship for which it was intended. When, for instance, a piece of timber was ready for the starboard side, it was marked with a capital "S." A piece for the larboard side was marked "L."; larboard forward was marked "L. F.;" larboard aft was marked "L. A."; starboard aft, "S. A."; and starboard forward, "S. F." I soon learned these letters, and for what they were placed on the timbers.

My work now was to keep fire under the steam-box, and to watch the ship-yard while the carpenters had gone to dinner. This interval gave me a fine opportunity for copying the letters named. I soon astonished myself with the ease with which I made the letters, and the thought was soon present, "If I can make four letters I can make more." Having made these readily and easily, when I met boys about the Bethel church or on any of our play-grounds, I entered the lists with them in the art of writing, and would make the letters which I had been so fortunate as to learn, and ask them to "beat that if they could." With play-mates for my teachers, fences and pavements for my copy-books, and chalk for my pen and ink, I learned to write. I however adopted, afterward, various methods for improving my hand. The most successful was copying the italics in Webster's spelling-book until I could make them all without looking on the book. By this time my little "Master Tommy" had grown to be a big boy, and had written over a number of copy-books and brought them home. They had been shown to the neighbors, had elicited due praise, and had been laid carefully away. I got Master Tommy's copy-books and a pen and ink, and in the ample spaces between the lines I wrote other lines as nearly like his as possible. I was supported in my endeavors by renewed advice and by holy promises from the good father Lawson, with whom I continued to meet and pray and read the Scriptures. Although Master Hugh was aware of these meetings, I must say for his credit that he never executed his threats to whip me for having thus innocently employed my leisure time.

had been shown that I must preach the gospel. His words made a very deep impression upon me, and I verily felt that some such work was before me, though I could not see how I could ever engage in its performance. When I would tell him, "I am a slave, and a slave for life, how can I do anything?" he would quietly answer, "The Lord can make you free, my dear; all things are possible with Him; only have faith in God. 'Ask, and it shall be given you.' If you want liberty, ask the Lord for it in FAITH, and He will give it to you."

Thus assured and thus cheered on under the inspiration of hope, I worked and prayed with a light heart, believing that my life was under the guidance of a wisdom higher than my own. With all other blessings sought at the mercy seat, I always prayed that God would, of His great mercy, and in His own good time, deliver me from my bondage.

I went, one day, on the wharf of Mr. Waters, and seeing two Irishmen unloading a scow of stone or ballast, I went on board unasked, and helped them. When we had finished the work one of the men came to me, aside, and asked me a number of questions, and among them if I were a slave? I told him "I was a slave for life." The good Irishman gave a shrug, and seemed deeply affected. He said it was a pity so fine a little fellow as I should be a slave for life. They both had much to say about

CHAPTER XIII

THE VICISSITUDES OF SLAVE LIFE

DEATH OF OLD MASTER'S SON RICHARD SPEEDILY FOLLOWED BY THAT OF OLD MASTER—VALUATION AND DIVISION OF ALL THE PROPERTY, INCLUDING THE SLAVES—SENT FOR TO COME TO HILLSBOROUGH TO BE VALUED AND DIVIDED—SAD PROSPECTS AND GRIEF—SLAVES HAVE NO VOICE IN DECIDING THEIR OWN DESTINIES—GENERAL DREAD OF FALLING INTO MASTER ANDREW'S HANDS—GOOD FORTUNE IN FALLING TO MISS LUCRETIA—SHE ALLOWS MY RETURN TO BALTIMORE—JOY AT MASTER HUGH'S—DEATH OF MISS LUCRETIA—MASTER THOMAS AULD'S SECOND MARRIAGE—THE NEW WIFE UNLIKE THE OLD—AGAIN REMOVED FROM MASTER HUGH'S—REASONS FOR REGRET—PLAN OF ESCAPE.

I must now ask the reader to go back with me a little in point of time, in my humble story, and notice another circumstance that entered into my slavery experience, and which, doubtless, has had a share in deepening my horror of slavery and of my hostility toward those men and measures that practically uphold the slave system.

It has already been observed that though I was, after my removal from Col. Lloyd's plantation, in form the slave of Master Hugh Auld, I was in fact and in law the slave of my old master, Capt. Anthony. Very well. In a very short time after I went to Baltimore my old master's youngest son, Richard, died; and in three years and six months after, my old master himself died, leaving, to share the estate, only his daughter Lucretia and his son Andrew. The old man died while on a visit to his daughter in Hillsborough, where Capt. Auld and Mrs. Lucretia now lived. Master

Thomas, having given up the command of Col. Lloyd's sloop, was now keeping store in that town.

Cut off thus unexpectedly, Capt. Anthony died intestate, and his property must be equally divided between his two children, Andrew and Lucretia. On the death of old master I was immediately sent for to be valued and divided with the other property. What an assemblage! Men and women, young and old, married and single; moral and thinking human beings, in open contempt of their humanity, leveled at a low with horses, sheep, horned cattle, and swine. Horses and men, cattle and women, pigs and children—

Our destiny was to be fixed for life, and we had no more voice in the decision of the question than the oxen and cows that stood chewing at the hay-mow. One word of the appraisers, against all preferences and prayers, could sunder all the ties of friendship and affection, even to separating

A family being separated as the father is sold at auction.

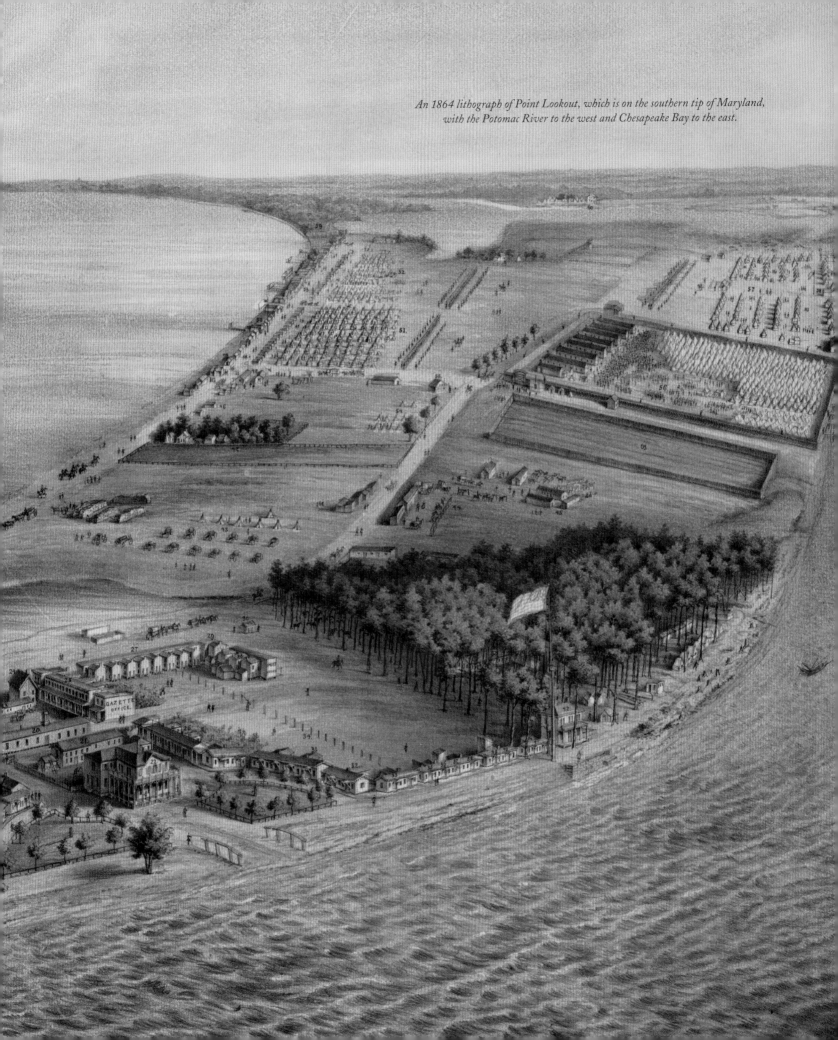

An 1864 lithograph of Point Lookout, which is on the southern tip of Maryland, with the Potomac River to the west and Chesapeake Bay to the east.

Shown here is a common, brutal method of whipping that used a paddle.

husbands and wives, parents and children. Added to this dread of separation, most painful to the majority of the slaves, we all had a decided
horror of falling into the hands of Master Andrew, who was distinguished for his cruelty and intemperance.

The thought of becoming the slave of Andrew Anthony—who but
a few days before the division, had, in my presence, seized my brother
Perry by the throat, dashed him on the ground, and with the heel of his
boot stamped him on the head, until the blood gushed from his nose
and ears—was terrible! This fiendish proceeding had no better apology
than the fact that Perry had gone to play when Master Andrew wanted
him for some trifling service. After inflicting this cruel treatment on
my brother, observing me, as I looked at him in astonishment, he said,
"That's the way I'll serve you, one of these days"; meaning, probably,
when I should come into his possession.

At last the anxiety and suspense were ended; and ended, thanks to
a kind Providence, in accordance with my wishes. I fell to the portion
of Mrs. Lucretia, the dear lady who bound up my head in her father's
kitchen, and shielded me from the maledictions of Aunt Katy.

Capt. Thomas Auld and Mrs. Lucretia at once decided on my
return to Baltimore. They knew how warmly Mrs. Hugh Auld was
attached to me, and how delighted Tommy would be to see me, and
withal, having no immediate use for me, they willingly concluded this
arrangement.

I need not stop to narrate my joy on finding myself back in Baltimore.
I was just one month absent, but the time seemed fully six months.

I had returned to Baltimore but a short time when the tidings
reached me that my kind friend, Mrs. Lucretia, was dead. She left one
child, a daughter, named Amanda, of whom I shall speak again. Shortly
after the death of Mrs. Lucretia, Master Andrew died, leaving a wife
and one child. Thus the whole family of Anthonys, as it existed when
I went to Col. Lloyd's place, was swept away during the first five years'
time of my residence at Master Hugh Auld's in Baltimore.

A print for a theatrical performance of Uncle Tom's Cabin.

The bullwhip became infamous as the overseer's
preferred instrument of cruelty.

No especial alternation took place in the condition of the slaves, in consequence of these deaths, yet I could not help the feeling that I was less secure now that Mrs. Lucretia was gone. While she lived, I felt that I had a strong friend to plead for me in any emergency.

Two years after the death of Mrs. Lucretia, Master Thomas married his second wife. Her name was Rowena Hamilton, the eldest daughter of Mr. William Hamilton, a rich slaveholder on the Eastern Shore of Maryland, who lived about five miles from St. Michaels, the then place of Master Thomas Auld's residence.

Not long after his marriage, Master Thomas had a misunderstanding with Master Hugh, and, as a means of punishing him, ordered him to send me home. As the ground of the misunderstanding will serve to illustrate the character of Southern chivalry and Southern humanity, fifty years ago, I will relate it.

Among the children of my Aunt Milly was a daughter named Henny. When quite a child, Henny had fallen into the fire and had burnt her hands so badly that they were of very little use to her. This unprofitable piece of property, ill-shapen, and disfigured, Capt. Auld sent off to Baltimore.

After giving poor Henny a fair trial, Master Hugh and his wife came to the conclusion that they had no use for the poor cripple, and they sent her back to Master Thomas. This the latter took as an act of ingratitude on the part of his brother and, as a mark of his displeasure, required him to send me immediately to St. Michaels, saying, "if he cannot keep Hen., he shan't have Fred."

A change had taken place, both in Master Hugh and in his once pious and affectionate wife. The influence of brandy and bad company on him, and of slavery and social isolation on her, had wrought disastrously upon the characters of both. Thomas was no longer "little Tommy," but was a big boy and had learned to assume towards me the airs of his class. My condition, therefore, in the house of Master Hugh was not by any means so comfortable as in former years. My attachments were now outside of our family. They were to those to whom I imparted instruction, and to those little white boys from whom I received instruction. There, too, was my dear old father, the pious Lawson, who was in all the Christian graces the very counterpart of "Uncle Tom"—the resemblance so perfect that he might have been the original of Mrs. Stowe's Christian hero.

In addition to the pain of parting from friends, as I supposed, forever, I had the added grief of neglected chances of escape to brood over.

In addition to the pain of parting from friends, as I supposed, forever, I had the added grief of neglected chances of escape to brood over. I had put off running away until I was now to be placed where opportunities for escape would be much more difficult, and less frequent.

As we sailed down the Chesapeake bay, on board the sloop *Amanda*, I formed many a plan for my future, beginning and ending in the same determination—to find some way yet of escape from slavery.

CHAPTER XIV

EXPERIENCE IN ST. MICHAELS

St. Michaels and its inhabitants—Capt. Auld—His new wife—Sufferings from hunger—Forced to steal—Argument in vindication thereof—Southern camp-meeting—What Capt. Auld did there—Hopes—Suspicions—The result—Faith and works at variance—Position in the church—Poor Cousin Henny—Methodist Preachers—Their disregard of the slaves—One exception—Sabbath-school—How and by whom broken up—Sad change in my prospects—Covey, the negro-breaker.

St. Michaels, the village in which was now my new home, compared favorably with villages in slave States generally, at this time—1833. There were a few comfortable dwellings in it, but the place as a whole wore a dull, slovenly, enterprise-forsaken aspect.

St. Michaels had, in former years, enjoyed some reputation as a ship-building community, but that business had almost entirely given place to oyster-fishing for the Baltimore and Philadelphia markets, a course of life highly unfavorable to morals, industry, and manners. Miles river was broad, and its oyster-fishing grounds were extensive, and the fishermen were, during autumn, winter and spring, often out all day and a part of the night. This exposure was an excuse for carrying with them, in considerable quantities, spirituous liquors, the then supposed best antidote for cold. This drinking habit, in an ignorant population, fostered coarseness, vulgarity, and an indolent disregard for the social improvement of the place, so that it was admitted by the few sober thinking people who remained there, that St. Michaels was an unsaintly, as well as unsightly place.

I went to St. Michaels to live in March, 1833. It was now more than seven years since I had lived with Master Thomas Auld, in the family of my old master, Capt. Anthony, on the home plantation of Col. Lloyd. I knew him then as the husband of old master's daughter; I had now to know him as my master. All my lessons concerning his temper and disposition, and the best methods of pleasing him, were yet to be learned. Slaveholders, however, were not very ceremonious in approaching a slave, and my ignorance of the new material in the shape of a master was but transient. Nor was my new mistress long in making known her animus. Unlike Miss Lucretia, whom I remembered with the tenderness which departed blessings leave, Mrs. Rowena Auld was as

This house in St. Michaels, Maryland, dates back to 1690.

A group of freed children in front of their school in South Carolina, circa 1862.

cold and cruel as her husband was stingy, and possessed the power to make him as cruel as herself, while she could easily descend to the level of his meanness.

As long as I lived in Mr. Hugh Auld's family, in whatever changes came over them there had always been a bountiful supply of food. Now, for the first time in seven years, I realized the pitiless pinchings of hunger. So wretchedly starved were we that we were compelled to live at the expense of our neighbors, or to steal from the home larder. We were often-times severely pinched with hunger, when meat and bread were mouldering under lock and key.

It was necessary that the right to steal from others should be established; and this could only rest upon a wider range of generalization than that which supposed the right to steal from my master. It was some time before I arrived at this clear right. As society has marked me out as privileged plunder, on the principle of self-preservation, I am justified in plundering in turn.

When I lived with Capt. Auld I thought him incapable of a noble action. His leading characteristic was intense selfishness. I think he was himself fully aware of this fact, and often tried to conceal it. Capt. Auld was not born a slaveholder. He was not a birthright member of the slaveholding oligarchy. The luxury of having slaves to wait upon him was new to Master Thomas, and for it he was wholly unprepared. He was a slaveholder, without the ability to hold or manage his slaves. Failing to command their respect, both himself and wife were ever on the alert lest some indignity should be offered them by the slaves.

It was in the month of August, 1833, when I had become almost desperate under the treatment of Master Thomas, and entertained more strongly than ever the oft-repeated determination to run away, that a circumstance occurred which seemed to promise brighter and better days for us all. At a Methodist camp-meeting, held in the Bay side (a famous place for camp-meetings), about eight miles from St. Michaels, Master Thomas came out with a profession of religion. He had long been an object of interest to the church; a fish quite worth catching, for he had money and standing. In the community of St. Michaels he was equal to the best citizen. He was strictly temperate, and there was little to do for him in order to give him the appearance of piety and to make him a pillar of the church. Well, the camp-meeting continued a week; people gathered from all parts of the country, and two steamboats came loaded from Baltimore. After the preaching was over, at every service, an invitation was given to mourners to come forward into the pen; and in some cases, ministers went out to persuade men and women to come in. By one of these ministers Master Thomas was persuaded to go inside the pen. I was deeply interested in that matter, and followed; and though colored people were not allowed either in the pen, or in front of the preacher's stand, I ventured to take my stand at a sort of half-way place between the blacks and whites, where I could distinctly see the movements of the mourners, and especially the progress of Master Thomas. "If he has got religion," thought I, "he will emancipate his slaves; or, if he should not do so much as this, he will at any rate behave towards us more kindly, and feed us more generously than he has heretofore done." But in my expectations I was doubly disappointed: Master Thomas was Master Thomas still. The fruits of his righteousness were to show themselves in no such way as I had anticipated. His conversion was not to change his relation toward men—at any rate not toward BLACK men—but toward God.

There was always a scarcity of good-nature about the man; but now his whole countenance was soured all over with the seemings of piety, and he became more rigid and stringent in his exactions. If religion had any effect at all on him, it made him more cruel and hateful in all his ways. His house, being one of the holiest in St. Michaels, became the "preachers' home." They evidently liked to share his hospitality; for while he starved us, he stuffed them— three or four of these "ambassadors" not unfrequently being there at a time and all living on the fat of the land while we in the kitchen were worse than hungry. Not often did we get a smile of recognition from these holy men. They seemed about as unconcerned about our getting to heaven as about our getting out of slavery. To this general charge I must make one exception—the Reverend George Cookman. There was not a slave in our neighborhood who did not love and venerate Mr. Cookman. It was pretty generally believed that he had been instrumental in bringing one of the largest slaveholders in that neighborhood—Mr. Samuel Harrison—to emancipate all his slaves, and the general impression about Mr. Cookman was, that whenever he met slaveholders he labored faithfully with them, as a religious duty, to induce them to liberate their bondmen. When this good man was at our house, we were all sure to be called in to prayers in the morning; and he was not slow in making inquiries as to the state of our minds, nor in giving us a word of exhortation and of encouragement.

But to my experience with Master Thomas after his conversion. In Baltimore I could occasionally get into a Sabbath-school amongst the free children and receive lessons with the rest; but having already learned to read and write I was more a teacher than a scholar, even there. When, however, I went back to the eastern shore and was at the house of Master Thomas, I was not allowed either to teach or to be taught. The whole community among the whites, with but one single exception, frowned upon everything like imparting instruction, either to slaves or to free colored persons. That single exception, a pious young man named Wilson, asked me one day if I would like to assist him in teaching a little Sabbath-school at the house of a free colored man named James Mitchell. The idea to me was a delightful one and I told him that I would gladly devote to that most laudable work as many of my Sabbaths as I could command. I learned there were some objections to the existence of our school; and, surely enough, we had scarcely got to work—good work, simply teaching a few colored children how to read the gospel of the Son of God—when in rushed a mob, headed by two class-leaders, Mr. Wright Fairbanks and Mr. Garrison West, and with them Master Thomas. They were armed with sticks and other missiles and drove us off, commanding us never again to meet for such a purpose. Thus ended the Sabbath-school; and the reader will not be surprised that this conduct, on the part of class-leaders and professedly holy men, did not serve to strengthen my religious convictions. The cloud over my St. Michaels home grew heavier and blacker than ever.

The many differences springing up between Master Thomas and myself, owing to the clear perception I had of his character, and the boldness with which I defended myself against his capricious complaints, led him to declare that I was unsuited to his wants; that my city life had affected me perniciously; that in fact it had almost ruined me for every good purpose, and had fitted me for everything bad. Master Thomas at last resolved to endure my behavior no longer. I had lived with him nearly nine months and he had given me a number of severe whippings, without any visible improvement in my character or conduct, and now he was resolved to put me out, as he said, "to be broken."

There was, in the Bay-side, very near the camp-ground where my master received his religious impressions, a man named Edward Covey, who enjoyed the reputation of being a first rate hand at breaking young negroes. This Covey was a poor man, a farm renter; and his reputation of being a good hand to break in slaves was of immense pecuniary advantage to him, since it enabled him to get his farm tilled with very little expense, compared with what it would have cost him otherwise. Some slaveholders thought it an advantage to let Mr. Covey have the government of their slaves a year or two, almost free of charge, for the sake of the excellent training they had under his management. Like some horse-breakers noted for their skill, who ride the best horses in the country without expense, Mr. Covey could have under him the most fiery bloods of the neighborhood, for the simple reward of returning them to their owners well broken.

CHAPTER XV

COVEY, THE NEGRO BREAKER

JOURNEY TO COVEY'S—COVEY'S HOUSE—FAMILY—AWKWARDNESS AS A FIELD HAND—A CRUEL BEATING—WHY GIVEN—DESCRIPTION OF COVEY—FIRST ATTEMPT AT DRIVING OXEN—HAIR-BREADTH ESCAPE—OX AND MAN ALIKE PROPERTY—HARD LABOR MORE EFFECTIVE THAN THE WHIP FOR BREAKING DOWN THE SPIRIT—CUNNING AND TRICKERY OF COVEY—FAMILY WORSHIP—SHOCKING AND INDECENT CONTEMPT FOR CHASTITY—ANGUISH BEYOND DESCRIPTION.

The morning of January 1, 1834, with its chilling wind and pinching frost, quite in harmony with the winter in my own mind, found me, with my little bundle of clothing on the end of a stick swung across my shoulder, on the main road bending my way towards Covey's, whither I had been imperiously ordered by Master Thomas. He had been as good as his word, and had committed me without reserve to the mastery of that hard man. Eight or ten years had now passed since I had been taken from my grandmother's cabin in Tuckahoe; and these years, for the most part, I had spent in Baltimore, where, as the reader has already seen, I was treated with comparative tenderness. I was now about to sound profounder depths in slave life. Starvation made me glad to leave Thomas Auld's, and the cruel lash made me dread to go to Covey's. Escape, however, was impossible; so, heavy and sad, I paced the seven miles which lay between his house and St. Michaels, thinking much by the solitary way, of my adverse condition.

The good clothes I had brought with me from Baltimore were now worn thin, and had not been replaced; for Master Thomas was as little careful to provide against cold as against hunger. Met here by a north wind sweeping through an open space of forty miles, I was glad to make any port, and, therefore, I speedily pressed on to the wood-colored house. The family consisted of Mr. and Mrs. Covey; Mrs. Kemp (a broken-backed woman), sister to Mrs. Covey; William Hughes, cousin to Mr. Covey; Caroline, the cook; Bill Smith, a hired man, and myself. Bill Smith, Bill Hughes, and myself were the working force of the farm, which comprised three or four hundred acres. I was now for the first time in my life to be a field-hand; and in my new employment I found myself even more awkward than a green country boy may be supposed to be upon his first entrance into the bewildering scenes of city life. My awkwardness gave me much trouble. Strange and unnatural as it may seem, I had been in my new home but three days before Mr.

This now-famous image shows the astounding and atrocious punishment overseers inflicted on enslaved people.

Covey (my brother in the Methodist church) gave me a bitter foretaste of what was in reserve for me. I presume he thought that, since he had but a single year in which to complete his work, the sooner he began the better. Perhaps he thought that by coming to blows at once we should mutually better understand our relations to each other. But to whatever motive, direct or indirect, the cause may be referred, I had not been in his possession three whole days before he subjected me to a most brutal chastisement. Under his heavy blows blood flowed freely, and wales were left on my back as large as my little finger. The sores from this flogging continued for weeks, for they were kept open by the rough and coarse cloth which I wore for shirting. The occasion and details of this first chapter of my experience as a field-hand must be told, that the reader may see how unreasonable, as well as how cruel, my new Master Covey was. The whole thing I found to be characteristic of the man, and I was probably treated no worse by him than had been scores of lads previously committed to him. But here are the facts connected with the affair, precisely as they occurred.

On one of the coldest mornings of the whole month of January, 1834, I was ordered at daybreak to get a load of wood, from a forest about two miles from the house. In order to perform this work, Mr. Covey gave me a pair of unbroken oxen, for it seemed that his breaking abilities had not been turned in that direction. In due form, and with all proper ceremony, I was introduced to this huge yoke of unbroken oxen, and was carefully made to understand which was "Buck," and which was "Darby,"—which was the "in hand" ox, and which was the "off hand." The master of this important ceremony was no less a person than Mr. Covey himself, and the introduction was the first of the kind I had ever had.

My life, hitherto, had been quite away from horned cattle, and I had no knowledge of the art of managing them. After initiating me into the use of the "whoa," "back," "gee," "Lither,"—the entire language spoken between oxen and driver,—Mr. Covey took a rope about ten feet long and one inch thick, and placed one end of it around the horns of the "in hand ox," and gave the other end to me, telling me that if the oxen started to run away (as the scamp knew they would), I must hold on to the rope and stop them. With his directions, and without stopping to question, I started for the woods. The distance from the house to the wood's gate—a full mile, I should think—was passed over with little

difficulty: for, although the animals ran, I was fleet enough in the open field to keep pace with them, especially as they pulled me along at the end of the rope; but on reaching the woods, I was speedily thrown into a distressing plight. The animals took fright, and started off ferociously into the woods, carrying the cart full tilt against trees, over stumps, and dashing from side to side in a manner altogether frightful. As I held the rope I expected every moment to be crushed between the cart and the huge trees, among which they were so furiously dashing. After running thus for several minutes, my oxen were finally brought to a stand, by a tree, against which they dashed themselves with great violence, upsetting the cart, and entangling themselves among sundry young saplings. By the shock the body of the cart was flung in one direction and the wheels and tongue in another, and all in the greatest confusion. There I was, all alone in a thick wood to which I was a stranger; my cart upset and shattered, my oxen, wild and enraged, were entangled, and I, poor soul, was but a green hand to set all this disorder right.

After standing a few minutes, surveying the damage, and not without a presentiment that this trouble would draw after it others, even more distressing, I took one end of the cart-body and, by an extra outlay of strength, I lifted it toward the axle-tree, from which it had been violently flung. After much pulling and straining, I succeeded in getting the body of the cart in its place. The cart was provided with an ax—with this I cut down the saplings by which my oxen were entangled, and again pursued my journey. On reaching the part of the forest where I had, the day before, been chopping wood, I filled the cart with a heavy load.

Half of the day was already gone and I had not yet turned my face homeward. It required only two days' experience and observation to teach me that no such apparent waste of time would be lightly overlooked by Covey. I therefore hurried toward home; but in reaching the lane gate I met the crowning disaster of the day. This gate was a fair specimen of southern handicraft, so hung on one that it opened only about half the proper distance. On arriving here it was necessary for me to let go the end of the rope on the horns of the "in-hand ox";

Jim Crow, dressed in rags, was an offensive caricature of an enslaved African American man. A white actor, Thomas Rice (1880–1860), was the original performer to play this role, though not the first to perform in blackface.

A circa 1830 engraving of an overseer whipping an enslaved man.

and as soon as the gate was open and I let go of it to get the rope again, off went my oxen, full tilt; making nothing of their load, as, catching the huge gate between the wheel and the cart-body, they literally crushed it to splinters and came within only a few inches of subjecting me to a similar catastrophe, for I was just in advance of the wheel when it struck the left gate-post. With these two hair-breadth escapes I thought I could successfully explain to Mr. Covey the delay and avert punishment. On coming to him his countenance assumed an aspect of rigid displeasure, and as I gave him a history of the casualties of my trip, his wolfish face, with his greenish eyes, became intensely ferocious. "Go back to the woods again," he said, muttering something else about wasting time. I hastily obeyed, but I had not gone far on my way when I saw him coming after me. My oxen now behaved themselves with singular propriety, contrasting their present conduct to my representation of their former antics, readily obeying orders, and seeming to understand them quite as well as I did myself. On reaching the woods, my tormenter, who seemed all the time to be remarking to himself upon the good behavior of the oxen, came up to me and ordered me to stop the cart, accompanying the same with the threat that he would now teach me how to break gates and idle

This 1868 lithograph by Currier & Ives depicts an idealized American farm.

This historic photograph shows enslaved people being kept at cabins while they were being raised for the market.

consisted, I should think, in this species of cunning. We were never secure. He was, to us, behind every stump, tree, bush, and fence on the plantation. He carried this kind of trickery so far that he would sometimes mount his horse and make believe he was going to St. Michaels, and in thirty minutes afterwards you might find his horse tied in the woods, and the snake-like Covey lying flat in the ditch with his head lifted above its edge, or in a fence-corner, watching every movement of the slaves.

But with Mr. Covey trickery was natural. Everything in the shape of learning or religion which he possessed was made to conform to this semi-lying propensity. He did not seem conscious that the practice had anything unmanly, base or contemptible about it. It was with him a part of an important system essential to the relation of master and slave.

I have already implied that Mr. Edward Covey was a poor man. He was, in fact, just commencing to lay the foundation of his fortune, as fortune was regarded in a slave state. The first condition of wealth and respectability there being the ownership of human property, every nerve was strained by the poor man to obtain it, with little regard sometimes as to the means. In pursuit of this object, pious as Mr. Covey was, he proved himself as unscrupulous and base as the worst of his neighbors. In the beginning he was only able—as he said—"to buy one slave"; and scandalous and shocking as is the fact, he boasted that he bought her simply "as a breeder." But the worst of this is not told in this naked statement. This young woman (Caroline was her name) was virtually compelled by Covey to abandon herself to the object for which he had purchased her; and the result was the birth of twins at the end of the year. At this addition to his human stock Covey and his wife were ecstatic with joy. No one dreamed of reproaching the woman or of finding fault with the hired man, Bill Smith, the father of the children, for Mr. Covey himself had locked the two up together every night, thus inviting the result.

I shall never be able to narrate half the mental experience through which it was my lot to pass, during my stay at Covey's. I was completely wrecked, changed, and bewildered; goaded almost to madness at one time, and at another reconciling myself to my wretched condition. All the kindness I had received at Baltimore, all my former hopes and aspirations for usefulness in the world, and even the happy moments spent in the exercises of religion, contrasted with my then present lot, served but to increase my anguish.

I suffered bodily as well as mentally. I had neither sufficient time in which to eat, or to sleep, except on Sundays. The over-work, and the brutal chastisements of which I was the victim, combined with that ever-gnawing and soul-devouring thought—"I am a slave—a slave for life—a slave with no rational ground to hope for freedom"—rendered me a living embodiment of mental and physical wretchedness.

away my time when he sent me to the woods. This flogging was the first of a series of floggings, and though very severe, it was less so than many which came after it, and these for offences far lighter than the gate-breaking.

I remained with Mr. Covey one year (I cannot say I lived with him), and during the first six months that I was there I was whipped, either with sticks or cow-skins, every week. Aching bones and a sore back were my constant companions. Frequent as the lash was used, Mr. Covey thought less of it as a means of breaking down my spirit than that of hard and continued labor. He worked me steadily up to the point of my powers of endurance. From the dawn of day in the morning till the darkness was complete in the evening, I was kept hard at work in the field or the woods. Covey would attend us in the field and urge us on with words or blows, as it seemed best to him. It was, however, scarcely necessary for Mr. Covey to be really present in the field to have his work go on industriously. He had the faculty of making us feel that he was always present. By a series of adroitly managed surprises which he practiced, I was prepared to expect him at any moment. One-half of his proficiency in the art of negro-breaking

CHAPTER XVI

ANOTHER PRESSURE OF THE TYRANT'S VISE

EXPERIENCE AT COVEY'S SUMMED UP—FIRST SIX MONTHS SEVERER THAN THE REMAINING SIX—PRELIMINARIES TO THE CHANGE—REASONS FOR NARRATING THE CIRCUMSTANCES—SCENE IN THE TREADING-YARD—AUTHOR TAKEN ILL—ESCAPES TO ST. MICHAELS—THE PURSUIT—SUFFERING IN THE WOODS—TALK WITH MASTER THOMAS—DRIVEN BACK TO COVEY'S—THE SLAVE'S NEVER SICK—NATURAL TO EXPECT THEM TO FEIGN SICKNESS—LAZINESS OF SLAVEHOLDERS.

The reader has but to repeat, in his mind, once a week the scene in the woods, where Covey subjected me to his merciless lash, to have a true idea of my bitter experience, during the first six months of the breaking process through which he carried me. I have no heart to repeat each separate transaction. Such a narration would fill a volume much larger than the present one. I aim only to give the reader a truthful impression of my slave-life, without unnecessarily affecting him with harrowing details.

You have, dear reader, seen me humbled, degraded, broken down, enslaved, and brutalized; and you understand how it was done; now let us see the converse of all this, and how it was brought about; and this will take us through the year 1834. On one of the hottest days of the month of August of the year just mentioned, had the reader been passing through Covey's farm, he might have seen me at work in what was called the "treading-yard"—a yard upon which wheat was trodden out from the straw by the horses' feet. About three o'clock, while the sun was pouring down his burning rays, and not a breeze was stirring, I broke down; my strength failed me; I was seized with a violent aching of the head, attended with extreme dizziness, and trembling in every limb. Finding what was coming, and feeling that it would never do to stop work, I nerved myself up and staggered on, until I fell by the side of the wheat fan, with a feeling that the earth had fallen in upon me. This brought the entire work to a dead stand. There was work for four: each one had his part to perform, and each part depended on the other, so that when one stopped, all were compelled to stop. Covey, who had become my dread, was at the house, about a hundred yards from where I was fanning, and instantly, upon hearing the fan stop, he came down to the treading-yard to inquire into the cause of the interruption. Bill Smith told him that I was sick and unable longer to bring wheat to the fan.

African Americans working a cotton field.

This photo shows an auction house in Atlanta, Georgia, that was put out of use by General Sherman at the end of the Civil War.

I had by this time crawled away in the shade, under the side of a post-and-rail fence, and was exceedingly ill. In this condition Covey, finding out where I was, came to me, and after standing over me a while asked what the matter was. I told him as well as I could, for it was with difficulty that I could speak. He gave me a savage kick in the side which jarred my whole frame, and commanded me to get up. I made an effort to rise, but fell back in the attempt before gaining my feet. While down in this sad condition, and perfectly helpless, the merciless negro-breaker took up the hickory slab (a very hard weapon), and, with the edge of it, he dealt me a heavy blow on my head which made a large gash, and caused the blood to run freely, saying at the same time, "If you have got the headache I'll cure you." This done, he ordered me again to rise, but I made no effort to do so, for I had now made up my mind that it was useless and that the heartless villain might do his worst. He could but kill me and that might put me out of my misery. Finding me unable to rise, Covey left me, with a view to getting on with the work without me. I was bleeding very freely, and my face was soon covered with my warm blood. Cruel and merciless as was the motive that dealt that blow, the wound was a fortunate one for me. Bleeding was never more efficacious. The pain in my head speedily abated, and I was soon able to rise. Covey had, as I have said, left me to my fate, and the question was, shall I return to my work, or shall I find my way to St. Michaels and make Capt. Auld acquainted with the atrocious cruelty of his brother Covey, and beseech him to get me another master? Remembering the object he had in view in placing me under the management of Covey, and further, his cruel treat-ment of my poor crippled cousin Henny, and his meanness in the matter of feeding and clothing his slaves, there was little ground to hope for a favorable reception at the hands of Capt. Thomas Auld. Nevertheless, I resolved to go straight to him, thinking that, if not animated by motives of humanity, he might be induced to interfere on my behalf from selfish considerations. "He cannot," I thought, "allow his property to be thus bruised and battered, marred and defaced, and I will go to him about the matter." I watched my chance while the cruel and cunning Covey was looking in an opposite direction, and started off across the field for St. Michaels. This was a daring step. If it failed it would only exasperate Covey and increase during the remainder of my term of service under him, the rigors of my bondage. But the step was taken and I must go for-ward. I succeeded in getting nearly half way across the broad field toward the woods, when Covey observed me. I was still bleeding and the exertion of running had started the blood afresh. "Come back! Come back!" he vociferated, with threats of what he would do if I did not instantly return. But, disregarding his calls and threats, I pressed on toward the woods as fast as my feeble state would allow. Seeing no signs of my stopping, he caused his horse to be brought out and saddled, as if he intended to pur-sue me. The race was now to be an unequal one, and thinking I might be overhauled by him if I kept the main road, I walked nearly the whole dis-tance in the woods, keeping far enough from the road to avoid detection

This print idealizes the American slave system to an absurd degree. In the full illustration there is dialogue in which the old man says, "God Bless you massa! you feed and clothe us. When we are sick you nurse us, and when too old to work, you provide for us!" The master states, "These poor creatures are a sacred legacy from my ancestors and while a dollar is left me, nothing shall be spared to increase their comfort and happiness."

and pursuit. But I had not gone far before my little strength again failed me, and I was obliged to lie down. After lying there about three-quarters of an hour, I again took up my journey toward St. Michaels. I was barefooted, bare-headed, and in my shirt-sleeves. The way was through briers and bogs, and I tore my feet often during the journey. I was full five hours in going the seven or eight miles; partly because of the difficulties of the way, and partly because of the feebleness induced by my illness, bruises, and loss of blood.

On gaining my master's store, I presented an appearance of wretchedness and woe calculated to move any but a heart of stone. From the crown of my head to the sole of my feet, there were marks of blood. My hair was all clotted with dust and blood, and the back of my shirt was literally stiff with the same. Briers and thorns had scarred and torn my feet and legs. In this plight I appeared before my professedly Christian master, humbly to invoke the interposition of his power and authority, to protect me from further abuse and violence. But I had jumped from a sinking ship into the sea. At first Master Thomas seemed somewhat affected by the story of my wrongs, but he soon repressed whatever feeling he may have had, and became as cold and hard as iron. He began moderately by finding excuses for Covey, and ended with a full justification of him, and a passionate condemnation of me. He had no doubt I deserved the flogging. He did not believe I was sick; I was only endeavoring to get rid of work. With such a knock-down to all my hopes, and feeling as I did my entire subjection to his power, I had very little heart to reply. Calming down a little, in view of my silence and hesitation,

and perhaps a little touched at my forlorn and miserable appearance, he inquired again, what I wanted him to do? Thus invited a second time, I told him I wished him to allow me to get a new home, and to find a new master; that as sure as I went back to live again with Mr. Covey, I should be killed by him; that he would never forgive my coming home with complaints; that since I had lived with him he had almost crushed my spirit, and I believed he would ruin me for future service and that my life was not safe in his hands. This Master Thomas (my brother in the church) regarded as "non-sense." "You belong to Mr. Covey for one year, and you must go back to him, come what will; and you must not trouble me with any more stories; and if you don't go immediately home, I'll get hold of you myself." This was just what I expected when I found he had prejudged the case against me. "But, sir," I said, "I am sick and tired, and I cannot get home to-night." At this he somewhat relented, and finally allowed me to stay the night, but said I must be off early in the morning, and concluded his directions by making me swallow a huge dose of Epsom salts, which was about the only medicine ever administered to slaves.

It was quite natural for Master Thomas to presume I was feigning sickness to escape work, for he probably thought that were he in the place of a slave, with no wages for his work, no praise for well-doing, no motive for toil but the lash, he would try every possible scheme by which to escape labor. These men did indeed literally "bind heavy burdens, grievous to be borne, and laid them upon men's shoulders, but they themselves would not move them with one of their fingers."

CHAPTER XVII

THE LAST FLOGGING

A SLEEPLESS NIGHT—RETURN TO COVEY'S—PUNISHED BY HIM—
THE CHASE DEFEATED—VENGEANCE POSTPONED—MUSINGS IN THE
WOODS—THE ALTERNATIVE—DEPLORABLE SPECTACLE—NIGHT IN THE
WOODS—EXPECTED ATTACK—ACCOSTED BY SANDY—A FRIEND, NOT A
MASTER—SANDY'S HOSPITALITY—THE ASH-CAKE SUPPER—INTERVIEW
WITH SANDY—HIS ADVICE—SANDY A CONJUROR AS WELL AS A
CHRISTIAN—THE MAGIC ROOT—STRANGE MEETING WITH COVEY—HIS
MANNER—COVEY'S SUNDAY FACE—AUTHOR'S DEFENSIVE RESOLVE—
THE FIGHT—THE VICTORY, AND ITS RESULTS.

I remained—sleep I did not—all night at St. Michaels, and in the morning (Saturday) I started off, obedient to the order of Master Thomas, feeling that I had no friend on earth, and doubting if I had one in heaven. I reached Covey's about nine o'clock; and just as I stepped into the field, before I had reached the house, true to his snakish habits, Covey darted out at me from a fence corner, in which he had secreted himself for the purpose of securing me. He was provided with a cowskin and a rope, and he evidently intended to tie me up, and wreak his vengeance on me to the fullest extent. I should have been an easy prey had he succeeded in getting his hands upon me, for I had taken no refreshment since noon on Friday; and this, with the other trying circumstances, had greatly reduced my strength. I, however, darted back into the woods before the ferocious hound could reach me, and buried myself in a thicket, where he lost sight of me.

Life in itself had almost become burdensome to me. I was weak from the toils of the previous day and from want of food and sleep, and I had been so little concerned about my appearance that I had not yet washed the blood from my garments. That day, in the woods, I would have exchanged my manhood for the brutehood of an ox.

Night came. I was still in the woods, and still unresolved what to do. I had come to the conclusion that Covey relied upon hunger to drive me home, and in this I was quite correct, for he made no effort to catch me after the morning. During the night I heard the step of a man in the woods. I hid myself in the leaves to prevent discovery. But as the night rambler in the woods drew nearer I found him to be a friend, not an enemy; a slave of Mr. William Groomes of Easton, a kind-hearted fellow named "Sandy." Sandy lived that year with Mr. Kemp, about four miles from St. Michaels. He, like myself, had been hired out, but unlike myself had not been hired out to be broken. He was the husband of a free woman who lived in the lower part of "Poppie Neck," and he was now on his way through the woods to see her and to spend the Sabbath with her.

Enslaved people in Santo Domingo rising up against the white masters in 1791.

This Zulu African witch doctor, circa 1920 but much unchanged since the time when people were captured in Africa for slavery in America, personifies the roots of Sandy's magical practices.

As soon as I had ascertained that the disturber of my solitude was not an enemy, but the good-hearted Sandy, I came out from my hiding-place and made myself known to him. I explained the circumstances of the past two days which had driven me to the woods, and he deeply compassionated my distress. It was a bold thing for him to shelter me, for had I been found in his hut he would have suffered the penalty of thirty-nine lashes on his bare back, if not something worse. But Sandy was too generous to permit the fear of punishment to prevent his relieving a brother bondman from hunger and exposure, and therefore, on his own motion, I accompanied him home to his wife—for the house and lot were hers, as she was a free woman. It was about midnight, but his wife was called up, a fire was made, some Indian meal was soon mixed with salt and water, and an ash-cake was baked in a hurry, to relieve my hunger. Sandy's wife was not behind him in kindness; both seemed to esteem it a privilege to succor me, for although I was hated by Covey and by my master I was loved by the colored people, because they thought I was hated for my knowledge, and persecuted because I was feared. I was the only slave in that region who could read or write. The supper was soon ready, and though over the sea I have since feasted with honorables, lord mayors and aldermen, my supper on ash-cake and cold water, with Sandy, was the meal of all my life most sweet to my taste and now most vivid to my memory.

I found Sandy an old adviser. He was not only a religious man, but he professed to believe in a system for which I have no name. He was a genuine African, and had inherited some of the so-called magical powers said to be possessed by the eastern nations. He told me that he could help me; that in those very woods there was an herb which in the morning might be found, possessing all the powers required for my protection (I put his words in my own language), and that if I would take his advice he would procure me the root of the herb of which he spoke. He told me, further, that if I would take that root and wear it on my right side it would be impossible for Covey to strike me a blow, and that, with this root about my person, no white man could whip me.

Now all this talk about the root was to me very absurd and ridiculous, if not positively sinful. I at first rejected the idea that the simple carrying a root on my right side (a root, by the way, over which I walked every time I went into the woods) could possess any such magic power as he ascribed to it, and I was, therefore, not disposed to cumber my pocket with it. I had a positive aversion to all pretenders to "divination." But Sandy was so earnest and so confident of the good qualities of this weed that, to please him, I was induced to take it.

This was of course Sunday morning. Sandy now urged me to go home with all speed, and to walk up bravely to the house, as though nothing had happened. I saw in Sandy, with all his superstition, too deep an insight into human nature not to have some respect for his advice; and perhaps, too, a slight gleam or shadow of his superstition had fallen on me. At any rate, I started off toward Covey's, as directed. Singularly enough, just as I entered the yard-gate I met him and his wife on their way to church, dressed in their Sunday best, and looking as smiling as angels. His manner perfectly astonished me. There was something really benignant in his countenance. He spoke to me as never before, told me that the pigs had got into the lot and he wished me to go to drive them out; inquired how I was, and seemed an altered man. This extraordinary conduct really made me begin to think that Sandy's herb had more virtue in it than I, in my pride, had been willing to allow. I suspected, however, that the Sabbath, not the root, was the real explanation of the change.

All went well with me till Monday morning; and then, whether the root had lost its virtue, or whether my tormentor had gone deeper into the black art than I had (as was sometimes said of him), or whether he had obtained a special indulgence for his faithful Sunday's worship, it is not necessary for me to know or to inform the reader; but this much I may say, the pious and benignant smile which graced the face of Covey on Sunday wholly disappeared on Monday.

Long before daylight I was called up to go feed, rub, and curry the horses. I obeyed the call, as I should have done had it been made at an earlier hour, for I had brought my mind to a firm resolve during that Sunday's reflection to obey every order, however unreasonable, if it were possible, and if Mr. Covey should then undertake to beat me to defend and protect myself to the best of my ability.

While I was obeying his order to feed and get the horses ready for the field, and when I was in the act of going up the stable-loft, for the purpose of throwing down some blades, Covey sneaked into the stable, in his peculiar way, and seizing me suddenly by the leg, he brought me to the stable-floor, giving my newly-mended body a terrible jar. I now forgot all about my roots, and remembered my pledge to stand up in my own defense. The brute was skillfully endeavoring to get a slip-knot on my legs, before I could draw up my feet. As soon as I found what he was up to, I gave a sudden spring (my two days' rest had been of much service to me) and by that means, no doubt, he was able to bring me to the floor so heavily. I was resolved to fight, and what was better still, I actually was hard at it. The fighting madness had come upon me, and I found my strong fingers firmly attached to the throat of the tyrant, as heedless of consequences, at the moment, as if we stood as equals before the law. But the conflict did not long remain equal. Covey soon cried lustily for help; not that I was obtaining any marked advantage over him, or was injuring him but because he was gaining none over me, and was not able, single-handed, to conquer me. He called for his cousin Hughes to come to his assistance, and now the scene was changed. I was compelled to give blows, as well as to parry them, and since I was in any case to suffer for resistance, I felt (as the musty proverb goes) that I "might as well be hanged for an old sheep as a lamb." I was still defensive toward Covey, but aggressive toward Hughes, on whom, at his first approach, I dealt a blow which fairly sickened him. He went off, bending over with pain, and manifesting no disposition to come again within my reach.

Taken completely by surprise, Covey seemed to have lost his usual strength and coolness. He was frightened, and stood puffing and blowing, seemingly unable to command words or blows. When he saw that Hughes was standing half bent with pain, his courage quite gone, the cowardly tyrant asked if I "meant to persist in my resistance." I told him I "did mean to resist, come what might; that I had been treated like a brute during the last six months, and that I should stand it no longer." With that he attempted to drag me toward a stick of wood. He meant to knock me down with it; but, just as he leaned over to get the stick, I seized him with both hands, by the collar, and with a vigorous and sudden snatch brought my assailant harmlessly, his full length, on the not over-clean ground, for we were now in the cow-yard.

By this time Bill, the hired man, came home. Covey and I had been skirmishing from before daybreak till now. The sun was shooting his beams almost over the eastern woods, and we were still at it. I could not see where the matter was to terminate. He evidently was afraid to let me go, lest I should again make off to the woods, otherwise he would probably have obtained arms from the house to frighten me. Holding me, he called upon Bill to assist him. The scene here had something comic about it. Bill, who knew precisely what Covey wished him to do, affected ignorance, and pretended he did not know what to do. "What shall I do, Master Covey?" said Bill. "Take hold of him!—take hold of him!" cried Covey. With a toss of his head, peculiar to Bill, he said: "Indeed, Master Covey, I want to go to work." "This is your work," said Covey; "take hold of him." Bill replied, with spirit: "My master hired me here to work, and not to help you whip Frederick." It was my turn to speak. "Bill," said I, "don't put your hands on me." To which he replied: "My God, Frederick, I ain't goin' to tech ye"; and Bill walked off, leaving Covey and myself to settle our differences as best we might.

But my present advantage was threatened when I saw Caroline (the slave woman of Covey) coming to the cow-yard to milk, for she was a powerful woman, and could have mastered me easily, exhausted as I was. As soon as she came near, Covey attempted to rally her to his aid.

This turn-of-the-century scene of an African American couple in a cabin in rural Virginia resembles the home of Sandy and his wife.

Strangely and fortunately, Caroline was in no humor to take a hand in any such sport. We were all in open rebellion that morning.

At length (two hours had elapsed) the contest was given over. Letting go of me, puffing and blowing at a great rate, Covey said: "Now, you scoundrel, go to your work; I would not have whipped you half so hard if you had not resisted." The fact was, he had not whipped me at all. He had not, in all the scuffle, drawn a single drop of blood from me. I had drawn blood from him, and should even without this satisfaction have been victorious, because my aim had not been to injure him, but to prevent his injuring me.

During the whole six months that I lived with Covey after this transaction, he never again laid the weight of his finger on me in anger. He would occasionally say he did not want to have to get hold of me again—a declaration which I had no difficulty in believing; and I had a secret feeling which answered, "You had better not wish to get hold of me again, for you will be likely to come off worse in a second fight than you did in the first."

This battle with Mr. Covey, undignified as it was and as I fear my narration of it is, was the turning-point in my "life as a slave." It rekindled in my breast the smouldering embers of liberty. It brought up my Baltimore dreams and revived a sense of my own manhood. I was a changed being after that fight. I was nothing before; I was a man now.

The reader may like to know why, after I had so grievously offended Mr. Covey, he did not have me taken in hand by the authorities; indeed, why the law of Maryland, which assigned hanging to the slave who resisted his master, was not put in force against me, at any rate why I was not taken up, as was usual in such cases, and publicly whipped as an example to other slaves, and as a means of deterring me from again committing the same offence. I confess that the easy manner in which I got off was always a surprise to me, and even now I cannot fully explain the cause, though the probability is that Covey was ashamed to have it known that he had been mastered by a boy of sixteen.

CHAPTER XVIII

NEW RELATIONS AND DUTIES

CHANGE OF MASTERS—BENEFITS DERIVED BY CHANGE—FAME OF THE FIGHT WITH COVEY—RECKLESS UNCONCERN—AUTHOR'S ABHORRENCE OF SLAVERY—ABILITY TO READ A CAUSE OF PREJUDICE—EFFECTS OF HOLIDAYS—DIFFERENCE BETWEEN COVEY AND FREELAND—IMPROVED CONDITION DOES NOT BRING CONTENTMENT—CONGENIAL SOCIETY AT FREELAND'S—AUTHOR'S SABBATH-SCHOOL—CONFIDENCE AND FRIENDSHIP AMONG SLAVES—SLAVERY THE INVITER OF VENGEANCE.

My term of service with Edward Covey expired on Christmas day, 1834. I gladly-enough left him, although he was by this time as gentle as a lamb. My home for the year 1835 was already secured, my next master selected. There was always more or less excitement about the changing of hands, but determined to fight my way, I had become somewhat reckless and cared little into whose hands I fell. The report got abroad that I was hard to whip; that I was guilty of kicking back, and that, though generally a good-natured negro, I sometimes "got the devil in me." This made me a marked lad among the slaves, and a suspected one among slaveholders. A knowledge also of my ability to read and write got pretty widely spread, which was very much against me.

The days between Christmas day and New Year's were allowed the slaves as holidays. During these days all regular work was suspended, and there was nothing to do but to keep fires and look after the stock. We regarded this time as our own by the grace of our masters, and we therefore used it or abused it as we pleased. Those who had families at a distance were expected to visit them and spend with them the entire week. The younger slaves or the unmarried ones were expected to see to the animals and attend to incidental duties at home.

To enslave men successfully and safely it is necessary to keep their minds occupied with thoughts and aspirations short of the liberty of which they are deprived. A certain degree of attainable good must be kept before them. These holidays served the purpose of keeping the minds of the slaves occupied with prospective pleasure within the limits of slavery. The young man could go wooing, the married man to see his wife, the father and mother to see their children, the industrious and money-loving could make a few dollars, the great wrestler could win laurels, the young people meet and enjoy each other's society, the drinking man could get plenty of whisky, and the religious man could hold prayer-meetings, preach, pray, and exhort.

Winter on a farm.

The Lord Is My Shepherd *by Eastman Johnson (1824–1906) was painted shortly after the Emancipation Proclamation to comfort white Americans who feared newly freed people but also to touch on the issue of reading, as in the South, teaching enslaved people to read had been a crime.*

This circa 1801 engraving, A Negro Festival drawn from Nature in the Island of St. Vincent, *perpetuated the myth that enslaved people were happy as well as well clothed and fed.*

On the first of January, 1835, I proceeded from St. Michaels to Mr. William Freeland's—my new home. Mr. Freeland lived only three miles from St. Michaels, on an old, worn-out farm, which required much labor to render it anything like a self-supporting establishment.

I found Mr. Freeland a different man from Covey. Though not rich, he was what might have been called a well-bred Southern gentleman. Though a slaveholder and sharing in common with them many of the vices of his class, he seemed alive to the sentiment of honor, and had also some sense of justice, and some feelings of humanity. He was fretful, impulsive, and passionate, but free from the mean and selfish characteristics which distinguished the creature from which I had happily escaped. Mr. Freeland was open, frank, and imperative. He practiced no concealments and disdained to play the spy. He was, in all these qualities, the opposite of Covey.

At Mr. Freeland's my condition was every way improved. [He] held every man individually responsible for his own conduct. Mr. Freeland, like Mr. Covey, gave his hands enough to eat, but, unlike Mr. Covey, he gave them time to take their meals. He worked us hard during the day, but gave us the night for rest. We were seldom in the field after dark in the evening,

or before sunrise in the morning. Our implements of husbandry were of the most improved pattern, and much superior to those used at Covey's.

Thus elevated a little at Freeland's, the dreams called into being by that good man, Father Lawson, when in Baltimore, began to visit me again. Shoots from the tree of liberty began to put forth buds, and dim hopes of the future began to dawn.

I found myself in congenial society. There were Henry Harris, John Harris, Handy Caldwell, and Sandy Jenkins (this last, of the root-preventive memory). Henry and John Harris were brothers, and belonged to Mr. Freeland. They were both remarkably bright and intelligent, though neither of them could read. As summer came on and the long Sabbath days stretched themselves over our idleness, I became uneasy and wanted a Sabbath-school in which to exercise my gifts and to impart to my brother-slaves the little knowledge I possessed. A house was hardly necessary in the summer time; I could hold my school under the shade of an old oak tree as well as any where else. The thing was to get the scholars, and to have them thoroughly imbued with the idea to learn. Two such boys were quickly found in Henry and John, and from them the contagion spread. I was not long in bringing around me twenty or thirty young men, who enrolled themselves gladly in my Sabbath-school, and were willing to meet me regularly under the trees or elsewhere, for the purpose of learning to read.

For much of the happiness, or absence of misery, with which I passed this year, I am indebted to the genial temper and ardent friendship of my brother slaves. They were every one of them manly, generous and brave. Yes, I say they were brave, and I will add, fine-looking. It is seldom the lot of any one to have truer and better friends than were the slaves on this farm. It was not uncommon to charge slaves with great treachery toward each other, but I must say I never loved, esteemed, or confided in men more than I did in these.

CHAPTER XIX

THE RUNAWAY PLOT

NEW YEAR'S THOUGHTS AND MEDITATIONS—AGAIN HIRED BY FREELAND—KINDNESS NO COMPENSATION FOR SLAVERY—INCIPIENT STEPS TOWARD ESCAPE—CONSIDERATIONS LEADING THERETO—HOSTILITY TO SLAVERY—SOLEMN VOW TAKEN—PLAN DIVULGED TO SLAVES—SCHEME GAINS FAVOR—DANGER OF DISCOVERY—SKILL OF SLAVE-HOLDERS—CONSULTATION—IGNORANCE OF GEOGRAPHY—SANDY A DREAMER—ROUTE TO THE NORTH MAPPED OUT—OBJECTIONS—FRAUDS—PASSES—ANXIETIES—FEAR OF FAILURE—STRANGE PRESENTIMENT—COINCIDENCE—BETRAYAL—ARRESTS—RESISTANCE—PRISON—BRUTAL JESTS—PASSES EATEN—DENIAL—SANDY—DRAGGED BEHIND HORSES—SLAVE-TRADERS—ALONE IN PRISON—SENT TO BALTIMORE.

I am now at the beginning of the year 1836. At the opening year the mind naturally occupies itself with the mysteries of life in all its phases—the ideal, the real, and the actual. Sober people then look both ways, surveying the errors of the past and providing against the possible errors of the future. I, too, was thus exercised. I had little pleasure in retrospect, and the future prospect was not brilliant.

Mr. Freeland renewed the purchase of my services of Mr. Auld for the coming year. I was not through the first month of my second year with the kind and gentlemanly Mr. Freeland before I was earnestly considering and devising plans for gaining that freedom which, when I was but a mere child, I had ascertained to be the natural and inborn right of every member of the human family. The desire for this freedom had been benumbed while I was under the brutalizing dominion of Covey, and it had been postponed and rendered inoperative by my truly pleasant Sunday-school

engagements with my friends during the year at Mr. Freeland's. It had, however, never entirely subsided. I hated slavery always, and my desire for freedom needed only a favorable breeze to fan it to a blaze at any moment.

Accordingly, at the beginning of this year 1836, I took upon me a solemn vow, that the year which had just now dawned upon me should not close without witnessing an earnest attempt, on my part, to gain my liberty. This vow only bound me to make good my own individual escape, but my friendship for my brother-slaves was so affectionate and confiding that I felt it my duty, as well as my pleasure, to give them an opportunity to share in my determination. Toward Henry and John Harris I felt a friendship as strong as one man can feel for another, for I could have died with and for them. To them, therefore, with suitable caution, I began to disclose my sentiments and plans, sounding them the while on the subject of running away, provided a good chance should offer.

This illustration from Lydia Maria Child's 1833 book An Appeal in Favor of That Class of Americans Called Africans *shows the shackles used on slave ships to bind prisoners together and prevent them from escaping.*

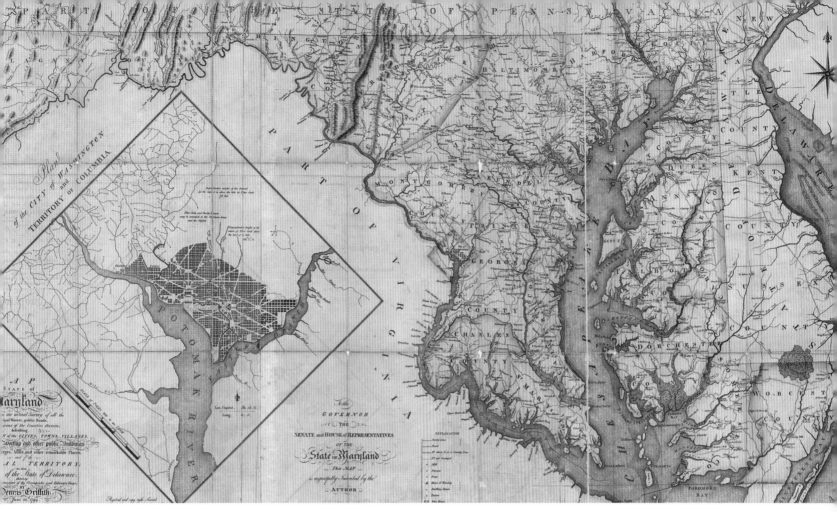

A late-eighteenth-century map of the Eastern Shore of Maryland, showing its proximity to Delaware and Pennsylvania.

It was the interest and business of slaveholders to study human nature, and the slave nature in particular, with a view to practical results; and many of them attained astonishing proficiency in this direction. They had to deal not with earth, wood, and stone, but with men; and by every regard they had for their own safety and prosperity they had need to know the material on which they were to work. So much intellect as that surrounding them, required watching. Their safety depended on their vigilance. Suspicion and torture were there the approved methods of getting at the truth. It was necessary, therefore, for me to keep a watch over my deportment, lest the enemy should get the better of me. But with all our caution and studied reserve, I am not sure that Mr. Freeland did not suspect that all was not right with us. It did seem that he watched us more narrowly after the plan of escape had been conceived and discussed amongst us. Men seldom see themselves as others see them; and while to ourselves everything connected with our contemplated escape appeared concealed, Mr. Freeland may, with the peculiar prescience of a slaveholder, have mastered the huge thought which was disturbing our peace. As I now look back, I am the more inclined to think that he suspected us, because, prudent as we were, I can see that we did many silly things well calculated to awaken suspicion. We were at times remarkably buoyant, singing hymns, and making joyous exclamations, almost as triumphant in their tone as if we had reached a land of freedom and safety.

I had succeeded in winning to my scheme a company of five young men, the very flower of the neighborhood, each one of whom would have commanded one thousand dollars in the home market. At New Orleans they would have brought fifteen hundred dollars apiece, and perhaps more. Their names were as follows: Henry Harris, John Harris, Sandy Jenkins, Charles Roberts, and Henry Bailey. I was the youngest but one of the party. I had, however, the advantage of them all in experience, and in a knowledge of letters. This gave me a great influence over them. As for Mr. Freeland, we all liked him, and would gladly have remained with him as free men. Liberty was our aim, and we had now come to think that we had a right to it against every obstacle, even against the lives of our enslavers.

To look at the map and observe the proximity of Eastern Shore, Maryland, to Delaware and Pennsylvania, it may seem to the reader quite absurd to regard the proposed escape as a formidable undertaking. The real distance was great enough, but the imagined distance was, to our ignorance, much greater. Our notions of the geography of the country were very vague and indistinct. The distance, however, was not the chief trouble, for the nearer were the lines of a slave state to the borders of a free state the greater was the trouble. Hired kidnappers infested the borders. Then, too, we knew that merely reaching a free state did not free us, that wherever caught we could be returned to slavery.

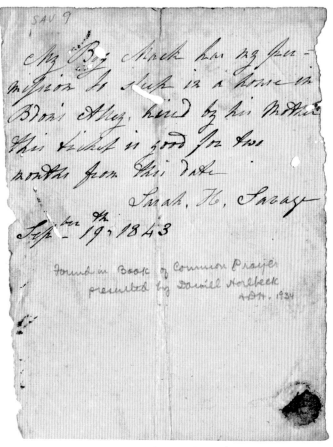

*This slave pass from 1843 granting a
boy to visit his mother was found in a prayer book.*

In the progress of our preparations Sandy (the root man) became troubled. He began to have distressing dreams, but I showed no concern, attributing it to the general excitement and perturbation consequent upon our contemplated plan to escape.

The plan for our escape, which I recommended and to which my comrades consented, was to take a large canoe owned by Mr. Hamilton, and on the Saturday night previous to the Easter holidays launch out into the Chesapeake bay and paddle with all our might for its head, a distance of seventy miles. On reaching this point we were to turn the canoe adrift and bend our steps toward the north-star till we reached a free state.

There were several objections to this plan. In rough weather the waters of the Chesapeake are much agitated, and there would be danger, in a canoe, of being swamped by the waves. Another objection was that the canoe would soon be missed, the absent slaves would at once be suspected of having taken it, and we should be pursued by some of the fast-sailing craft out of St. Michaels. Then again, if we reached the head of the bay and turned the canoe adrift, she might prove a guide to our track and bring the hunters after us. These and other objections were set aside by the stronger ones, which could be urged against every other plan that could then be suggested.

The week before our intended start, I wrote a pass for each of our party, giving him permission to visit Baltimore during the Easter holidays. The pass ran after this manner:

"This is to certify that I, the undersigned, have given the bearer, my servant John, full liberty to go to Baltimore to spend the Easter holidays. W. H. NEAR ST. MICHAELS, Talbot Co., Md."

Although we were not going to Baltimore, and were intending to land east of North Point, in the direction I had seen the Philadelphia steamers go, these passes might be useful to us in the lower part of the bay, while steering towards Baltimore. These were not, however, to be shown by us until all our answers had failed to satisfy the inquirer. We were all fully alive to the importance of being calm and self-possessed when accosted, if accosted we should be; and we more than once rehearsed to each other how we should behave in the hour of trial.

I cannot describe the tempest and tumult of my brain that morning. The reader will please bear in mind that in a slave State an unsuccessful runaway was not only subjected to cruel torture, and sold away to the far South, but he was frequently execrated by the other slaves. He was charged with making the condition of the other slaves intolerable by laying them all under the suspicion of their masters—subjecting them to greater vigilance, and imposing greater limitations on their privileges. I dreaded murmurs from this quarter. It was difficult, too, for a slave-master to believe that slaves escaping had not been aided in their flight by some one of their fellow-slaves. When, therefore, a slave was missing, every slave on the place was closely examined as to his knowledge of the undertaking.

Our anxiety grew more and more intense, as the time of our intended departure drew nigh. I appealed to the pride of my comrades by telling them that if, after having solemnly promised to go, as they had done, they now failed to make the attempt, they would in effect brand themselves with cowardice, and might well sit down, fold their arms, and acknowledge themselves fit only to be slaves. This detestable character all were unwilling to assume. Every man except Sandy (he, much to our regret, withdrew) stood firm, and pledged ourselves afresh. This meeting was in the middle of the week, at the end of which we were to start.

Early on the appointed morning we went as usual to the field, but with hearts that beat quickly and anxiously. Any one intimately acquainted with us might have seen that all was not well with us, and that some monster lingered in our thoughts. Our work that morning was the same that it had been for several days past—drawing out and spreading manure. While thus engaged, I had a sudden presentiment, which flashed upon me like lightning in a dark night, revealing to the lonely traveler the gulf before and the enemy behind. I instantly turned to Sandy Jenkins, who was near me, and said: "Sandy, we are betrayed!—something has just told me so." I felt as sure of it as if the officers were in sight. Sandy said: "Man, dat is strange; but I feel just as you do."

In a few minutes after this, the long, low, and distant notes of the horn summoned us from the field to breakfast. I felt as one may be supposed to feel before being led forth to be executed for some great offense. I wanted no breakfast, but for form's sake I went with the other slaves toward the house. My feelings were not disturbed as to the right of running away; on that point I had no misgiving whatever, but from a sense of the consequences of failure.

In thirty minutes after that vivid impression came the apprehended crash. On reaching the house, and glancing my eye toward the lane gate, the worst was at once made known. The lane gate to Mr. Freeland's house was nearly half a mile from the door, and much shaded by the heavy wood which bordered the main road. I was, however, able to descry four white men and two colored men approaching. The white men were on horseback, and the colored men were walking behind, and seemed to be tied. "It is indeed all over with us; we are surely betrayed," I thought to myself. I became composed, or at least comparatively so, and calmly awaited the result. I watched the ill-omened company entering the gate. Successful flight was impossible, and I made up my mind to stand and meet the evil, whatever it might be, for I was not altogether without a slight hope that things might turn differently from what I had at first feared. In a few moments in came Mr. William Hamilton, riding very rapidly and evidently much excited. He was in the habit of riding very slowly, and was seldom known to gallop his horse. This time his horse was nearly at full speed, causing the dust to roll thick behind him. Mr. Hamilton, though one of the most resolute men in the whole neighborhood, was, nevertheless, a remarkably mild-spoken man, and even when greatly excited his language was cool and circumspect. He came to the door, and inquired if Mr. Freeland was in. I told him that Mr. Freeland was at the barn. Off the old gentleman rode toward the barn, with unwonted speed. In a few moments Mr. Hamilton and Mr. Freeland came down from the barn to the house, and just as they made their appearance in the front-yard, three men, who proved to be constables, came dashing into the lane on horse-back, as if summoned by a sign requiring quick work. A few seconds brought them into the front-yard, where they hastily dismounted and tied their horses. This done, they joined Mr. Freeland and Mr. Hamilton, who were standing a short distance from the kitchen. A few moments were spent as if in consulting how to proceed, and then the whole party walked up to the kitchen-door. There was now no one in the kitchen but myself and John Harris; Henry and Sandy were yet in the barn. Mr. Freeland came inside the kitchen-door, and, with an agitated voice, called me by name, and told me to come forward; that there were some gentlemen who wished to see me. I stepped toward them at the door, and asked what they wanted; when the constables grabbed me, and told me that I had better not resist; that I had been in a scrape, or was said to have been in one; that they were merely going to take me where I

Eastman Johnson (1824–1906) claimed to have painted A Ride for Liberty—The Fugitive Slaves *based on events he witnessed near Manassas, Virginia.*

could be examined; that they would have me brought before my master at St. Michaels, and if the evidence against me was not proved true I should be acquitted. I was now firmly tied, and completely at the mercy of my captors. Resistance was idle. They were five in number and armed to the teeth. When they had secured me, they turned to John Harris and in a few moments succeeded in tying him as firmly as they had tied me. They next turned toward Henry Harris, who had now returned from the barn. "Cross your hands," said the constable to Henry. "I won't," said Henry, in a voice so firm and clear, and in a manner so determined, as for a moment to arrest all proceedings. "Won't you cross your hands?" said Tom Graham, the constable. "No, I won't," said Henry, with increasing emphasis. Mr. Hamilton, Mr. Freeland, and the officers now came near to Henry. Each of these hired ruffians now cocked his pistol, and, with fingers apparently on the triggers, presented his deadly weapon to the breast of the unarmed slave, saying, that if he did not cross his hands, he would "blow his d—d heart out of him." "Shoot me, shoot me," said Henry; "you can't kill me but once. Shoot, shoot, and be damned! I won't be tied!" This the brave fellow said in a voice as defiant and heroic in its tone as was the language itself; and at the moment of saying it, with the pistols at his very breast, he quickly raised his arms and dashed them from the puny hands of his assassins, the weapons flying in all directions. Now came the struggle. All hands rushed upon the brave fellow and after beating him for some time succeeded in overpowering and tying him. Henry put me to shame; he fought, and fought bravely. John and I had made no resistance. Yet there was something almost providential in the resistance made by Henry. But for that resistance every soul of us would have been hurried off to the far South. Just a moment previous to the trouble with Henry, Mr. Hamilton mildly said,—and this gave me the unmistakable clue to the cause of our arrest,—"Perhaps we had now better make a search for those protections, which we understand Frederick has written for himself and the rest." Had these passes been found, they would have been point-blank evidence against us, and would have confirmed all the statements of our betrayer. Thanks to the resistance of Henry, the excitement produced by the scuffle drew all attention in that direction, and I succeeded in flinging my pass, unobserved, into the fire. The confusion attendant on the scuffle, and the apprehension of still further trouble, perhaps, led our captors to forego, for the time, any search for "those protections which Frederick was said to have written for his companions"; so we were not yet convicted of the purpose to run away, and it was evident that there was some doubt on the part of all whether we had been guilty of such purpose.

"Perhaps we had now better make a search for those protections, which we understand Frederick has written for himself and the rest."

Could the kind reader have been riding along the main road to or from Easton that morning, his eye would have met a painful sight. He would have seen five young men, guilty of no crime save that of preferring liberty to slavery, drawn along the public highway—firmly bound together, tramping through dust and heat, bare-footed and bare-headed—fastened to three strong horses, whose riders were armed with pistols and daggers, and on their way to prison like felons, and suffering every possible insult from the crowds of idle, vulgar people who clustered round, and heartlessly made their failure to escape the occasion for all manner of ribaldry and sport.

Some said "I ought to be hanged," and others, "I ought to be burned"; others, I ought to have the "hide" taken off my back; while no one gave us a kind word or sympathizing look, except the poor slaves who were lifting their heavy hoes, and who cautiously glanced at us through the post-and-rail fences, behind which they were at work. Our sufferings that morning can be more easily imagined than described. Our hopes were all blasted at one blow. While the constables were looking forward, Henry and I being fastened together, could occasionally exchange a word without being observed by the kidnappers who had us in charge. "What shall I do with my pass?" said Henry. "Eat it with your biscuit," said I; "it won't do to tear it up." We were now near St. Michaels. The direction concerning the passes was passed around, and executed. "Own nothing," said I. "Own nothing" was passed round, enjoined, and assented to. Our confidence in each other was unshaken, and we were quite resolved to succeed or fail together; as much after the calamity which had befallen us as before.

On reaching St. Michaels we underwent a sort of examination at my master's store, and it was evident to my mind that Master Thomas suspected the truthfulness of the evidence upon which they had acted in arresting us, and that he only affected, to some extent, the positiveness with which he asserted our guilt. From something which dropped, in the course of the talk, it appeared that there was but one witness against us, and that that witness could not be produced. Master Thomas would not tell us who his informant was, but we suspected, and suspected one person only. Several circumstances seemed to point Sandy out as our betrayer, and yet we could not suspect him. We all loved him too well to think it possible that he could have betrayed us. So we rolled the guilt on other shoulders.

We were literally dragged, that morning, behind horses, a distance of fifteen miles, and placed in the Easton jail. We were glad to reach the end of our journey, for our pathway had been full of insult and mortification. In jail we were placed under the care of Mr. Joseph Graham, the sheriff of the county. Henry and John and myself were placed in one room, and Henry Bailey and Charles Roberts in another by themselves. This separation was intended to deprive us of the advantage of concert, and to prevent trouble in jail.

Once shut up, a new set of tormentors came upon us. A swarm of imps in human shape—the slave-traders and agents of slave-traders—who gathered in every country town of the State watching for chances to buy human flesh (as buzzards watch for carrion), flocked in upon us to ascertain if our masters had placed us in jail to be sold. I felt as if surrounded by a pack of fiends fresh from perdition. They laughed, leered, and grinned at us, saying, "Ah, boys, we have got you, haven't we? So you were going to make your escape? Where were you going to?"

Aside from these slave-buyers who infested the prison from time to time, our quarters were much more comfortable than we had any right to expect them to be. Our allowance of food was small and coarse, but our room was the best in the jail—neat and spacious, and with nothing about it necessarily reminding us of being in prison but its heavy locks and bolts and the black iron lattice-work at the windows.

A slave jail in Maryland.

Soon after the holidays were over, contrary to all our expectations, Messrs. Hamilton and Freeland came up to Easton; not to make a bargain with "Georgia traders," nor to send us up to Austin Woldfolk, as was usual in the case of runaway-slaves, but to release, from prison, Charles, Henry Harris, Henry Bailey and John Harris, and this, too, without the infliction of a single blow. I was left alone in prison. The innocent had been taken and the guilty left. My friends were separated from me, and apparently forever. This circumstance caused me more pain than any other incident connected with our capture and imprisonment.

Not until this last separation, dear reader, had I touched those profounder depths of desolation which it is the lot of slaves often to reach. I was solitary and alone within the walls of a stone prison, left to a fate of life-long misery. I had hoped and expected much, for months before, but my hopes and expectations were now withered and blasted. The ever-dreaded slave life in Georgia, Louisiana, and Alabama—from which escape was next to impossible—now in my loneliness stared me in the face. The possibility of ever becoming anything but an abject slave, a mere machine in the hands of an owner, had now fled, and it seemed to me it had fled forever. A life of living death, beset with the innumerable horrors of the cotton-field and the sugar-plantation, seemed to be my doom.

After remaining in this life of misery and despair about a week, which seemed a month, Master Thomas, very much to my surprise and greatly to my relief, came to the prison and took me out, for the purpose, as he said, of sending me to Alabama with a friend of his, who would emancipate me at the end of eight years. I was glad enough to get out of prison, but I had no faith in the story that his friend would emancipate me. Besides, I had never heard of his having a friend in Alabama, and I took the announcement simply as an easy and comfortable method of shipping me off to the far south.

After lingering about St. Michaels a few days, Master Thomas decided to send me back again to Baltimore, to live with his brother Hugh, with whom he was now at peace. Possibly he became so by his profession of religion at the camp-meeting in the Bay-side. Master Thomas told me that he wished me to go to Baltimore and learn a trade; and that if I behaved myself properly he would emancipate me at twenty-five. Thanks for this one beam of hope in the future! The promise had but one fault—it seemed too good to be true.

CHAPTER XX

APPRENTICESHIP LIFE

NOTHING LOST IN MY ATTEMPT TO RUN AWAY—COMRADES AT HOME—
REASONS FOR SENDING ME AWAY—RETURN TO BALTIMORE—TOMMY
CHANGED—CAULKING IN GARDINER'S SHIP-YARD—DESPERATE FIGHT—
ITS CAUSES—CONFLICT BETWEEN WHITE AND BLACK LABOR—OUTRAGE—
TESTIMONY—MASTER HUGH—SLAVERY IN BALTIMORE—MY CONDITION
IMPROVES—NEW ASSOCIATIONS—SLAVEHOLDER'S RIGHT TO THE
SLAVE'S WAGES.

Well, dear reader, I am not, as you have probably inferred, a loser by the general upstir described in the foregoing chapter. The little domestic revolution, notwithstanding the sudden snub it got by the treachery of somebody, did not, after all, end so disastrously as when in the iron cage at Easton I conceived it would. The prospect from that point did look about as dark as any that ever cast its gloom over the vision of the anxious, out-looking human spirit. "All's well that ends well!" My affectionate friends, Henry and John Harris, are still with Mr. Freeland. Charles Roberts and Henry Bailey are safe at their homes. I have not, therefore, anything to regret on their account. My friends had nothing to regret, either: for while they were watched more closely, they were doubtless treated more kindly than before, and got new assurances that they should some day be legally emancipated, provided their behavior from that time forward should make them deserving. Not a blow was struck any one of them. As for Master Freeland, good soul, he did not believe we were intending to run away at all. Having given—as he thought—no occasion to his boys to leave him, he could not think it probable that they had entertained a design so grievous. My "Cousin Tom" told me that while I was in jail Master Thomas was very unhappy, and that the night before his going up to release me he had walked the floor nearly all night, evincing great distress; that very tempting offers had been made to him by the negro-traders, but he had rejected them all, saying that money could not tempt him to sell me to the far south. I can easily believe all this, for he seemed quite reluctant to send me away at all. He told me that he only consented to do so because of the very strong prejudice against me in the neighborhood, and that he feared for my safety if I remained there.

Thus, after three years spent in the country, roughing it in the field, and experiencing all sorts of hardships, I was again permitted to return to Baltimore, the very place of all others, short of a free State, where I most desired to live. The three years spent in the country had made some difference in me, and in the household of Master Hugh.

The Levering Coffee House on Chase's Wharf at Fell's Point, Baltimore, Maryland, was built circa 1806.

A trading brig, contemporaneous to the Tweed.

"Little Tommy" was no longer little Tommy, and I was not the slender lad who had left the Eastern Shore just three years before. The loving relations between Master Tommy and myself were broken up. So we were cold to each other, and parted. It was a sad thing to me, that, loving each other as we had done, we must now take different roads. To him a thousand avenues were open. He had grown and become a man: I, though grown to the stature of manhood, must all my life remain a minor—a mere boy. Thomas Auld, junior, obtained a situation on board the brig *Tweed*, and went to sea. I have since heard of his death.

There were few persons to whom I was more sincerely attached than to him.

Very soon after I went to Baltimore to live, Master Hugh succeeded in getting me hired to Mr. William Gardiner, an extensive ship-builder on Fell's Point. I was placed there to learn to calk, a trade of which I already had some knowledge, gained while in Mr. Hugh Auld's ship-yard. Gardiner's, however, proved a very unfavorable place for the accomplishment of the desired object. Mr. Gardiner was that season engaged in building two large man-of-war vessels, professedly for the Mexican government. These vessels were to be launched in the month

of July of that year, and in failure thereof Mr. Gardiner would forfeit a very considerable sum of money. So, when I entered the ship-yard, all was hurry and driving. There were in the yard about one hundred men; of these, seventy or eighty were regular carpenters—privileged men. There was no time for a raw hand to learn anything. Every man had to do that which he knew how to do, and in entering the yard Mr. Gardiner had directed me to do whatever the carpenters told me to do. This was placing me at the beck and call of about seventy-five men. I was to regard all these as my masters. Their word was to be my law. My situation was a trying one. I was called a dozen ways in the space of a single minute. I needed a dozen pairs of hands. Three or four voices would strike my car ear at the same moment. At the end of eight months Master Hugh refused longer to allow me to remain with Gardiner. The circumstance which led to this refusal was the committing of an outrage upon me, by the white apprentices of the ship-yard. The fight was a desperate one, and I came out of it shockingly mangled. I was cut and bruised in sundry places, and my left eye was nearly knocked out of its socket. The facts which led to this brutal outrage upon me illustrate a phase of slavery which was destined to become an important element in

Emancipated men working as laborers at Quartermaster's Wharf, Alexandria, Virginia, circa 1863.

Mr. Walter Price and Mr. Robb. Nobody seemed to see any impropriety in it. Some of the blacks were first-rate workmen and were given jobs requiring the highest skill. All at once, however, the white carpenters swore that they would no longer work on the same stage with negroes. My fellow-apprentices very soon began to feel it to be degrading to work with me. They began to put on high looks and to talk contemptuously and maliciously of "the niggers," saying that they would take the "country," and that they "ought to be killed." Encouraged by workmen who, knowing me to be a slave, made no issue with Mr. Gardiner about my being there, these young men did their utmost to make it impossible for me to stay. They seldom called me to do anything without coupling the call with a curse, and Edward North, the biggest in everything, rascality included, ventured to strike me, whereupon I picked him up and threw him into the dock. Whenever any of them struck me I struck back again, regardless of consequences. I could manage any of them singly, and so long as I could keep them from combining I got on very well. In the conflict which ended my stay at Mr. Gardiner's I was beset by four of them at once. Two of them were as large as myself, and they came near killing me, in broad daylight. One came in front, armed with a brick; there was one at each side and one behind, and they closed up all around me. I was struck on all sides; and while I was attending to those in front I received a blow on my head from behind, dealt with a heavy hand-spike. I was completely stunned by the blow, and fell heavily on the ground among the timbers. Taking advantage of my fall they rushed upon me and began to pound me with their fists. They had done me little damage, so far; but finally getting tired of that sport I gave a sudden surge, and despite their weight I rose to my hands and knees. Just as I did this one of their number planted a blow with his boot in my left eye, which for a time seemed to have burst my eye-ball. When they saw my eye completely closed, my face covered with blood, and I staggering under the stunning blows they had given me, they left me. As soon as I gathered strength I picked up the hand-spike and madly enough attempted to pursue them; but there the carpenters interfered and compelled me to give up my pursuit. It was impossible to stand against so many.

Dear reader, you can hardly believe the statement, but it is true and therefore I write it down; that no fewer than fifty white men stood by and saw this brutal and shameful outrage committed, and not a man of them all interposed a single word of mercy. After the united attack, finding that the carpenters were as bitter toward me as the apprentices, and that the latter were probably set on by the former, I found my only chance for life was in flight. I succeeded in getting away without an additional blow. After making my escape from the ship-yard I went straight home and related my story to Master Hugh; and to his credit I say it, that his conduct, though he was not a religious man, was every way more humane than that of his brother Thomas, when I went to him in a somewhat similar plight, from the hands of his "Brother Edward

the overthrow of the slave system, and I may therefore state them with some minuteness. That phase was this—the conflict of slavery with the interests of white mechanics and laborers. In the country this conflict was not so apparent; but in cities, such as Baltimore, Richmond, New Orleans, Mobile, etc., it was seen pretty clearly. The slaveholders, with a craftiness peculiar to themselves, by encouraging the enmity of the poor laboring white man against the blacks, succeeded in making the said white man almost as much a slave as the black slave himself. The impression was cunningly made that slavery was the only power that could prevent the laboring white man from falling to the level of the slave's poverty and degradation. To make this enmity deep and broad between the slave and the poor white man, the latter was allowed to abuse and whip the former without hindrance. But, as I have said, this state of affairs prevailed mostly in the country. In the city of Baltimore there were not unfrequent murmurs that educating slaves to be mechanics might, in the end, give slave-masters power to dispense altogether with the services of the poor white man.

Until a very little while before I went there, white and black carpenters worked side by side in the shipyards of Mr. Gardiner, Mr. Duncan,

This historic house located on Chapel Street in Fell's Point, Baltimore, Maryland, was built circa 1800.

Covey." Master Hugh listened attentively to my narration of the circumstances leading to the ruffianly assault, and gave many evidences of his strong indignation at what was done. He was a rough but manly-hearted fellow, and at this time his best nature showed itself.

The heart of my once kind mistress Sophia was again melted in pity towards me. My puffed-out eye and my scarred and blood-covered face moved the dear lady to tears. She kindly drew a chair by me, and with friendly and consoling words, she took water and washed the blood from my face. No mother's hand could have been more tender than hers. She bound up my head and covered my wounded eye with a lean piece of fresh beef.

As for Master Hugh, he was furious, and gave expression to his feelings in the forms of speech usual in that locality. He poured curses on the whole of the ship-yard company, and swore that he would have satisfaction. Just as soon as I got a little the better of my bruises Master Hugh took me to Esquire Watson's office on Bond street, Fell's Point, with a view to procuring the arrest of those who had assaulted me. He gave to the magistrate an account of the outrage as I had related it to him, and seemed to expect that a warrant would at once be issued for the arrest of the lawless ruffians. Mr. Watson heard all that he had to say, then coolly inquired, "Mr. Auld, who saw this assault of which you speak?" "It was done, sir, in the presence of a ship-yard full of hands."

This promissory bank note was issued in 1840, by which time Douglass would be able to keep all the money he made.

"Sir," said Mr. Watson, "I am sorry, but I cannot move in this matter, except upon the oath of white witnesses." "But here's the boy; look at his head and face," said the excited Master Hugh; "they show what has been done." But Watson insisted that he was not authorized to do anything, unless white witnesses of the transaction would come forward and testify to what had taken place. He could issue no warrant, on my word, against white persons, and if I had been killed in the presence of a thousand blacks, their testimony combined would have been insufficient to condemn a single murderer. Master Hugh was compelled to say, for once, that this state of things was too bad, and he left the office of the magistrate disgusted.

Master Hugh, on finding that he could get no redress for the cruel wrong, withdrew me from the employment of Mr. Gardiner and took me into his own family, Mrs. Auld kindly taking care of me and dressing my wounds until they were healed and I was ready to go to work again.

While I was on the Eastern Shore, Master Hugh had met with reverses which overthrew his business and had given up ship-building in his own yard, on the City Block, and was now acting as foreman of Mr. Walter Price. The best that he could do for me was to take me into Mr. Price's yard, and afford me the facilities there for completing the trade which I began to learn at Gardiner's. Here I rapidly became expert in the use of calkers' tools, and in the course of a single year, I was able to command the highest wages paid to journeymen calkers in Baltimore.

The reader will observe that I was now of some pecuniary value to my master. During the busy season I was bringing six and seven dollars per week. I have sometimes brought him as much as nine dollars a week, for wages were a dollar and a half per day.

Many of the young calkers could read, write, and cipher. Some of them had high notions about mental improvement, and the free ones on Fell's Point organized what they called the "East Baltimore Mental Improvement Society." To this society, notwithstanding it was intended that only free persons should attach themselves, I was admitted, and was several times assigned a prominent part in its debates. I owe much to the society of these young men.

The reader already knows enough of the ill effects of good treatment on a slave to anticipate what was now the case in my improved condition. It was not long before I began to show signs of disquiet with slavery, and to look around for means to get out of it by the shortest route. I was living among freemen, and was in all respects equal to them by nature and attainments. Why should I be a slave? There was no reason why I should be the thrall of any man. Besides, I was now getting, as I have said, a dollar and fifty cents per day. I contracted for it, worked for it, collected it; it was paid to me, and it was rightfully my own; and yet upon every returning Saturday night, this money—my own hard earnings, every cent of it—was demanded of me and taken from me by Master Hugh. I became more and more dissatisfied with this state of things, and in so becoming I only gave proof of the same human nature which every reader of this chapter in my life—slaveholder, or non-slaveholder—is conscious of possessing.

CHAPTER XXI

ESCAPE FROM SLAVERY

CLOSING INCIDENTS IN MY "LIFE AS A SLAVE"—DISCONTENT—
SUSPICIONS—MASTER'S GENEROSITY—DIFFICULTIES IN THE WAY OF
ESCAPE—PLAN TO OBTAIN MONEY—ALLOWED TO HIRE MY TIME—A GLEAM
OF HOPE—ATTEND CAMP-MEETING—ANGER OF MASTER HUGH—THE
RESULT—PLANS OF ESCAPE—DAY FOR DEPARTURE FIXED—HARASSING
DOUBTS AND FEARS—PAINFUL THOUGHTS OF SEPARATION FROM FRIENDS.

My condition during the year of my escape (1838) was comparatively a free and easy one, so far, at least, as the wants of the physical man were concerned; but the reader will bear in mind that my troubles from the beginning had been less physical than mental, and he will thus be prepared to find that slave life was adding nothing to its charms for me as I grew older, and became more and more acquainted with it. The practice of openly robbing me, from week to week, of all my earnings, kept the nature and character of slavery constantly before me. I could be robbed by indirection, but this was too open and barefaced to be endured. I could see no reason why I should, at the end of each week, pour the reward of my honest toil into the purse of my master. My obligation to do this vexed me, and the manner in which Master Hugh received my wages vexed me yet more. Carefully counting the money, and rolling it out dollar by dollar, he would look me in the face, as if he would search my heart as well as my pocket, and reproachfully ask me, "Is that all?"—implying that I had perhaps kept back part of my wages.

Held to a strict account, and kept under a close watch—the old suspicion of my running away not having been entirely removed—to accomplish my escape seemed a very difficult thing. The railroad from Baltimore to Philadelphia was under regulations so stringent that even free colored travelers were almost excluded. They must have free papers; they must be measured and carefully examined before they could enter the cars, and could go only in the day time, even when so examined. The steamboats were under regulations equally stringent. And still more, and worse than all, all the great turnpikes leading northward were beset with kidnappers; a class of men who watched the newspapers for advertisements for runaway slaves, thus making their living by the accursed reward of slave-hunting.

My discontent grew upon me, and I was on a constant look-out for means to get away. With money I could easily have managed the matter, and from this consideration I hit upon the plan of soliciting the privilege of hiring my time. It was quite common in Baltimore to allow slaves this privilege, and was the practice also in New Orleans. A slave who was considered trustworthy could, by regularly paying his master a definite sum at the end of each week, dispose of his time as he liked. It so happened that I was not in very good odor, and was far from being a trustworthy slave. Nevertheless, I watched my opportunity when Master Thomas came to Baltimore (for I was still his property, Hugh only acting as

The coins from Douglass's time bore the much sought after "Liberty" promised by the United States Bill of Rights.

The steamship docks at Washington, D.C., in 1839, the year after Douglass's escape.

his agent) in the spring of 1838, to purchase his spring supply of goods, and applied to him directly for the much-coveted privilege of hiring my time. This request Master Thomas unhesitatingly refused to grant and charged me, with some sternness, with inventing this stratagem to make my escape.

About two months after applying to Master Thomas for the privilege of hiring my time, I applied to Master Hugh for the same liberty, supposing him to be unacquainted with the fact that I had made a similar application to Master Thomas and had been refused. My boldness in making this request fairly astounded him at first. He gazed at me in amazement.

After mature reflection, as I suppose it was, Master Hugh granted me the privilege in question, on the following terms: I was to be allowed all my time; to make all bargains for work, and to collect my own wages; and in return for this liberty, I was required or obliged to pay him three dollars at the end of each week, and to board and clothe myself, and buy my own calking tools. This was a hard bargain. The wear and tear of clothing, the losing and breaking of tools, and the expense of board, made it necessary for me to earn at least six dollars per week to keep even with the world.

Master Hugh seemed, for a time, much pleased with this arrangement; and well he might be, for it was decidedly in his favor. It relieved him of all anxiety concerning me. His money was sure. He had armed my love of liberty with a lash and a driver far more efficient than any I had before known; for, while by this arrangement, he derived all the benefits of slaveholding without its evils, I endured all the evils of being a slave, and yet suffered all the care and anxiety of a responsible freeman.

I was not only able to meet my current expenses, but also to lay by a small sum at the end of each week. All went on thus from the month of May till August; then, for reasons which will become apparent as I proceed, my much-valued liberty was wrested from me.

During the week previous to this calamitous event, I had made arrangements with a few young friends to accompany them on Saturday night to a camp-meeting, to be held about twelve miles from Baltimore. On the evening of our intended start for the camp-ground, something occurred in the ship-yard where I was at work which detained me unusually late, and compelled me either to disappoint my friends, or to neglect carrying my weekly dues to Master Hugh. Knowing that I had the money and could hand it to him on another day, I decided to go to camp-meeting and, on my return, to pay him the three dollars for the past week. But as soon as I returned I went directly to his home on Fell street to hand him his (my) money. Unhappily the fatal mistake had been made. I found him exceedingly angry. "You rascal! I have a great mind to give you a sound whipping. How dare you go out of the city without first asking and obtaining my permission?" After reflecting a few moments, he became somewhat cooled down, but, evidently greatly troubled, said: "Now, you scoundrel, you have done for yourself; you shall hire your time no longer.

The next thing I shall hear of will be your running away. Bring home your tools at once. I'll teach you how to go off in this way."

Thus ended my partial freedom. I could hire my time no longer. I obeyed my master's orders at once. Punished by Master Hugh, it was now my turn to punish him. So, instead of going to look for work on Monday morning, as I had formerly done, I remained at home during the entire week, without the performance of a single stroke of work. Saturday night came, and he called upon me as usual for my wages. I, of course, told him I had done no work, and had no wages. Here we were at the point of coming to blows. His wrath had been accumulating during the whole week; for he evidently saw that I was making no effort to get work, but was most aggravatingly awaiting his orders in all things. Master Hugh raved, and swore he would "get hold of me," but wisely for him, and happily for me, his wrath employed only those harmless. He closed his reproofs by telling me that hereafter I need give myself no uneasiness about getting work; he "would himself see to getting work for me, and enough of it at that." This threat, I confess, had some terror in it, and on thinking the matter over during the Sunday, I resolved not only to save him the trouble of getting me work, but that on the third day of September I would attempt to make my escape. His refusal to allow me to hire my time therefore hastened the period of my flight. I had three weeks in which to prepare for my journey.

Once resolved, I felt a certain degree of repose, and on Monday morning, instead of waiting for Master Hugh to seek employment for me, I was up by break of day, and off to the ship-yard of Mr. Butler, on the City Block, near the draw-bridge. I was a favorite with Mr. Butler, and, young as I was, I had served as his foreman, on the float-stage, at calking. Of course I easily obtained work, and at the end of the week, which, by the way, was exceedingly fine, I brought Master Hugh nine dollars. The effect of this mark of returning good sense on my part was excellent. He was very much pleased; he took the money, commended me and told me that I might have done the same thing the week before. He probably thought that I was never better satisfied with my condition than at the very time I was planning my escape. The second week passed, and I again carried him my full week's wages—nine dollars; and so well pleased was he that he gave me twenty-five cents! and bade me "make good use of it." I told him I would do so, for one of the uses to which I intended to put it was to pay my fare on the "underground railroad."

Things without went on as usual; but I was passing through the same internal excitement and anxiety which I had experienced two years and a half before. The last two days of the week, Friday and Saturday, were spent mostly in collecting my things together for my journey. Having worked four days that week for my master, I handed him six dollars on Saturday night. I seldom spent my Sundays at home, and for fear that something might be discovered in my conduct, I kept up my custom and absented myself all day. On Monday, the third day of September, 1838, in accordance with my resolution, I bade farewell to the city of Baltimore, and to that slavery which had been my abhorrence from childhood.

A poster for the Philadelphia, Wilmington & Baltimore railroad.

SECOND PART

Charles T. Webber (1825–1911) painted The Underground Railroad *to celebrate the heroism of abolitionists and those escaping slavery. Shown here are Cincinnati abolitionists Levi Coffin, his wife Catharine, and Hannah Haydock.*

CHAPTER I

ESCAPE FROM SLAVERY

REASONS FOR NOT HAVING REVEALED THE MANNER OF ESCAPE—NOTHING OF ROMANCE IN THE METHOD—DANGER—FREE PAPERS—UNJUST TAX—PROTECTION PAPERS—"FREE TRADE AND SAILORS' RIGHTS"—AMERICAN EAGLE—RAILROAD TRAIN—UNOBSERVING CONDUCTOR—CAPT. MCGOWAN—HONEST GERMAN—FEARS—SAFE ARRIVAL IN PHILADELPHIA—DITTO IN NEW YORK.

In the first narrative of my experience in slavery, written nearly forty years ago, and in various writings since, I have given the public what I considered very good reasons for withholding the manner of my escape. In substance these reasons were, first, that such publication at any time during the existence of slavery might be used by the master against the slave, and prevent the future escape of any who might adopt the same means that I did. The second reason was publication of details would certainly have put in peril the persons and property of those who assisted. I shall now, however, cease to avail myself of this formula, and, as far as I can, endeavor to satisfy this very natural curiosity. I should perhaps have yielded to that feeling sooner, had there been anything very heroic or thrilling in the incidents connected with my escape, for

I am sorry to say I have nothing of that sort to tell; and yet the courage that could risk betrayal and the bravery which was ready to encounter death if need be, in pursuit of freedom, were essential features in the undertaking. My success was due to address rather than to courage; to good luck rather than to bravery. My means of escape were provided for me by the very men who were making laws to hold and bind me more securely in slavery. It was the custom in the State of Maryland to require of the free colored people to have what were called free papers. This instrument they were required to renew very often, and by charging a fee for this writing, considerable sums from time to time were collected by the State. In these papers the name, age, color, height and form of the free man were described, together with any scars or other marks upon his person which could

A daguerreotype of Douglass, likely made in the late 1840s.

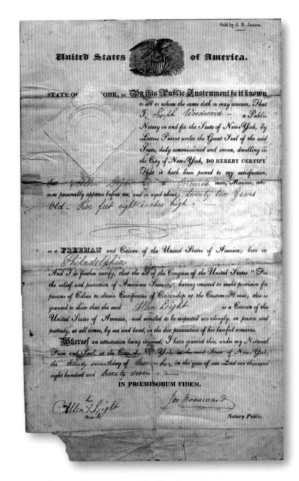

Left: An African American sailor in the 1860s. Right: This protective certificate proved the freedom of an African American seaman and is much like the document Douglass used to escape.

assist in his identification. I was not so fortunate as to sufficiently resemble any of my free acquaintances as to answer the description of their papers. But I had one friend—a sailor—who owned a sailor's protection, which answered somewhat the purpose of free papers—describing his person and certifying to the fact that he was a free American sailor. The instrument had at its head the American eagle, which at once gave it the appearance of an authorized document. This protection did not, when in my hands, describe its bearer very accurately. Indeed, it called for a man much darker than myself, and close examination of it would have caused my arrest at the start. In order to avoid this fatal scrutiny on the part of the railroad official, I had arranged with Isaac Rolls, a hackman, to bring my baggage to the train just on the moment of starting, and jumped upon the car myself when the train was already in motion. One element in my favor was the kind feeling which prevailed in Baltimore and other seaports at the time, towards "those who go down to the sea in ships." "Free trade and sailors' rights" expressed the sentiment of the country just then. In my clothing I was rigged out in sailor

style. I had on a red shirt and a tarpaulin hat and black cravat, tied in sailor fashion, carelessly and loosely about my neck. My knowledge of ships and sailor's talk came much to my assistance, for I knew a ship from stem to stern, and from keelson to cross-trees, and could talk sailor like an "old salt." On sped the train, and I was well on the way to Havre de Grace before the conductor came into the negro car to collect tickets and examine the papers of his black passengers. This was a critical moment in the drama. My whole future depended upon the decision of this conductor. Agitated I was while this ceremony was proceeding, but still, externally at least, I was apparently calm and self-possessed. He went on with his duty—examining several colored passengers before reaching me. He was somewhat harsh in tone and peremptory in manner until he reached me, when, strangely enough, and to my surprise and relief, his whole manner changed. Seeing that I did not readily produce my free papers, as the other colored persons in the car had done, he said to me in a friendly contrast with that observed towards the others: "I suppose you have your free papers?" To which I answered: "No, sir; I never carry my

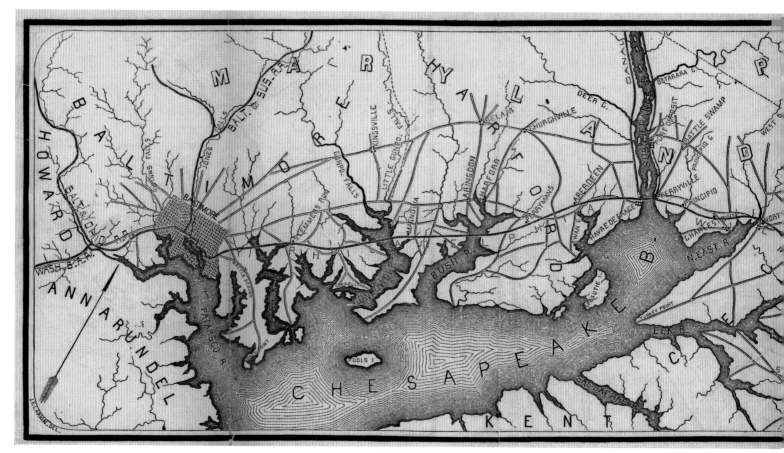

*A sketch map showing the area between Philadelphia and Baltimore indicating drainage,
cities and towns, roads, and railroad connections.*

free papers to sea with me." "But you have something to show that you are a free man, have you not?" "Yes, sir," I answered; "I have a paper with the American eagle on it, that will carry me round the world." The merest glance at the paper satisfied him, and he took my fare and went on about his business. This moment of time was one of the most anxious I ever experienced. When he left me with the assurance that I was all right, though much relieved, I realized that I was still in great danger: I was still in Maryland, and subject to arrest at any moment. I saw on the train several persons who would have known me in any other clothes, and I feared they might recognize me, even in my sailor "rig," and report me to the conductor.

The train was moving at a very high rate of speed for that time of railroad travel, but to my anxious mind, it was moving far too slowly. After Maryland I was to pass through Delaware—another slave State, where slave-catchers generally awaited their prey. The passage of the Susquehanna river at Havre de Grace was at that time

made by ferry-boat, on board of which I met a young colored man by the name of Nichols, who came very near betraying me. He was a "hand" on the boat, but instead of minding his business, he insisted upon knowing me, and asking me dangerous questions as to where I was going, and when I was coming back, etc. I got away from my old and inconvenient acquaintance as soon as I could decently do so, and went to another part of the boat. Once across the river I encountered a new danger. Only a few days before I had been at work on a revenue cutter, in Mr. Price's ship-yard, under the care of Captain McGowan. On the meeting at this point of the two trains, the one going south stopped on the track just opposite to the one going north, and it so happened that this Captain McGowan sat at a window where he could see me very distinctly, and would certainly have recognized me had he looked at me but for a second. Fortunately, in the hurry of the moment, he did not see me, and the trains soon passed each other on their respective ways. But this was

not the only hair-breadth escape. A German blacksmith, whom I knew well, was on the train with me, and looked at me very intently, as if he thought he had seen me somewhere before in his travels. I really believe he knew me, but had no heart to betray me. At any rate he saw me escaping and held his peace.

The last point of imminent danger, and the one I dreaded most, was Wilmington. Here we left the train and took the steam-boat for Philadelphia. In making the change I again apprehended arrest, but no one disturbed me, and I was soon on the broad and beautiful Delaware, speeding away to the Quaker City. On reaching Philadelphia in the afternoon I inquired of a colored man how I could get on to New York? He directed me to the Willow street depot, and thither I went, taking the train that night. I reached New York Tuesday morning, having completed the journey in less than twenty-four hours. Such is briefly the manner of my escape from slavery—and the end of my experience as a slave.

Escaping from slavery involved mortal risk—especially after the Fugitive Slave Act was passed in 1850, which increased federal and state responsibility to recover fugitive slaves. The danger is condemned in this print of four fugitive men being pursued by an armed gang.

CHAPTER II

LIFE AS A FREEMAN

Loneliness and Insecurity—"Allender's Jake"—Succored by a sailor—David Ruggles—Marriage—Steamer *J. W. Richmond*—Stage to New Bedford—Arrival there—Driver's detention of baggage—Nathan Johnson—Change of name—Obtaining work—The *Liberator* and its editor.

My free life began on the third of September, 1838. On the morning of the 4th of that month, after an anxious and most perilous but safe journey, I found myself in the big city of New York, a free man; one more added to the mighty throng which, like the confused waves of the troubled sea, surged to and fro between the lofty walls of Broadway. Though dazzled with the wonders which met me on every hand, my thoughts could not be much withdrawn from my strange situation. The bonds that had held me to "old master" were broken. No man now had a right to call me his slave or assert mastery over me. If life is more than breath, and the "quick round of blood," I lived more in one day than in a year of my slave life. It was a time of joyous excitement which words can but tamely describe.

I soon found that New York was not quite so free or so safe a refuge as I had supposed, and a sense of loneliness and insecurity again oppressed me most sadly. I chanced to meet on the street, a few hours after my landing, a fugitive slave whom I had once known well in slavery. The information received from him alarmed me. The fugitive in question was known in Baltimore as "Allender's Jake," but in New York he wore the more respectable name of "William Dixon." Jake, in law, was the property of Doctor Allender, and Tolly Allender, the son of the doctor, had once made an effort to recapture Mr. Dixon, but had failed for want of evidence to support his claim. He told me that New York was then full of southerners returning from the watering-places north; that the colored people of New York were not to be trusted; that there were hired men of my own color who would betray me for a few dollars; that there were hired men ever on the lookout for fugitives; that I must trust no man with my secret; that I must not think of going either upon the wharves, or into any colored boarding-house, for all such places were closely watched; that he was himself unable to help me; and, in fact, he seemed while speaking to me, to fear lest I myself might be a spy and a betrayer. While wandering about the streets of New York, and lodging at least one night among the barrels on one of the wharves, I was indeed free—from slavery, but free from food and shelter as well. I kept my secret to myself as long as I could, but was compelled at last to seek some one who should befriend me without taking advantage of my destitution

Douglass's first wife, Anna Murray-Douglass.

Left: An illustration from an original edition of Narrative of the Life of Frederick Douglass, an American Slave.
Right: "The Tombs" is a detention center in lower Manhattan. The original building is shown here, circa 1896.

to betray me. Such an one I found in a sailor named Stuart, a warm-hearted and generous fellow, who, from his humble home on Center street, saw me standing on the opposite sidewalk, near "The Tombs." As he approached me I ventured a remark to him which at once enlisted his interest in me. He took me to his home to spend the night, and in the morning went with me to Mr. David Ruggles, the secretary of the New York vigilance committee, a co-worker with Isaac T. Hopper, Lewis and Arthur Tappan, Theodore S. Wright, Samuel Cornish, Thomas Downing, Philip A. Bell, and other true men of their time. Once in the hands of these brave and wise men, I felt comparatively safe. With Mr. Ruggles, on the corner of Lispenard and Church streets, I was hidden several days, during which time my intended wife came on from Baltimore at my call, to share the burdens of life with me. She was a free woman, and came at once on getting the good news of my safety. We were married by Rev. J. W. C. Pennington, then a well-known and respected Presbyterian minister. I had no money with which to pay the marriage fee, but he seemed well pleased with our thanks.

Mr. Ruggles was the first officer on the underground railroad with whom I met after coming North, and was indeed the only one with whom I had anything to do, till I became such an officer myself. Learning that my trade was that of a calker, he promptly decided that the best place for me was in New Bedford, Mass. So, on the day of the marriage ceremony, we took our little luggage to the steamer *John W. Richmond*, which at that time was one of the line running between New York and Newport, R. I. We arrived at Newport the next morning, and soon after an old-fashioned stage-coach with "New Bedford" in large, yellow letters on its sides, came down to the wharf. I had not money enough to pay our fare and stood hesitating to know what to do. Fortunately for us, there were two Quaker gentlemen who were about to take passage on the stage—Friends William C. Taber and Joseph Ricketson—who at once discerned our true situation, and in a peculiarly quiet way, addressing me, Mr. Taber said: "Thee get in." I never obeyed an order with more alacrity, and we were soon on our way to our new home. When we reached "Stone Bridge" the passengers alighted for breakfast and paid their fares to the driver. We took no breakfast, and when asked for our fares I told the driver I would make it right with him when we reached New Bedford. When, however, we reached New Bedford he took our baggage, including three music books—two of them collections by Dyer, and one by Shaw—and held them until I was able to redeem them by paying to him the sums due for our rides. This was soon done, for Mr. Nathan Johnson not only received me kindly and hospitably, but, on being informed about our baggage, at once loaned me the two dollars with which to square accounts with the stage-driver.

New York City in the mid-nineteenth century.

Once initiated into my new life of freedom and assured by Mr. Johnson that I need not fear recapture in that city, a comparatively unimportant question arose, as to the name by which I should be known thereafter, in my new relation as a free man. The name given me by my dear mother was no less pretentious and long than Frederick Augustus Washington Bailey. I had, however, while living in Maryland, disposed of the Augustus Washington, and retained only Frederick Bailey. Between Baltimore and New Bedford, the better to conceal myself from the slave-hunters. Nathan Johnson, mine host, wished me to allow him to select a name for me. I consented, and he called me by my present name, Frederick Douglass.

I saw in New Bedford the nearest approach to freedom and equality that I had ever seen.

Living in Baltimore as I had done for many years, the reader may be surprised, when I tell the honest truth of the impressions I had in some way conceived of the social and material condition of the people at the north. I had no proper idea of the wealth, refinement, enterprise, and high civilization of this section of the country. I was not long in finding the cause of the difference, in these respects, between the people of the north and south. It was the superiority of educated mind over mere brute force. I will not detain the reader by extended illustrations as to how my understanding was enlightened on this subject. On the wharves of New Bedford I received my first light. I saw there industry without bustle, labor without noise, toil—honest, earnest and exhaustive—without the whip. I saw in New Bedford the nearest approach to freedom and equality that I had ever seen. I was amazed when Mr. Johnson told me that there was nothing in the laws or constitution of Massachusetts that would prevent a colored man from being governor of the State, if the people should see fit to elect him. There, too, the black man's children attended the same public schools with the white man's children, and apparently without objection from any quarter.

The fifth day after my arrival I put on the clothes of a common laborer, and went upon the wharves in search of work. On my way down Union street I saw a large pile of coal in front of the house of Rev. Ephraim Peabody, the Unitarian minister. I went to the kitchen-door and asked the privilege of bringing in and putting away this coal. "What will you charge?" said the lady. "I will leave that to you, madam." "You may put it away," she said. I was not long in accomplishing the job, when

New Bedford Harbor.

The Johnson House in New Bedford was the first place Douglass lived after his escape. On the left is the house and on the right is Johnsons' Quaker meetinghouse.

the dear lady put into my hand two silver half-dollars. To understand the emotion which swelled my heart as I clasped this money, realizing that I had no master who could take it from me—that it was mine—that my hands were my own, and could earn more of the precious coin—one must have been in some sense himself a slave.

The season was growing late and work was plenty. Ships were being fitted out for whaling, and much wood was used in storing them. The sawing this wood was considered a good job. With the help of old Friend Johnson I got a "saw" and "buck" and went at it. It was new business to me, but I never, in the same space of time, did for Covey, the negro-breaker, better work, or more of it, than I did for myself in these earliest years of my freedom.

Notwithstanding the just and humane sentiment of New Bedford three-and-forty years ago, the place was not entirely free from race and color prejudice. It so happened that Mr. Rodney French, a wealthy and enterprising citizen, distinguished as an anti-slavery man, was fitting out a vessel for a whaling voyage, upon which there was a heavy job of calking and coppering to be done. I had some skill in both branches, and applied to Mr. French for work. He, generous man that he was,

told me he would employ me, and I might go at once to the vessel. I obeyed him, but upon reaching the float-stage, where other calkers were at work, I was told that every white man would leave the ship in her unfinished condition if I struck a blow at my trade upon her. Slavery had inured me to hardships that made ordinary trouble sit lightly upon me. Could I have worked at my trade I could have earned two dollars a day, but as a common laborer I received but one dollar. The difference was of great importance to me, but if I could not get two dollars I was glad to get one; and so I went to work for Mr. French as a common laborer. The consciousness that I was free—no longer a slave—kept me cheerful under this and many similar proscriptions which I was destined to meet in New Bedford and elsewhere on the free soil of Massachusetts.

Becoming satisfied that I could not rely on my trade in New Bedford to give me a living, I prepared myself to do any kind of work that came to hand. I sawed wood, shoveled coal, dug cellars, moved rubbish from back-yards, worked on the wharves, loaded and unloaded vessels, and scoured their cabins.

This was an uncertain and unsatisfactory mode of life, for it kept me too much of the time in search of work. Fortunately it was not to last long. One of the gentlemen of whom I have spoken as being in company with Mr. Taber on the Newport wharf when he said to me, "Thee get in," was Mr. Joseph Ricketson, and he was the proprietor of a large candle-works in the south part of the city. By the kindness of Mr. Ricketson I found in this "candle-works," as it was called, though no candles were manufactured there, what is of the utmost importance to a young man just starting in life—constant employment and regular wages.

I had been living four or five months in New Bedford when there came a young man to me with a copy of the *Liberator*, the paper edited by William Lloyd Garrison and published by Isaac Knapp, and asked me to subscribe for it. I told him I had but just escaped from slavery and was of course very poor, and had no money then to pay for it. He was very willing to take me as a subscriber, notwithstanding, and from this time I was brought into contact with the mind of Mr. Garrison, and his paper took a place in my heart second only to the Bible.

Soon after becoming a reader of the *Liberator*, it was my privilege to listen to a lecture in Liberty Hall by Mr. Garrison, its editor. He was then a young man of a singularly pleasing countenance, and earnest and impressive manner. His Bible was his text-book—held sacred as the very word of the Eternal Father. Prejudice against color was rebellion against God. Of all men beneath the sky, the slaves, because most neglected and despised, were nearest and dearest to his great heart. I had not long been a reader of the *Liberator*, and a listener to its editor, before I got a clear comprehension of the principles of the anti-slavery movement. All the anti-slavery meetings held in New Bedford I promptly attended, my heart bounding at every true utterance against the slave system and every rebuke of its friends and supporters. Thus passed the first three years of my free life.

CHAPTER III

INTRODUCED TO THE ABOLITIONISTS

ANTI-SLAVERY CONVENTION AT NANTUCKET—FIRST SPEECH—MUCH SENSATION—EXTRAORDINARY SPEECH OF MR. GARRISON—ANTI-SLAVERY AGENCY—YOUTHFUL ENTHUSIASM—FUGITIVE SLAVESHIP DOUBTED—EXPERIENCE IN SLAVERY WRITTEN—DANGER OF RECAPTURE.

In the summer of 1841 a grand anti-slavery convention was held in Nantucket, under the auspices of Mr. Garrison and his friends. I had taken no holiday since establishing myself in New Bedford, and feeling the need of a little rest, I determined on attending the meeting, though I had no thought of taking part in any of its proceedings. Indeed, I was not aware that any one connected with the convention so much as knew my name. Mr. William C. Coffin, a prominent abolitionist in those days of trial, had heard me speaking to my colored friends in the little school-house on Second street, where we worshiped. He sought me out in the crowd and invited me to say a few words to the convention. Thus sought out, and thus invited, I was induced to express the feelings inspired by the occasion, and the fresh recollection of the scenes through which I had passed as a slave. I trembled in every limb. I am not sure that my embarrassment was not the most effective part of my speech, if speech it could be called. The audience sympathized with me at once, and from having been remarkably quiet, became much excited. Mr. Garrison followed me, taking me as his text, and now, whether I had made an eloquent plea in behalf of freedom, or not, his was one, never to be forgotten. Those who had heard him oftenest and had known him longest, were astonished at his masterly effort. For the time he possessed that almost fabulous inspiration often referred to, but seldom attained, in which a public meeting is transformed, as it were, into a single individuality, the orator swaying a thousand heads and hearts at once and, by the simple majesty of his all-controlling thought, converting his hearers into the express image of his own soul. That night there were at least a thousand Garrisonians in Nantucket!

At the close of this great meeting I was duly waited on by Mr. John A. Collins, then the general agent of the Massachusetts Anti-Slavery Society, and urgently solicited by him to become an agent of that society and publicly advocate its principles. I was reluctant to take the proffered position. I had not been quite three years from slavery and was honestly distrustful of my ability, and I wished to be excused. Besides, publicity might discover me to my master, and many other objections presented themselves. But Mr. Collins was not to be refused, and I finally consented to go out

John A. Collins (1810–1879).

FREDERICK DOUGLASS AND OTHER BLACK ABOLITIONISTS

From *Before the Mayflower* by Lerone Bennett Jr.

For fifty years, from 1845 to 1895, the apostle-militant stood on the watchtower of American freedom, championing the cause of all oppressed men and women. In these years, which spanned the Abolitionist movement, the Civil War, Reconstruction, and the post-Reconstruction period, Douglass helped define the roads and boundaries of black protest, earning the title of "Father of the Protest movement." Like W. E. B. DuBois, he ranged all over the landscape, changing his tactics as the terrain changed. But from first to last, he held to the philosophy of reform that informed the great speech he made at the West India Emancipation Celebration at Canandaigua, New York, on August 4, 1857. The burden of the speech is in one word: struggle. "The whole history of the progress of human liberty," he said, "shows that all concessions yet made to her august claims, have been born of earnest struggle. . . . If there is no struggle there is no progress. Those who profess to favor freedom and yet deprecate agitation, are men who want crops without plowing up the ground, they want rain without thunder and lightning. They want the ocean without the awful roar of its many waters."

What kind of struggle was Douglass talking about?

Was this a moral struggle or a physical struggle? "This struggle," he said, coming to close grips with the subject, "may be a moral one, or it may be a physical one, and it may be both moral and physical, but it must be a struggle. Power concedes nothing without a demand. It never did and it never will. Find out just what any people will quietly submit to and you have found out the exact measure of injustice and wrong which will be imposed upon them, and these will continue till they are resisted with either words or blows, or with both. The limits of tyrants are prescribed by the endurance of those whom they oppress." As for the concrete grievances of blacks, he said: "Negroes will be hunted at the North, and held and flogged at the South so long as they submit to those devilish outrages, and make no resistance, either moral or physical. Men may not get all they pay for in this world, but they must certainly pay for all they get. If we ever get free from the oppressions and wrongs heaped upon us, we must pay for their removal. We must do this by labor, by suffering, by sacrifice, and if needs be, by our lives and the lives of others."

W. E. B. DuBois (1868–1963) was one of the most important African American protest leaders in the struggle that continued into the twentieth century. One of his most notable roles was as a creator of the National Association for the Advancement of Colored People (NAACP).

Such, then, was the gospel of struggle preached by the black edge of the varicolored and variegated abolitionist procession. Douglass was unquestionably the major black actor in that procession, but he shared the spotlight with a number of men and women, who covered the spectrum from pre–Martin Luther King Jr. passive resisters to prototypical Malcolm X's.

*Charles Lenox Remond (1810–1873) was the first
major black abolitionist.*

*Samuel Ringgold Ward (1817– circa 1866). This portrait is from the
frontispiece of his 1855 book,* Autobiography of a Fugitive Negro: His
Anti-Slavery Labours in the United States, Canada, & England.

Charles Lenox Remond, the first major black abolitionist, leaned toward the Garrison tenets of nonviolence and nonvoting. Born in Salem, Massachusetts, the son of a free West Indian hairdresser who got on a boat and paid his way to America, Remond was an elegant little man in elegant clothes—a lover of fine horses and the New England air, fastidious, spare, with a long, deeply furrowed face and an aquiline nose. He began his career as a professional abolitionist in 1838 and shot to fame after a triumphant tour of England. Although Remond was a devoted Garrisonian he later abandoned nonviolence and championed slave revolts. One of the seventeen members of the first antislavery society in America, Remond later served as vice-president of the New England Anti-Slavery Society and president of his county unit. A bitter foe of intolerance, he lectured against slavery until its abolition. In the forties and fifties, however, he was overshadowed by the rising star of Frederick Douglass—and he was human enough to resent it. Remond was not a lucky man; and history, largely the story of lucky people, has passed him by. He did not have the firsthand knowledge of slavery that Douglass had and his speeches lacked Douglass's concreteness and fire. In Remond's later years illness, bad luck and frustration made him somewhat peevish. When Douglass broke with Garrison, Remond supported Garrison and publicly thanked God that he was not a slave or the son of a slave. Douglass, stung to the quick, retorted; "I thank God that I am neither a barber nor the son of a barber."

Samuel Ringgold Ward, one of the most eloquent men of an age of eloquence, was a fugitive slave and the son of a fugitive slave. Unlike Remond, who was a major supporter of the Massachusetts Garrisonians, Ward was a New Yorker who advocated a militant, political brand of abolitionism. Born in 1817 in Maryland, he was carried to New York at an early age by his fugitive slave parents. He was educated there, became a Presbyterian minister and pastored a white church in South Butler, New York. He became a professional antislavery agent in 1839 and was one of the first blacks to join the Liberty party. Big-framed, eloquent, "so black that when he closed his eyes you could not see him," Ward was an imposing presence on abolitionist platforms. He was advertised as "The Black Daniel Webster," but some experts thought he was a better speaker than either Webster or Frederick Douglass. In 1851, after passage of the Fugitive Slave Law, Ward fled America, going first to England and then to Jamaica, where he died in poverty.

for three months, supposing I should in that length of time come to the end of my story and my consequent usefulness.

Here opened for me a new life—a life for which I had had no preparation. Mr. Collins used to say when introducing me to an audience, I was a "graduate from the peculiar institution, with my diploma written on my back." Among the first duties assigned me on entering the ranks was to travel in company with Mr. George Foster to secure subscribers to the *Anti-Slavery Standard* and the *Liberator*. With him I traveled and lectured through the eastern counties of Massachusetts. Much interest was awakened—large meetings assembled. Many came, no doubt from curiosity to hear what a negro could say in his own cause. I was generally introduced as a "chattel"—a "thing"—a piece of southern property—the chairman assuring the audience that it could speak. Fugitive slaves were rare then, and as a fugitive slave lecturer, I had the advantage of being a "bran new fact"—the first one out. The only precaution I took at the beginning, to prevent Master Thomas from knowing where I was and what I was about, was the withholding my former name, my master's name, and the name of the State and county from which I came. During the first three or four months my speeches were almost exclusively made up of narrations of my own personal experience as a slave. "Let us have the facts," said the people. So also said Friend George Foster, who always wished to pin me down to a simple narrative. "Give us the facts," said Collins, "we will take care of the philosophy." "Tell your story, Frederick," would whisper my revered friend, Mr. Garrison, as I stepped upon the platform. It did not entirely satisfy me to narrate wrongs; I felt like denouncing them. I could not always curb my moral indignation for the perpetrators of slaveholding villainy long enough for a circumstantial statement of the facts which I felt almost sure everybody must know. Besides, I was growing and needed room. "People won't believe you ever were a slave, Frederick, if you keep on this way," said friend Foster. "Be yourself," said Collins, "and tell your story." "Better have a little of the plantation speech than not," was said to me; "it is not best that you seem too learned."

This collection box for the Massachusetts Anti-Slavery Society was meant to sit in "the most public room in your dwelling" to collect funds for the group's lectures, newspapers, and pamphlets.

At last the apprehended trouble came. People doubted if I had ever been a slave. They said I did not talk like a slave, look like a slave, or act like a slave, and that they believed I had never been south of Mason and Dixon's line. Thus I was in a pretty fair way to be denounced as an impostor. The committee of the Massachusetts Anti-Slavery Society knew all the facts in my case and agreed with me thus far in the prudence of keeping them private; but going down the aisles of the churches in which my meetings were held, and hearing the outspoken Yankees repeatedly saying, "He's never been a slave, I'll warrant you," I resolved that at no distant day, and by such a revelation of facts as could not be made by any other than a genuine fugitive, I would dispel all doubt. In a little less than four years, therefore, after becoming a public lecturer, I was induced to write out the leading facts connected with my experience in slavery, giving names of persons, places, and dates, thus putting it in the power of any who doubted, to ascertain the truth or falsehood of my story. This statement soon became known in Maryland, and I had reason to believe that an effort would be made to recapture me.

It is not probable that any open attempt to secure me as a slave could have succeeded further than the obtainment by my master of the money value of my bones and sinews. Fortunately for me, in the four years of my labors in the abolition cause I had gained many friends who would have suffered themselves to be taxed to almost any extent to save me from slavery. It was felt that I had committed the double offense of running away and exposing the secrets and crimes of slavery and slaveholders. There was a double motive for seeking my re-enslavement—avarice and vengeance; and while, as I have said, there was little probability of successful recapture, if attempted openly, I was constantly in danger of being spirited away at a moment when my friends could render me no assistance. Thus the reader will observe that the overcoming of one difficulty only opened the way for another, and that though I had reached a free State, and had attained a position for public usefulness, I was still under the liability of losing all I had gained.

CHAPTER IV

RECOLLECTIONS OF OLD FRIENDS

In the State of Rhode Island, under the leadership of Thomas W. Dorr, an effort was made in 1841 to set aside the old colonial charter, under which that State had lived and flourished since the Revolution, and to replace it with a new constitution having such improvements as it was thought that time and experience had shown to be wise and necessary. This new constitution was especially framed to enlarge the basis of representation so far as the white people of the State were concerned—to abolish an odious property qualification and to confine the right of suffrage to white male citizens only. Anti-slavery men wanted a new constitution, but they did not want a defective instrument which required reform at the start. The result was that abolitionists of the State decided that the time had come when the people of Rhode Island might be taught a more comprehensive gospel of human rights than had gotten itself into this Dorr constitution. The public mind was awake, and one class of its people at least was ready to work with us to the extent of seeking to defeat the proposed constitution, though their reasons for such work were far different from ours. Stephen S. Foster, Parker Pillsbury, Abby Kelley, James Monroe, and myself were called into the State to advocate equal rights as against this narrow and proscriptive constitution. We cared nothing for the Dorr party on the one hand, nor the "law and order party" on the other. What we wanted, and what we labored to obtain, was a constitution free from the narrow, selfish, and senseless limitation of the word white. Naturally enough, when we said a strong and striking word against the Dorr Constitution the conservatives were pleased and applauded, while the Dorr men were disgusted and indignant. I think that our labors in Rhode Island during this Dorr excitement did more to abolitionize the State than any previous or subsequent work. It was the "tide," "taken at the flood." One effect of those labors was to induce the old "Law and Order" party, when it set about making its new constitution, to avoid the narrow folly of the Dorrites, and make a constitution which should not abridge any man's rights on account of race or color. Such a constitution was finally adopted.

While thus remembering the noble anti-slavery men and women of Rhode Island, I do not forget that I suffered much rough usage within her borders. It was like all the northern States at that time, under the influence of slave power, and often showed a proscriptive and persecuting spirit, especially upon its railways, steamboats, and in its public houses.

Wendell Phillips (1811–1884), a good friend of Douglass, was an activist for abolitionism, women's rights, and Native Americans.

The harbor view of Providence, Rhode Island, circa 1858.

The Stonington route was a "hard road" for a colored man "to travel" in that day. I was several times dragged from the cars for the crime of being colored.

There is something in the world above fixed rules and the logic of right and wrong, and there is some foundation for recognizing works, which may be called works of supererogation. Wendell Phillips, James Monroe, and William White, were always dear to me for their nice feeling at this point. I have known James Monroe to pull his coat about him and crawl upon the cotton bales between decks and pass the night with me, without a murmur. Wendell Phillips would never go into a first-class car while I was forced into what was called the Jim Crow car. True men they were, who could accept welcome at no man's table where I was refused. I speak of these gentlemen, not as singular or exceptional cases, but as representatives of a large class of the early workers for the abolition of slavery. As a general rule there was in New England after 1840, little difficulty in obtaining suitable places where I could plead the cause of my people. The abolitionists had passed the Red Sea of mobs and had conquered the right to a respectful hearing.

CHAPTER V

ONE HUNDRED CONVENTIONS

ANTI-SLAVERY CONVENTIONS HELD IN PARTS OF NEW ENGLAND AND IN SOME OF THE MIDDLE AND WESTERN STATES—MOBS—INCIDENTS, ETC.

The year 1843 was one of remarkable anti-slavery activity. The New England Anti-Slavery Society, at its annual meeting held in the spring of that year, resolved, under the auspices of Mr. Garrison and his friends, to hold a series of one hundred conventions. The territory embraced in this plan for creating anti-slavery sentiment included New Hampshire, Vermont, New York, Ohio, Indiana, and Pennsylvania. I had the honor to be chosen one of the agents to assist in these proposed conventions, and I never entered upon any work with more heart and hope. All that the American people needed, I thought, was light. Could they know slavery as I knew it, they would hasten to the work of its extinction.

Our first convention was held in Middlebury, [Vermont's] chief seat of learning and the home of William Slade, who was for years the co-worker with John Quincy Adams in Congress; and yet in this town the opposition to our anti-slavery convention was intensely bitter and violent. Few people attended our meeting, and apparently little was accomplished by it. The several towns visited showed that Vermont was surprisingly under the influence of the slave power. Her proud boast that within

her borders no slave had ever been delivered up to his master, did not hinder her hatred to anti-slavery. What was in this respect true of the Green Mountain State was most discouragingly true of New York, the State next visited. All along the Erie canal, from Albany to Buffalo, there was evinced apathy, indifference, aversion, and sometimes a mobocratic spirit. Even Syracuse would not at that time furnish us with church, market, house, or hall in which to hold our meetings. Discovering this state of things, some of our number were disposed to turn our backs upon the town and to shake its dust from our feet, but of these, I am glad to say, I was not one. I had somewhere read of a command to go into the hedges and highways and compel men to come in. Mr. Stephen Smith, under whose hospitable roof we were made at home, thought as I did. The house of our friend Smith stood on the southwest corner of the park. Taking my stand under a small tree in the southeast corner of this park I began to speak in the morning to an audience of five persons, and before the close of my afternoon meeting I had before me not less than five hundred. In the evening I was waited upon by officers of the Congregational church and tendered the use of an old wooden building which they

Henry Highland Garnet (1815–1882).

Left: An illustration from an original edition of Narrative of the Life of Frederick Douglass, an American Slave. *Right: Theodore S. Wright (1797–1847).*

had deserted for a better, but still owned, and here our convention was continued during three days. I believe there has been no trouble to find places in Syracuse in which to hold anti-slavery meetings since.

In the growing city of Rochester we had in every way a better reception. Abolitionists of all shades of opinion were broad enough to give the Garrisonians (for such we were) a hearing. Pleased with our success in Rochester, we—that is, Mr. Bradburn and myself—made our way to Buffalo, then a rising city of steamboats, bustle, and business. Buffalo was too busy to attend to such matters as we had in hand. For nearly a week I spoke every day in this old post-office to audiences constantly increasing in numbers and respectability, till the Baptist church was thrown open to me; and when this became too small I went on Sunday into the open Park and addressed an assembly of four or five thousand persons. After this my colored friends, Charles L. Remond, Henry Highland Garnet, Theodore S. Wright, Amos G. Beaman, Charles M. Ray, and other well-known colored men held a convention here, and then Remond and myself left for our next meeting in Clinton county, Ohio. This was held under a great shed, built for this special purpose by the abolitionists, of whom Dr. Abram Brook and Valentine Nicholson were the most noted. Thousands gathered here and were addressed by

Bradburn, White, Monroe, Remond, Gay, and myself. The influence of this meeting was deep and wide-spread.

From Ohio we divided our forces and went into Indiana. At our first meeting we were mobbed, and some of us had our good clothes spoiled by evil-smelling eggs. At Pendleton this mobocratic spirit was even more pronounced. It was found impossible to obtain a building in which to hold our convention, and our friends erected a platform in the woods, where quite a large audience assembled. As soon as we began to speak a mob of about sixty of the roughest characters I ever looked upon ordered us, through its leaders, to "be silent," threatening us, if we were not, with violence. We attempted to dissuade them, but they had not come to parley but to fight, and were well armed. Undertaking to fight my way through the crowd with a stick which I caught up in the mêlée, I attracted the fury of the mob, which laid me prostrate on the ground under a torrent of blows. Leaving me thus, with my right hand broken, and in a state of unconsciousness, the mobocrats hastily mounted their horses and rode to Andersonville, where most of them resided. As the bones broken were not properly set, my hand has never recovered its natural strength and dexterity.

CHAPTER VI

IMPRESSIONS ABROAD

DANGER TO BE AVERTED—A REFUGE SOUGHT ABROAD—VOYAGE ON THE STEAMSHIP *CAMBRIA*—REFUSAL OF FIRST-CLASS PASSAGE—ATTRACTIONS OF THE FORECASTLE-DECK—EXPERIENCES ABROAD—ATTENTIONS RECEIVED—IMPRESSIONS OF DIFFERENT MEMBERS OF PARLIAMENT AND OF OTHER PUBLIC MEN—CONTRAST WITH LIFE IN AMERICA—KINDNESS OF FRIENDS—THEIR PURCHASE OF MY PERSON AND THE GIFT OF THE SAME TO MYSELF—MY RETURN.

As I have before intimated, the publishing of my "Narrative" was regarded by my friends with mingled feelings of satisfaction and apprehension. They were glad to have the doubts and insinuations which the advocates and apologists of slavery had made against me proved to the world to be false, but they had many fears lest this very proof would endanger my safety, and make it necessary for me to leave a position which in a signal manner had opened before me, and one in which I had thus far been efficient in assisting to arouse the moral sentiment of the community against a system which had deprived me, in common with my fellow-slaves, of all the attributes of manhood.

I became myself painfully alive to the liability which surrounded me, and which might at any moment scatter all my proud hopes and return me to a doom worse than death. It was thus I was led to seek a refuge in monarchical England from the dangers of republican slavery.

My friend James N. Buffum of Lynn, Mass., who was to accompany me, applied on board the steamer *Cambria* of the Cunard line for tickets, and was told that I could not be received as a cabin passenger.

The insult was keenly felt by my white friends, but to me such insults were so frequent and expected that it was of no great consequence whether I went in the cabin or in the steerage. Moreover, I felt that if I could not go in the first cabin, first cabin passengers could come in the second cabin, and in this thought I was not mistaken, as I soon found myself an object of more general interest than I wished to be, and, so far from being degraded by being placed in the second cabin, that part of the ship became the scene of as much pleasure and refinement as the cabin itself. The effect was that with the majority of the passengers all color distinctions were flung to the winds, and I found myself treated with every mark of respect.

James N. Buffum (1807–1887).

This watercolor, painted in 1846 (the year after Douglass sailed on her in transatlantic voyage to England), is a view from the steamer Cambria *in Boston Harbor.*

A pediment of Free Trade Hall, Manchester, England.

My visit to England did much for me every way. Not the least among the many advantages derived from it was the opportunity it afforded me of becoming acquainted with educated people and of seeing and hearing many of the most distinguished men of that country. When I went to England that country was in the midst of a tremendous agitation. The people were divided by two great questions of "Repeal"—the repeal of the corn laws and the repeal of the union between England and Ireland.

Debate ran high in Parliament and among the people everywhere, especially concerning the corn laws. Of the anti-corn-law movement, Richard Cobden and John Bright, both then members of Parliament, were the leaders. They were the rising statesmen of England, and possessed a very friendly disposition toward America.

Wherever these two great men appeared, the people assembled in thousands. They could, at an hour's notice, pack the Town Hall of Birmingham, which would hold seven thousand persons, or the Free Trade Hall in Manchester, and Covent Garden theater, London, each of which was capable of holding eight thousand.

One of the first attentions shown me by these gentlemen was to make me welcome at the Free-Trade Club, in London.

I was not long in England before a crisis was reached in the anti-corn-law movement. The announcement that Sir Robert Peel, then prime minister of England, had become a convert to the views of Messrs. Cobden and Bright, came upon the country with startling effect, and formed the turning-point in the anti-corn-law question. Sir Robert had been the strong defense of the landed aristocracy of England, and his defection left them without a competent leader; and just here came the opportunity so Mr. Benjamin Disraeli, the Hebrew, since Lord Beaconsfield. To him it was in public affairs the "tide which led on to fortune." His ability was equal to the situation, and the world knows the result of his ambition. Despite all his ability and power, however, as the defender of the landed interests of England, his cause was already lost. The increasing power of the anti-corn-law league, the burden of the tax upon bread, the cry of distress coming from famine-stricken Ireland, and the adhesion of Peel to the views of Cobden and Bright, made the repeal of the corn laws speedy and certain.

The repeal of the union between England and Ireland was not so fortunate. It is still, under one name or another, the cherished hope and inspiration of her sons. It stands little better or stronger than it did six and thirty years ago, when its greatest advocate, Daniel

Top Left: Benjamin Disraeli (1804–1881). Top Right: Sir Robert Peel (1788–1850).
Bottom Left: Hans Christian Andersen (1805–1875). Bottom Right: Daniel O'Connell (1775–1847), "The Champion of Liberty."

Know all men by these prents that I Thomas Auld of Talbot County and State of Maryland, for and in consideration of the sum of one hundred dollars current money to me in hand paid by Hugh Auld of the City of Baltimore in the said State, at and before the sealing and delivering of these presents the receipt whereof, I the said Thomas Auld do hereby acknowledge, have granted, bargained, and sold, and by these prents do grant bargain, and sell unto the said Hugh Auld his executors administrators and assigns one negro man by the name of Frederick Bailey, he is now at this time about twenty seven years old. To have and to hold the said negro man for life, and I the said Thomas Auld, for myself my heirs, executors and administrators, all and singular the said Frederick Bailey unto the said Hugh Auld his executors, administrators and assigns, against me the said Thomas Auld my executors and administrators, and against all and every other person or persons whatsoever, shall and will warrant and forever defend by these presents, In witness whereof I set my hand and seal this 25th day of October eighteen hundred and forty five

Signed, sealed and delivered in presence of — *Wrightson Jones*

Thos Auld [Seal]
Hugh Auld [Seal]

State of Maryland. Talbot County, to wit. Be it remembered and it is hereby certified that on this 25th day of October Anno Domini, Eighteen hundred and forty five, before the subscriber a Justice of the Peace, of the state of Maryland, in and for Talbot County personally appeared Thomas Auld and Hugh Auld

A versoion of the "bill of sale" that transferred the legal ownership of Douglass from Thomas Auld to Hugh Auld. Hugh Auld then filed Douglass's manumission, which legally set him free.

cause, for, though he failed to effect the repeal of the union between England and Ireland, he fought out the battle of Catholic emancipation, and was clearly the friend of liberty the world over. In introducing me to an immense audience in Conciliation Hall he playfully called me the "Black O'Connell of the United States." Nor did he let the occasion pass without his usual word of denunciation of our slave system. No transatlantic statesman bore a testimony more marked and telling against the crime and curse of slavery than did Daniel O'Connell. He would shake the hand of no slaveholder, nor allow himself to be introduced to one if he knew him to be such. When the friends of repeal in the Southern States sent him money with which to carry on his work, he, with ineffable scorn, refused the bribe and sent back what he considered the blood-stained offering, saying he would "never purchase the freedom of Ireland with the price of slaves."

While in England, I saw few literary celebrities, except William and Mary Howitt, and Sir John Bowering. I was invited to breakfast by the latter in company with Wm. Lloyd Garrison, and spent a delightful morning with him, chiefly as a listener to their conversation. William and Mary Howitt were among the kindliest people I ever met. Their interest in America, and their well-known testimonies against slavery, made me feel much at home with them at their house in that part of London known as Clapham. Whilst stopping here, I met the Swedish poet and author—Hans Christian Andersen.

Whilst in Edinburgh, so famous for its beauty, its educational institutions, its literary men, and its history, I had a very intense desire

O'Connell, welcomed me to Ireland and to "Conciliation Hall," and where I first had a specimen of his truly wondrous eloquence. Until I heard this man I had thought that the story of his oratory and power were greatly exaggerated. I did not see how a man could speak to twenty or thirty thousand people at one time and be heard by any considerable portion of them, but the mystery was solved when I saw his ample person and heard his musical voice. His eloquence came down upon the vast assembly like a summer thunder-shower upon a dusty road. He could at will stir the multitude to a tempest of wrath or reduce it to the silence with which a mother leaves the cradle-side of her sleeping babe. He was called "The Liberator," and not without

gratified—and that was to see and converse with George Combe, the eminent mental philosopher, and author of "Combe's Constitution of Man," a book which had been placed in my hands a few years before. It would detain the reader too long, and make this volume too large, to tell of the many kindnesses shown me while abroad, or even to mention all the great and noteworthy persons who gave me a friendly hand and a cordial welcome; but there is one other, now long gone to his rest, of whom a few words must be spoken, and that one was Thomas Clarkson—the last of the noble line of Englishmen who inaugurated the anti-slavery movement for England and the civilized world— the life-long friend and co-worker with Granville Sharpe, William

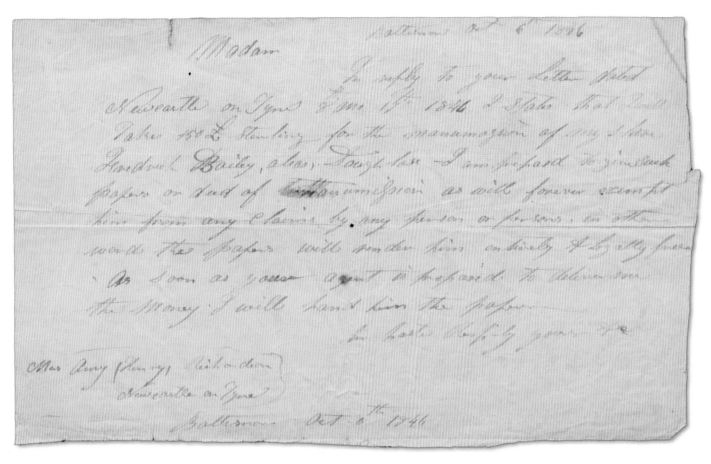

This is a letter from Hugh Auld to Anna Richardson in which Auld agrees to the manumission of Douglass.

Wilberforce, Thomas Fowell Buxton, and other leaders in that great reform which nearly put an end to slavery in all parts of the globe. We found the venerable object of our visit seated at a table where he had been busily writing a letter to America against slavery; for though in his eighty-seventh year, he continued to write. When we were presented to him, he rose to receive us. The scene was impressive. It was the meeting of two centuries. Garrison, Thompson, and myself were young men. After shaking hands with my two distinguished friends, and giving them welcome, he took one of my hands in both of his, and, in a tremulous voice, said, "God bless you, Frederick Douglass! I have given sixty years of my life to the emancipation of your people, and if I had sixty years more they should all be given to the same cause."

Another interesting circumstance connected with my visit to England was the position of the Free Church of Scotland, with the great Doctors Chalmers, Cunningham, and Candlish at its head. That Church had settled for itself the question which was frequently asked by the opponents of abolition at home, "What have we to do with slavery?" by accepting contributions from slaveholders; i.e., receiving the price of blood into its treasury with which to build churches and pay

ministers for preaching the gospel; and worse than this, when honest, anti-slavery men in Glasgow denounced the transaction as disgraceful, and shocking to the religious sentiment of Scotland, this church, through its leading divines, instead of repenting and seeking to amend the mistake into which it had fallen, caused that mistake to become a flagrant sin by undertaking to defend, in the name of God and the Bible, the principle not only of taking the money of slave-dealers to build churches and thus extend the gospel, but of holding fellowship with the traffickers in human flesh.

The general assembly of the Free Church was in progress at Cannon Mills, Edinburgh. The building would hold twenty-five hundred persons, and on this occasion was densely packed, notice having been given that Doctors Cunningham and Candlish would speak that day in defense of the relations of the Free Church of Scotland to slavery in America. Messrs. Thompson, Buffum, myself and a few other anti-slavery friends attended, but sat at such distance and in such position as not to be observed from the platform. The excitement was intense, having been greatly increased by a series of meetings held by myself and friends, in the most splendid hall in that most beautiful city, just previous to this meeting of the general assembly. "SEND BACK THE MONEY!" in large capitals stared from every street corner; "SEND BACK THE MONEY!" adorned the broad flags of the pavement; "SEND BACK THE MONEY!" was the chorus of the popular street-song; "SEND BACK THE MONEY!" was the heading of leading editorials in the daily newspapers. The Free Church held on to the blood-stained money, and continued to justify itself in its position.

One good result followed the conduct of the Free Church; it furnished an occasion for making the people thoroughly acquainted with the character of slavery and for arraying against it the moral and religious sentiment of that country; therefore, while we did not procure the sending back of the money, we were amply justified by the good which really did result from our labors.[1]

I felt it my duty to labor and suffer with my oppressed people in my native land.

Miss Ellen Richardson, an excellent member of the society of Friends, assisted by her sister-in-law, Mrs. Henry Richardson, a lady devoted to every good word and work, the friend of the Indian and the African, conceived the plan of raising a fund to effect my ransom from slavery. They corresponded with Hon. Walter Forward of Pennsylvania, and through him ascertained that Captain Auld would take one hundred and fifty pounds sterling for me; and this sum they promptly raised and paid for my liberation, placing the papers of my manumission into my hands before they would tolerate the idea of my return to my native land. To this commercial transaction, to this blood-money, I owe my immunity from the operation of the fugitive slave law of 1793, and also from that of 1850. The whole affair speaks for itself, and needs no comment, now that slavery has ceased to exist in this country, and is not likely ever again to be revived.

Some of my uncompromising anti-slavery friends in this country failed to see the wisdom of this commercial transaction, and were not pleased that I consented to it, even by my silence. They thought it a violation of anti-slavery principles, conceding the right of property in man, and a wasteful expenditure of money. For myself, viewing it simply in the light of a ransom, or as money extorted by a robber, and my liberty of more value than one hundred and fifty pounds sterling, I could not see either a violation of the laws of morality or of economy. It is true I was not in the possession of my claimants, and could have

remained in England, for my friends would have generously assisted me in establishing myself there. To this I could not consent. I felt it my duty to labor and suffer with my oppressed people in my native land. Considering all the circumstances, the fugitive bill included, I think now as then, that the very best thing was done in letting Master Hugh have the money, and thus leave me free to return to my appropriate field of labor.[1]

Having remained abroad nearly two years, and being about to return to America, not as I left it, a slave, but a freeman, prominent friends of the cause of emancipation intimated their intention to make me a testimonial, both on grounds of personal regard to me and also to the cause to which they were so ardently devoted. How such a project would have succeeded I do not know, but many reasons led me to prefer that my friends should simply give me the means of obtaining a printing-press and materials to enable me to start a paper advocating the interests of my enslaved and oppressed people. In my judgement, a tolerably well-conducted press in the hands of persons of the despised race would, by calling out and making them acquainted with their own latent powers, by enkindling their hope of a future and developing their moral force, prove a most powerful means of removing prejudice and awakening an interest in them. At that time there was not a single newspaper in the country, regularly published by the colored people, though many attempts had been made to establish such, and had from one cause or another failed.. The result was that nearly two thousand five hundred dollars were speedily raised toward my establishing such a paper as I had indicated.

Proposing to leave England and turning my face toward America in the spring of 1847, I was painfully reminded of the kind of life which awaited me on my arrival. For the first time in the many months spent abroad I was met with proscription on account of my color. While in London I had purchased a ticket and secured a berth for returning home in the *Cambria*—the steamer in which I had come from thence—and paid therefor the round sum of forty pounds nineteen shillings sterling. This was first-cabin fare; but on going on board I found that the Liverpool agent had ordered my berth to be given to another, and forbidden my entering the saloon.

This contemptible conduct met with stern rebuke from the British press. The *London Times* and other leading journals throughout the United Kingdom held up the outrage to unmitigated condemnation. So good an opportunity for calling out British sentiment on the subject had not before occurred, and it was fully embraced. The result was that Mr. Cunard came out in a letter expressive of his regret, and promising that the like indignity should never occur again on his steamers, which promise I believe has been faithfully kept.

CHAPTER VII

TRIUMPHS AND TRIALS

New experiences—Painful disagreement of opinion with old friends—Final decision to publish my paper in Rochester—Its fortunes and its friends—Change in my own views regarding the Constitution of the United States—Fidelity to conviction—Loss of old friends—Support of new ones—Loss of house, etc., by fire—Triumphs and trials—Underground railroad—Incidents.

Prepared as I was to meet with many trials and perplexities on reaching home, one of which I little dreamed was awaiting me. My plans for future usefulness, as indicated in the last chapter, were all settled, and in imagination I already saw myself wielding my pen as well as my voice in the great work of renovating the public mind, and building up a public sentiment, which should send slavery to the grave, and restore to "liberty and the pursuit of happiness" the people with whom I had suffered.

My friends in Boston had been informed of what I was intending, and I expected to find them favorably disposed toward my cherished enterprise. In this I was mistaken. They had many reasons against it. First, no such paper was needed; secondly, it would interfere with my usefulness as a lecturer; thirdly, I was better fitted to speak than to write; fourthly, the paper could not succeed. This opposition from a quarter so highly esteemed, and to which I had been accustomed to look for advice and direction, caused me not only to hesitate, but inclined me to abandon the undertaking. The unsuccessful projectors of all former attempts had been my superiors in point of education, and if they had failed how could I hope for success? Yet I did hope for success, and persisted in the undertaking, encouraged by my English friends to go forward.

From motives of peace, instead of issuing my paper in Boston, among New England friends, I went to Rochester, N. Y., among strangers, where the local circulation of my paper—"THE NORTH STAR"—would not interfere with that of the *Liberator* or the *Anti-Slavery Standard*, for I was then a faithful disciple of Wm. Lloyd Garrison, and fully committed to his doctrine touching the pro-slavery character of the Constitution of the United States, also the non-voting principle of which he was the known and distinguished advocate. With him, I held it to be the first duty of the non-slaveholding States to dissolve the union with the slaveholding States, and hence my cry, like his, was "No union with slaveholders." After a time, a careful reconsideration of the subject convinced me that there was no necessity for dissolving the "union between the northern and southern States"; that to seek this dissolution was no

An 1848 issue of Douglass's paper the North Star.

The printing room for the North Star *in 1893.*

part of my duty as an abolitionist; that to abstain from voting was to refuse to exercise a legitimate and powerful means for abolishing slavery; and that the Constitution of the United States not only contained no guarantees in favor of slavery, but, on the contrary, was in its letter and spirit an anti-slavery instrument, demanding the abolition of slavery as a condition of its own existence as the supreme law of the land.

The *North Star* was a large sheet, published weekly, at a cost of $80 per week, and an average circulation of 3,000 subscribers. There were many times when, in my experience as editor and publisher, I was very hard pressed for money, but by one means or another I succeeded so well as to keep my pecuniary engagements, and to keep my anti-slavery banner steadily flying during all the conflict from the autumn of 1847 till the union of the States was assured and emancipation was a fact accomplished. I had friends abroad as well as at home who helped me liberally. But to no one person was I more indebted for substantial assistance than

Frederick Douglass, circa 1847, the year he founded the North Star.

to Mrs. Julia Griffiths Crofts. She came to my relief when my paper had nearly absorbed all my means, and I was heavily in debt, and when I had mortgaged my house to raise money to meet current expenses; and in a single year by her energetic and effective management enabled me to extend the circulation of my paper from 2,000 to 4,000 copies, pay off the debts and lift the mortgage from my house. During the first three or four years my paper was published under the name of the *North Star*. It was subsequently changed to *Frederick Douglass' Paper*, in order to distinguish it from the many papers with "Stars" in their titles.

Of course there were moral forces operating against me in Rochester, as well as material ones. There were those who regarded the publication of a "Negro paper" in that beautiful city as a blemish and a misfortune. The *New York Herald*, true to the spirit of the times, counselled the people of the place to throw my printing-press into Lake Ontario and to banish me to Canada, and, while they were not quite prepared for this violence, it was plain that many of them did not well relish my presence amongst them. This feeling, however, wore away gradually, as the people knew more of me and my works. I lectured every Sunday evening during an entire winter in the beautiful Corinthian Hall, then owned by Wm. R. Reynolds, Esq., who, though he was not an abolitionist, was a lover of fair play, and was willing to allow me to be heard.

The 2d of June, 1872, brought me a very grievous loss. My house in Rochester was burnt to the ground, and among other things of value, twelve volumes of my paper, covering the period from 1848 to 1860, were devoured by the flames. I have never been able to replace them, and the loss is immeasurable. Only a few weeks before, I had been invited to send these bound volumes to the library of Harvard University, where they would have been preserved in a fire-proof building, and the result of my procrastination attests the wisdom of more than one proverb. If I have at any time said or written that which is worth remembering or repeating, I must have said such things between the years 1848 and 1860, and my paper was a chron-icle of most of what I said during that time. Within that space we had the great Free-Soil Convention at Buffalo, the Nomination of Martin Van Buren, the Fugitive-Slave Law, the 7th of March Speech by Daniel Webster, the Dred Scott decision, the repeal of the Missouri Compromise, the Kansas Nebraska bill, the Border war in Kansas, the John Brown raid

This house-turned-furniture-store on Alexander Street is one of the many houses Douglass lived in in Rochester, New York.

upon Harper's Ferry, and a part of the War against the Rebellion, with much else, well calculated to fire the souls of men having one spark of liberty and patriotism within them. I have only fragments now of all the work accomplished during these twelve years, and must cover this chasm as best I can from memory, and the incidental items which I am able to glean from various sources.

One important branch of my anti-slavery work in Rochester, in addition to that of speaking and writing against slavery, must not be forgotten or omitted. My position gave me the chance of hitting that old enemy some telling blows, in another direction than these. I was on the southern border of Lake Ontario, and the Queen's dominions were right over the way—and my prominence as an abolitionist, and as the editor of an anti-slavery paper, naturally made me the station-master and conductor of the underground railroad passing through this goodly city. Secrecy and concealment were necessary conditions to the success-ful operation of this railroad, and hence its prefix "underground." My agency was all the more exciting and interesting, because not altogether

free from danger. I could take no step in it without exposing myself to fine and imprisonment, for these were the penalties imposed by the fugitive-slave law for feeding, harboring, or otherwise assisting a slave to escape from his master; but, in face of this fact, I can say I never did more congenial, attractive, fascinating, and satisfactory work.

So numerous were the fugitives passing through Rochester that I was obliged at last to appeal to my British friends for the means of sending them on their way, and when Mr. and Mrs. Carpenter and Mrs. Crofts took the matter in hand, I had never any further trouble in that respect. When slavery was abolished I wrote to Mrs. Carpenter, con-gratulating her that she was relieved of the work of raising funds for such purposes, and the characteristic reply of that lady was that she had been very glad to do what she had done, and had no wish for relief.

My pathway was not entirely free from thorns in Rochester, and the wounds and pains inflicted by them were perhaps much less eas-ily borne, because of my exemption from such annoyances while in England. A seminary for young ladies and misses, under the auspices

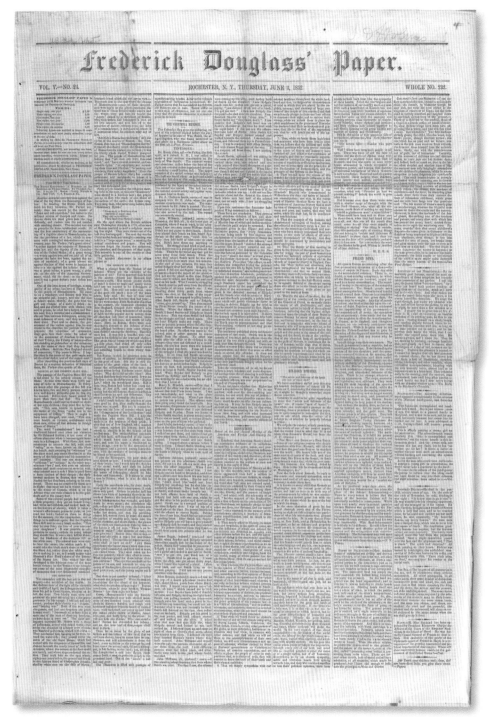

An 1895 printing of Frederick Douglass' Paper.

was lonely in that school; that she was in fact kept in solitary confinement; that she was not allowed in the room with the other girls, nor to go into the yard when they went out; that she was kept in a room by herself and not permitted to be seen or heard by the others. I went at once to Miss Tracy to ascertain if what I had heard was true, and was coolly told it was, and the miserable plea was offered that it would have injured her school if she had done otherwise.

My troubles attending the education of my children were not to end here. They were not allowed in the public school in the district in which I lived, owned property, and paid taxes, but were compelled, if they went to a public school, to go over to the other side of the city to an inferior colored school. I hardly need say that I was not prepared to submit tamely to this proscription, any more than I had been to submit to slavery, so I had them taught at home for a while by Miss Thayer. Meanwhile I went to the people with the question, and created considerable agitation. I sought and obtained a hearing before the Board of Education, and after repeated efforts with voice and pen the doors of the public schools were opened and colored children were permitted to attend them in common with others. There were barriers erected against colored people in most other places of instruction and amusement in the city, and until I went there they were imposed without any apparent sense of injustice and wrong, and submitted to in silence; but one by one they have gradually been removed, and colored people now enter freely, without hindrance or observation, all places of public resort.

Notwithstanding what I have said of the adverse feeling exhibited by some of its citizens at my selection of Rochester as the place in which to establish my paper, and the trouble in educational matters just referred to, that selection was in many respects very fortunate. The city was and still is the center of a virtuous, intelligent, enterprising, liberal, and growing population.

I now look back to my life and labors there with unalloyed satisfaction, and having spent a quarter of a century among its people, I shall always feel more at home there than anywhere else in this country.

of Miss Tracy, was near my house on Alexander street, and desirous of having my daughter educated like the daughters of other men, I applied to Miss Tracy for her admission to her school. All seemed fair, and the child was duly sent to "Tracy Seminary," and I went about my business happy in the thought that she was in the way of a refined and Christian education. Several weeks elapsed before I knew how completely I was mistaken. The little girl came home to me one day and told me she

CHAPTER VIII

JOHN BROWN AND MRS. STOWE

MY FIRST MEETING WITH CAPT. BROWN—THE FREE-SOIL MOVEMENT—
COLORED CONVENTION—*UNCLE TOM'S CABIN*—INDUSTRIAL SCHOOL
FOR COLORED PEOPLE.

About the time I began my enterprise in Rochester I chanced to spend a night and a day under the roof of a man whose character and conversation, and whose objects and aims in life, made a very deep impression upon my mind and heart. His name had been mentioned to me by several prominent colored men, among whom were the Rev. Henry Highland Garnet and J. W. Loguen. In speaking of him their voices would drop to a whisper, and what they said of him made me very eager to see and to know him. Fortunately, I was invited to see him in his own house.

In person he was lean, strong, and sinewy, of the best New England mold, built for times of trouble and fitted to grapple with the flintiest hardships. Clad in plain American woolen, shod in boots of cowhide leather, and wearing a cravat of the same substantial material, under six feet high, less than 150 pounds in weight, aged about fifty, he presented a figure straight and symmetrical as a mountain pine. His bearing was singularly impressive. His head was not large, but compact and high. His hair was coarse, strong, slightly gray and closely trimmed, and grew low on his forehead. His face was smoothly shaved,

and revealed a strong, square mouth, supported by a broad and prominent chin. His eyes were bluish-gray, and in conversation they were full of light and fire. When on the street, he moved with a long, springing, race-horse step, absorbed by his own reflections, neither seeking nor shunning observation. Such was the man whose name I had heard in whispers; such was Captain John Brown, whose name has now passed into history, as that of one of the most marked characters and greatest heroes known to American fame.

Captain Brown cautiously approached the subject which he wished to bring to my attention; for he seemed to apprehend opposition to his views. He denounced slavery in look and language fierce and bitter, thought that slaveholders had forfeited their right to live, that the slaves had the right to gain their liberty in any way they could, did not believe that moral suasion would ever liberate the slave, or that political action would abolish the system. He said that he had long had a plan which could accomplish this end, and he had invited me to his house to lay that plan before me. He said he had been for some time looking for colored men to whom he could safely reveal his secret, and at times he had almost despaired of finding

*John Brown (1800–1859) believed the only way to end
slavery was by an armed insurrection.*

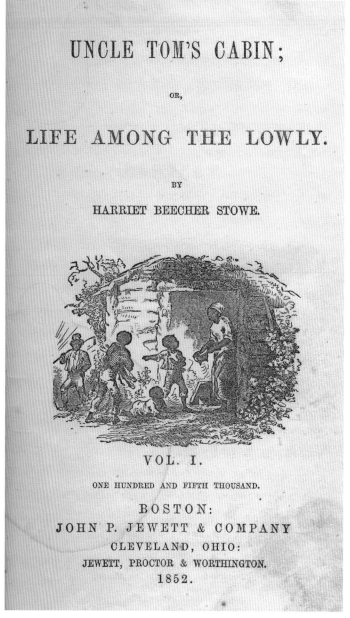

Left: Sojourner Truth (circa 1797– 1883). Right: The title page for an original edition of Uncle Tom's Cabin.

such men; but that now he was encouraged, for he saw heads of such rising up in all directions. He had observed my course at home and abroad, and he wanted my cooperation. His plan as it then lay in his mind had much to commend it. It did not, as some suppose, contemplate a general rising among the slaves, and a general slaughter of the slave-masters. An insurrection, he thought, would only defeat the object; but his plan did contemplate the creating of an armed force which should act in the very heart of the South. He was not averse to the shedding of blood, and thought the practice of carrying arms would be a good one for the colored people to adopt, as it would give them a sense of their manhood. No people, he said, could have self-respect, or be respected, who would not fight for their freedom. He called my attention to a map of the United States, and pointed out to me the far-reaching Alleghenies, which stretch away from the borders of New York into the Southern States. "These mountains," he said, "are the basis of my plan. God has given the strength of the hills to freedom; they were placed here for the emancipation of the negro race; they are full of natural forts, where one man for defense will be equal to a hundred for attack; they are full also of good hiding-places, where large numbers of brave men could be concealed, and baffle and elude pursuit for a long time. I know these mountains well, and could take a body of men into them and keep them there despite of all the efforts of Virginia to dislodge them. The true object to be sought is first of all to destroy the money value of slave property; and that can only be done by rendering such property insecure. My plan, then, is to take at first about twenty-five picked men, and begin on a small scale; supply them with arms and ammunition and post them in squads of fives on a line of twenty-five miles. The most persuasive and judicious of these shall go down to the fields from time to time, as opportunity offers, and induce the slaves to join them, seeking and selecting the most restless and daring."

With care and enterprise he thought he could soon gather a force of one hundred hardy men, men who would be content to lead the free and adventurous life. When I asked him how he would support these men, he said emphatically that he would subsist them upon the enemy. Slavery was a state of war, and the slave had a right to anything necessary to his freedom. "But," said I, "suppose you succeed in running off a few slaves, and thus impress the Virginia slaveholders with a sense of insecurity in their slaves, the effect will be only to make them sell their slaves further south." "That," said he, "will be what I want first to do; then I would follow them up. If we could drive slavery out of one county, it would be a great gain; it would weaken the system throughout the State." "But they would employ bloodhounds to hunt you out of the mountains." "That they might attempt," said he, "but the chances are, we should whip them, and when we should have whipped one squad, they would be careful how they pursued." When I suggested that we might convert the slaveholders, he became much excited, and said that could never be, "he knew their proud hearts and that they would never be induced to give up their slaves, until they felt a big stick about their heads."

From this night spent with John Brown in Springfield, Mass., 1847, while I continued to write and speak against slavery, I became all the same less hopeful of its peaceful abolition. My utterances became more and more tinged by the color of this man's strong impressions. Speaking at an anti-slavery convention in Salem,

Ohio, I expressed this apprehension that slavery could only be destroyed by blood-shed, when I was suddenly and sharply interrupted by my good old friend Sojourner Truth with the question, "Frederick, is God dead?" "No," I answered, "and because God is not dead slavery can only end in blood." My quaint old sister was of the Garrison school of non-resistants, and was shocked at my sanguinary doctrine, but she too became an advocate of the sword, when the war for the maintenance of the Union was declared.

In 1848 it was my privilege to attend, and in some measure to participate in the famous Free-Soil Convention held in Buffalo, New York.

A campaign banner for the Free-Soil Party's candidates Martin Van Buren and Charles Francis Adams. The short-lived party opposed slavery and was mostly absorbed by the Republican Party in the mid-1850s.

It was a vast and variegated assemblage, composed of persons from all sections of the North, and may be said to have formed a new departure in the history of forces organized to resist the growing and aggressive demands of slavery and the slave power. Until this Buffalo convention, anti-slavery agencies had been mainly directed to the work of changing public sentiment by exposing through the press and on the platform the nature of the slave system. The conviction became general that the time had come for a new organization which should embrace all who were in any manner opposed to slavery and the slave power, and this Buffalo Free-Soil convention was the result of that conviction. It is easy to say that this or that measure would have been wiser and better than the one adopted. But any measure is vindicated by its necessity and good results. It was impossible for the mountain to go to Mahomet, or for the Free-Soil element to go to the old Liberty party; so the latter went to the former. "All is well that ends well." This Buffalo convention of free-soilers, however low was their standard, did lay the foundation of a grand superstructure. It was a powerful link in the chain of events by which the slave system has been abolished, the slave emancipated and the country saved from dismemberment.

*Phillip's Inn and, next to it, Harriet Beecher Stowe's house in
Andover, Massachusetts.*

After the Free-Soil party, with "Free Soil," "Free Labor," "Free States," "Free Speech," and "Free Men" on its banner, had defeated the almost permanently victorious Democratic party under the leadership of so able and popular a standard-bearer as General Lewis Cass, Mr. Calhoun and other southern statesmen were more than ever alarmed at the rapid increase of anti-slavery feeling in the North, and devoted their energies more and more to the work of devising means to stay the torrents and tie up the storm. They clamored for more slave States, more power in the Senate and House of Representatives, and insisted upon the suppression of free speech. At the end of two years, in 1850, when Clay and Calhoun, two of the ablest leaders the South ever had, were still in the Senate, we had an attempt at a settlement of differences between the North and South which our legislators meant to be final. What those measures were I need not here enumerate, except to say that chief among them was the Fugitive Slave Bill, framed by James M. Mason of Virginia and supported by Daniel Webster of Massachusetts—a bill undoubtedly more designed to involve the North in complicity with slavery and deaden its moral sentiment than to procure the return of fugitives to their so-called owners.

Living, as I then did, in Rochester, on the border of Canada, I was compelled to see the terribly distressing effects of this cruel enactment. Fugitive slaves who had lived for many years safely and securely in western New York and elsewhere, some of whom had by industry and economy saved money and bought little homes for themselves and their children, were suddenly alarmed and compelled to flee to Canada for safety as from an enemy's land—a doomed city—and take up a dismal march to a new abode, empty-handed, among strangers. The hardships imposed by this atrocious and shameless law were cruel and shocking, and yet only a few of all the fugitives of the Northern States were returned to slavery under its infamously wicked provisions. As a means of recapturing their runaway property in human flesh the law was an utter failure. Its efficiency was destroyed by its enormity. Its chief effect was to produce alarm and terror among the class subject to its operation, and this it did most effectually and distressingly. Even colored people who had been free all their lives felt themselves very insecure in their freedom, for under this law the oaths of any two villains were sufficient to consign a free man to slavery for life. While the law was a terror to the free, it was a still greater terror to the escaped bondman. To him there was no peace. Asleep or awake, at work or at rest, in church or market, he was liable to surprise and capture. Happily this reign of terror did not continue long. Despite the efforts of Daniel Webster and Millard Fillmore and our Doctors of Divinity, the law fell rapidly into disrepute. The thing which more than all else destroyed the fugitive slave law was the resistance made to it by the fugitives themselves.

In the midst of these fugitive slave troubles came the book known as *Uncle Tom's Cabin*, a work of marvelous depth and power. Nothing

Left: Harriet Beecher Stowe (1811–1852), author of Uncle Tom's Cabin.
Right: Daniel Webster (1782–1852), a supporter of the Fugitive Slave Bill.

could have better suited the moral and humane requirements of the hour. Its effect was amazing, instantaneous, and universal. No book on the subject of slavery had so generally and favorably touched the American heart. It combined all the power and pathos of preceding publications of the kind, and was hailed by many as an inspired production. Mrs. Stowe at once became an object of interest and admiration. She had made fortune and fame at home, and had awakened a deep interest abroad. Eminent persons in England, roused to anti-slavery enthusiasm by her "Uncle Tom's Cabin," invited her to visit that country, and promised to give her a testimonial. Mrs. Stowe accepted the invitation and the proffered testimonial. Before sailing for England, however, she invited me from Rochester, N. Y., to spend a day at her house in Andover, Mass. Delighted with an opportunity to become personally acquainted with the gifted authoress, I lost no time in making my way to Andover. I was received at her home with genuine cordiality. There was no contradiction between the author and her book. Mrs. Stowe appeared in conversation equally as well as she appeared in her writing. She made to me a nice little speech in announcing her object in sending for me. "I have invited you here," she said, "because I wish to confer with you as to what can be done for the free colored people of the country. I am going to England and expect to have a considerable sum of money placed in my hands, and I intend to use it in some way for the permanent improvement of the

free colored people, and especially for that class which has become free by their own exertions. In what way I can do this most successfully is the subject about which I wish to talk with you. In any event I desire to have some monument rise after *Uncle Tom's Cabin*, which shall show that it produced more than a transient influence." What I thought of as best was a series of workshops, where colored people could learn some of the handicrafts, learn to work in iron, wood, and leather, and where a plain English education could also be taught. I argued that the want of money was the root of all evil to the colored people. After listening to me at considerable length, she was good enough to tell me that she favored my views, and would devote the money she expected to receive abroad to meeting the want I had described as the most important; by establishing an institution in which colored youth should learn trades as well as to read, write, and count.

After her return to this country I called again on Mrs. Stowe, and was much disappointed to learn from her that she had reconsidered her plan for the industrial school. I have never been able to see any force in the reasons for this change. It is enough, however, to say that they were sufficient for her, and that she no doubt acted conscientiously, though her change of purpose was a great disappointment, and placed me in an awkward position before the colored people of this country, as well as to friends abroad, to whom I had given assurances that the money would be appropriated in the manner I have described.

CHAPTER IX

INCREASING DEMANDS OF THE SLAVE POWER

INCREASED DEMANDS OF SLAVERY—WAR IN KANSAS—JOHN BROWN'S RAID—HIS CAPTURE AND EXECUTION—MY ESCAPE.

N otwithstanding the natural tendency of the human mind to weary of an old story, and to turn away from chronic abuses for which it sees no remedy, the anti-slavery agitation for thirty long years (from 1830 to 1860) was sustained with ever-increasing intensity and power. It was forever forcing itself into prominence. Unconscious, apparently, of its own deformity, it omitted no occasion for inviting disgust by seeking approval and admiration. It was noisiest when it should have been most silent and unobtrusive. Every effort made to put down agitation only served to impart to it new strength and vigor. Of this class was the "gag rule" attempted and partially enforced in Congress; the attempted suppression of the right of petition; the mobocratic demonstrations against the exercise of free speech; the display of pistols, bludgeons, and plantation manners in the Congress of the nation; the demand shamelessly made by our government upon England for the return of slaves who had won their liberty by their valor on the high seas; the bill for the recapture of runaway slaves; the annexation of Texas for the avowed purpose of increasing the number of slave States; the war with Mexico; the cold-blooded decision of Chief Justice Taney in the Dred Scott case,

wherein he states, as it were, a historical fact that "negroes are deemed to have no rights which white men are bound to respect"; the perfidious repeal of the Missouri compromise when all its advantages to the South had been gained and appropriated, and when nothing had been gained by the North; the armed and bloody attempt to force slavery upon Kansas; the rude attacks made upon Giddings, Hale, Chase, Wilson, Wm. H. Seward, and Charles Sumner; the effort to degrade these brave men and to drive them from positions of prominence; the summary manner in which Virginia hanged John Brown; in a word, whatever was done or attempted with a view to the support and security of slavery, only served as fuel to the fire, and heated the furnace of agitation to a higher degree than any before attained.

At no time during all the ten years preceding the war was the public mind at rest. In 1854, we had the Missouri compromise, which removed the only grand legal barrier against the spread of slavery over all the territory of the United States. From this time there was no pause, no repose. Everybody, however dull, could see that this was a phase of the slavery question which was not to be slighted or ignored. The people of the North had been accustomed to ask, in a tone of cruel

In 1857, Dred Scott sued for his freedom and lost, though he ultimately would become a free man through the work of abolitionists.

This cartoon shows presidential nominees Abraham Lincoln and Stephen Douglas in a footrace to the Capitol. Douglas carries a jug labeled "M.C." for the Missouri Compromise (a statute that prohibited slavery in the new territory), which he was largely responsible for repealing. The young black man taunts Douglas, that nominee won't be able to find him.

indifference, "What have we to do with slavery?" and now no labored speech was required in answer. Slaveholding aggression settled this question for us. The presence of slavery in a territory would certainly exclude the sons and daughters of the free States more effectually than statutes or yellow fever. Those who cared nothing for the slave, and were willing to tolerate slavery inside the slave States, were nevertheless not quite prepared to find themselves and their children excluded from the common inheritance of the nation.

As a measure of agitation, the repeal of the Missouri Compromise alluded to was perhaps the most effective. It was that which brought Abraham Lincoln into prominence, and into conflict with Stephen

A. Douglas (who was the author of that measure) and compelled the Western States to take a deeper interest than they ever had done before in the whole question. Pregnant words were now spoken on the side of freedom, words which went straight to the heart of the nation. It was Mr. Lincoln who told the American people at this crisis that the "Union could not long endure half slave and half free; that they must be all one or the other, and that the public mind could find no resting place but in the belief in the ultimate extinction of slavery." These were not the words of an abolitionist—branded a fanatic, and carried away by an enthusiastic devotion to the Negro—but the calm, cool, deliberate utterance of a statesman, comprehensive enough to take in the welfare

LIBERTY. THE FAIR MAID OF KANSAS_IN THE HANDS OF THE "BORDER RUFFIANS".

Left: This illustration bitterly blames the Democratic administration for the violence in Kansas in the wake of the Kansas-Nebraska Act, which effectively repealed the Missouri Compromise. Right: Chief Justice Roger Taney (1777–1864) ruled against Dred Scott in the belief that African Americans were never intended to be American citizens under the Constitution.

of the whole country. No wonder that the friends of freedom saw in this plain man of Illinois the proper standard-bearer of all the moral and political forces which could be united and wielded against the slave power. In a few simple words he had embodied the thought of the loyal nation, and indicated the character fit to lead and guide the country amid perils present and to come.

The South was not far behind the North in recognizing Abraham Lincoln as the natural leader of the rising political sentiment of the country against slavery, and it was equally quick in its efforts to counteract and destroy his influence. The situation during all the administration of President Pierce was only less threatening and stormy than that under the administration of James Buchanan. Intoxicated by their success in repealing the Missouri compromise—in divesting the native-born colored man of American citizenship—in harnessing both the Whig and Democratic parties to the car of slavery, and in holding continued possession of the national government, the propagandists of slavery threw off all disguises, abandoned all semblance of moderation, and very naturally and inevitably proceeded, under Mr. Buchanan, to avail themselves of all the advantages of their victories. Having legislated out of existence the great national wall, erected, in the better days of the republic, against the spread of slavery, and against the increase of its power—having blotted out all distinction, as they thought, between freedom and slavery in the law, theretofore, governing the Territories of the United States, and having left the whole question of the legislation or prohibition of slavery to be decided by the people of a Territory, the next thing in order was to fill up the Territory of Kansas—the one likely to be first organized—with a people friendly to slavery, and to keep out all such as were opposed to making that Territory a free State. Here was an open invitation to a fierce and bitter strife; and the history of the

times shows how promptly that invitation was accepted by both classes to which it was given, and shows also the scenes of lawless violence and blood that followed.

No wonder that the friends of freedom saw in this plain man of Illinois the proper standard-bearer of all the moral and political forces which could be united and wielded against the slave power.

All advantages were at first on the side of those who were for making Kansas a slave State. The moral force of the repeal of the Missouri compromise was with them; the strength of the triumphant Democratic party was with them; the power and patronage of the federal government was with them; the various governors, sent out under the Territorial government, were with them; and, above all, the proximity of the Territory to the slave State of Missouri favored them and all their designs. Those who opposed making Kansas a slave State, for the most part were far away from the battle-ground, residing chiefly in

This is a sketch of a mural called The Tragic Prelude *that appears in the Topeka State Capitol. It depicts John Brown looking wild and refers to the bloodshed of pro-slavery settlers in Kansas at the hands of Brown and his band of abolitionists at the time of the Kansas-Nebraska Act.*

New England, more than a thousand miles from the eastern border of the Territory, and their direct way of entering it was through a country violently hostile to them. With such odds against them, and only an idea—though a grand one—to support them, it will ever be a wonder that they succeeded in making Kansas a free State. The important point to me, as one desiring to see the slave power crippled, slavery limited and abolished, was the effect of this Kansas battle upon the moral sentiment of the North: how it made abolitionists of people before they themselves

became aware of it, and how it rekindled the zeal, stimulated the activity, and strengthened the faith of our old anti-slavery forces. The men who went to Kansas with the purpose of making it a free State were the heroes and martyrs. One of the leaders in this holy crusade for freedom, with whom I was brought into near relations, was John Brown, whose person, house, and purposes I have already described. This brave old man and his sons were amongst the first to hear and heed the trumpet of freedom calling them to battle. What they did and suffered, what they sought and gained, and by what means, are matters of history, and need not be repeated here.

When it became evident, as it soon did, that the war for and against slavery in Kansas was not to be decided by the peaceful means of words and ballots, but that swords and bullets were to be employed on both sides, Captain John Brown felt that now, after long years of waiting, his hour had come, and never did man meet the perilous requirements of any occasion more cheerfully, courageously, and disinterestedly than he.

The question was not merely which class should prevail in Kansas, but whether free-State men should live there at all. The border ruffians from Missouri had openly declared their purpose not only to make Kansas a slave State, but that they would make it impossible for free-State men to live there. They burned their towns, burned their farm-houses, and by assassination spread terror among them, until many of the free-State settlers were compelled to escape for their lives. John Brown was therefore the logical result of slaveholding per-secutions. Until the lives of tyrants and murderers shall become more precious in the sight of men than justice and liberty, John Brown will need no defender. In dealing with the ferocious enemies of the free-State cause in Kansas, he not only showed boundless courage but eminent military skill. With men so few, and odds against him so great, few cap-tains ever surpassed him in achievements. Before leaving Kansas he went into the border of Missouri and liberated a dozen slaves in a single night, and despite slave laws and marshals he brought these people through half a dozen States and landed them

John Brown was sentenced to hanging after his raid on the federal armory in Harper's Ferry. This painting by Thomas Dunmanway (1840–1895) is titled The Last Moments of John Brown *and shows him on the way to the gallows.*

safe in Canada. The successful efforts of the North in making Kansas a free State, despite all the sophistical doctrines and sanguinary measures of the South to make it a slave State, exercised a potent influence upon subsequent political forces and events in the then-near future.

Henceforth the favorite doctrine of the South was that the people of a territory had no voice in the matter of slavery whatever; and that the Constitution of the United States, of its own force and effect, carried slavery safely into any territory of the United States and protected the system there until it ceased to be a territory and became a State. This doctrine was in some sense supported by Chief-Justice Taney in the infamous Dred Scott decision. This new ground, however, was des-tined to bring misfortune to its inventors, for it divided for a time the Democratic party, one faction of it going with John C. Breckenridge

and the other espousing the cause of Stephen A. Douglas; the one held firmly to the doctrine that the United States Constitution, without any legislation, territorial, national, or otherwise, by its own force and effect, carried slavery into all the territories of the United States; the other held that the people of a territory had the right to admit slavery or reject slavery, as in their judgment they might deem best.

Now, while this war of words—this conflict of doctrines— was in progress, the portentous shadow of a stupendous civil war became more and more visible. Bitter complaints were raised by the slaveholders that they were about to be despoiled of their proper share in territory won by a common valor or bought by a common treasure. The North, on the other hand, or rather a large and growing party at the North, insisted that the complaint was unreasonable and groundless; that nothing properly considered as property was excluded or intended to be excluded from the territories; that Southern men could settle in any territory of the United States with some kinds of property, and on the same footing and with the same protection as citizens of the North; that men and women are not property in the same sense as houses, lands, horses, sheep and swine are property; that the fathers of the Republic neither intended the extension nor the perpetuity of slavery and that liberty is national and slavery is sectional. From 1856 to 1860 the whole land rocked with this great controversy. And when all hope of compromise had nearly vanished, as if to banish even the last glimmer of hope for peace between the sections, John Brown came upon the scene. On the night of the 16th of October, 1859, there appeared near the confluence of the Potomac and Shenandoah rivers a party of nineteen men—fourteen white and five colored. They were not only armed themselves, but they brought with them a large supply of arms for such persons as might join them. These men invaded the town of Harper's Ferry, disarmed the watchman, took possession of the arsenal, rifle factory, armory, and other government property at that place, arrested and made prisoners of nearly all the prominent citizens in the neighborhood, collected about fifty slaves, put bayonets into the hands of such as were able and willing to fight for their liberty, killed three men, proclaimed general emancipation, held the ground more than thirty hours, and were subsequently overpowered and nearly all killed, wounded, or captured by a body of United States troops under command of Col. Robert E. Lee, since famous as the rebel General Lee. At the time of his capture Capt. Brown was supposed to be mortally wounded, as he had several ugly gashes and bayonet wounds on his head and body, and, apprehending that he might speedily die, or that he might be rescued by his friends, and thus the opportunity to make him a signal example of slaveholding vengeance would be lost, his captors hurried him to Charlestown, 10 miles further within the border of Virginia, placed him in prison strongly guarded by troops, and, before his wounds were healed, he was brought into court, subjected to a nominal trial, convicted of high treason and inciting slaves to insurrection, and was executed.

His corpse was given up to his woe-stricken widow, and she, assisted by anti-slavery friends, caused it to be borne to North Elba, Essex county, N. Y., and there his dust now reposes amid the silent, solemn, and snowy grandeurs of the Adirondacks. This raid upon Harper's Ferry was as the last straw to the camel's back. What in the tone of Southern sentiment had been fierce before, became furious and uncontrollable now. A scream for vengeance came up from all sections of the slave States and from great multitudes in the North. All who were supposed to have been any way connected with John Brown were to be hunted down and surrendered to the tender mercies of slaveholding and panic-stricken Virginia, and there to be tried after the fashion of John Brown's trial, and, of course, to be summarily executed.

On the evening when the news came that John Brown had taken and was then holding the town of Harper's Ferry, it so happened that I was speaking to a large audience in National Hall, Philadelphia. The announcement came upon us with the startling effect of an earthquake. It was something to make the boldest hold his breath. I saw at once that my old friend had attempted what he had long ago resolved to do, and I felt certain that the result must be his capture and destruction. His carpet-bag had been secured by Governor Wise, and it was found to contain numerous letters and documents which directly implicated Gerritt Smith, Joshua R. Giddings, Samuel G. Howe, Frank P. Sanborn, and myself. This intelligence was soon followed by a telegram saying that we were all to be arrested. Knowing that I was then in Philadelphia, stopping with my friend Thomas J. Dorsey, Mr. John Hern, the telegraph operator, came to me and, with others, urged me to leave the city by the first train, as it was known through the newspapers that I was then in Philadelphia, and officers might even then be on my track. My friends for the most part were appalled at the thought of my being arrested then or there, or while on my way across the ferry from Walnut street wharf to Camden, for there was where I felt sure the arrest would be made, and asked some of them to go so far as this with me merely to see what might occur; but, upon one ground or another, they all thought it best not to be found in my company at such a time, except dear old Franklin Turner—a true man. The truth is, that in the excitement which prevailed my friends had reason to fear that the very fact that they were with me would be a sufficient reason for their arrest with me. The delay in the departure of the steamer seemed unusually long to me, for I confess I was seized with a desire to reach a more northern latitude. My friend Frank did not leave my side till "all ashore" was ordered and the paddles began to move. I reached New York at night, still under the apprehension of arrest at any moment, but no signs of such an event being made, I went at once to the Barclay street ferry, took the boat across the river, and went direct to Washington street, Hoboken, the home of Mrs. Marks, where I spent the night, and I may add without undue profession of timidity, an anxious night. It would not do to go to New York city and take the train, for that city was not less incensed against John Brown conspirators than many parts of the South. The course hit upon by my friends, Mr. Johnston and Miss Assing, was, to take me at night in a private conveyance from Hoboken to Paterson, where I could take the Erie railroad for home. This plan was carried out, and I reached home in safety, but had been there but a few moments when I was called upon by Samuel D. Porter, Esq., and my neighbor, Lieutenant-Governor Selden, who informed me that the governor of the State would certainly surrender me on a proper requisition from the governor of Virginia, and that while the people of Rochester would not permit me to be taken South, yet, in order to avoid collision with the government and consequent bloodshed, they advised me to quit the country, which I did—going to Canada.

CHAPTER X

THE BEGINNING OF THE END

MY CONNECTION WITH JOHN BROWN—TO AND FROM ENGLAND—
PRESIDENTIAL CONTEST—ELECTION OF ABRAHAM LINCOLN.

W hat was my connection with John Brown, and what I knew of his scheme for the capture of Harper's Ferry, I may now proceed to state. From the time of my visit to him in Springfield, Mass., in 1847, our relations were friendly and confidential. I never passed through Springfield without calling on him, and he never came to Rochester without calling on me. He often stopped over night with me, when we talked over the feasibility of his plan for destroying the value of slave property, and the motive for holding slaves in the border States.

After the close of his Kansas work, Captain Brown came to my house in Rochester, and said he desired to stop with me several weeks; "but," he added, "I will not stay unless you will allow me to pay board." Knowing that he was no trifler and meant all he said, and desirous of retaining him under my roof, I charged three dollars a week. While here, he spent most of his time in correspondence. He wrote often to George L. Stearns of Boston, Gerritt Smith of Peterboro, N. Y., and many others, and received many letters in return.

Once in a while he would say he could, with a few resolute men, capture Harper's Ferry, and supply himself with arms belonging to the government at that place;

but he never announced his intention to do so. It was, however, very evidently passing in his mind as a thing he might do. I paid but little attention to such remarks, though I never doubted that he thought just what he said.

While at my house, John Brown made the acquaintance of a colored man who called himself by different names—sometimes "Emperor," at other times, "Shields Green." He was a fugitive slave, who had made his escape from Charleston, South Carolina, a State from which a slave found it no easy matter to run away. John Brown saw at once what "stuff" Green "was made of," and confided to him his plans and purposes. Green easily believed in Brown, and promised to go with him whenever he should be ready to move. About three weeks before the raid on Harper's Ferry, John Brown wrote to me, informing me that a beginning in his work would soon be made, and that before going forward he wanted to see me, and appointed an old stone-quarry near Chambersburg, Penn., as our place of meeting. Mr. Kagi, his secretary, would be there, and they wished me to bring any money I could command, and Shields Green along with me. In the same letter, he said that his "mining tools" and stores were then at Chambersburg, and that he would be there to remove them. I obeyed the old man's summons.

*A campaign picture for Stephen A. Douglas, a Democratic
candidate for the 1860 presidential election.*

U.S. Marines storm the engine house where John Brown holed up after the Harper's Ferry insurrection.

He was passing under the name of John Smith. As I came near, he regarded me rather suspiciously, but soon recognized me, and received me cordially. We sat down among the rocks and talked over the enterprise which was about to be undertaken. The taking of Harper's Ferry, of which Captain Brown had merely hinted before, was now declared as his settled purpose, and he wanted to know what I thought of it. I at once opposed the measure with all the arguments at my command. To me such a measure would be fatal to running off slaves (as was the original plan), and fatal to all engaged in doing so. It would be an attack upon the federal government, and would array the whole country against us. Captain Brown did most of the talking on the other side of the question. He did not at all object to rousing the nation; it seemed to him that something startling was just what the nation needed. He had completely renounced his old plan, and thought that the capture of Harper's Ferry would serve as notice to the slaves that their friends had come, and as a trumpet to rally them to his standard. Our talk was long and earnest; we spent the most of Saturday and a part of Sunday in this debate—Brown for Harper's Ferry, and I against it; he for striking a blow which should instantly rouse the country, and I for the policy of gradually and unaccountably drawing off the slaves to the mountains, as at first suggested and proposed by him. When I found that he had fully made up his mind and could not be dissuaded, I turned to Shields Green and told him he heard what Captain Brown had said; his old plan

was changed, and that I should return home, and if he wished to go with me he could do so. Captain Brown urged us both to go with him, but I could not do so, and could but feel that he was about to rivet the fetters more firmly than ever on the limbs of the enslaved. In parting he put his arms around me in a manner more than friendly, and said: "Come with me, Douglass; I will defend you with my life. I want you for a special purpose. When I strike, the bees will begin to swarm, and I shall want you to help hive them." But my discretion or my cowardice made me proof against the dear old man's eloquence—perhaps it was something of both which determined my course. When about to leave I asked Green what he had decided to do, and was surprised by his coolly saying, in his broken way, "I b'leve I'll go wid de ole man." Here we separated; they to go to Harper's Ferry, I to Rochester.

Such then was my connection with John Brown, and it may be asked, if this is all, why I should have objected to being sent to Virginia to be tried for the offense charged. The explanation is not difficult. I knew that if my enemies could not prove me guilty of the offense of being with John Brown, they could prove that I was Frederick Douglass; they could prove that I was in correspondence and conspiracy with Brown against slavery; they could prove that I brought Shields Green, one of the bravest of his soldiers, all the way from Rochester to him at Chambersburg; they could prove that I brought money to aid him, and in what was then the state of the public mind I could not hope to make a

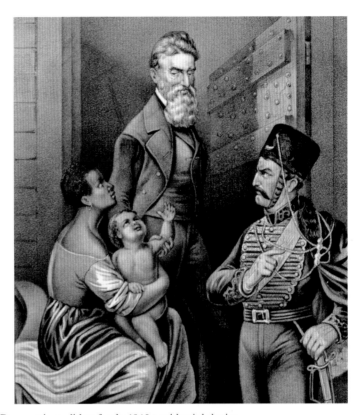

Left: A campaign picture for John C. Breckinridge, a Democratic candidate for the 1860 presidential election.
Right: John Brown depicted as a martyr in a Currier & Ives lithograph.

jury of Virginia believe I did not go the whole length he went, or that I was not one of his supporters; and I knew that all Virginia, were I once in her clutches, would say "Let him be hanged."

On the 12th of November, 1859, I took passage from Quebec on board the steamer *Scotia*, Captain Thompson, of the Allan line. My going to England was not at first suggested by my connection with John Brown, but the fact that I was now in danger of arrest on the ground of complicity with him made what I had intended a pleasure a necessity, for though in Canada, and under British law, it was not impossible that I might be kidnapped and taken to Virginia. England had given me shelter and protection when the slave-hounds were on my track fourteen years before, and her gates were still open to me now that I was pursued in the name of Virginia justice. I could but feel that I was going into exile, perhaps for life. Slavery seemed to be at the very top of its power; the national government, with all its powers and appliances, was in its hands, and it bade fair to wield them for many years to come. Nobody could then see that in the short space of four years this power would be broken and the slave system destroyed. Upon reaching Liverpool I learned that England was nearly as much alive to what had happened at Harper's Ferry as was the United States, and I was immediately called upon in different parts of the country to speak on the subject of slavery, and especially to give some account of the men who had thus flung away their lives in a desperate attempt to free the slaves. My own relation to

the affair was a subject of much interest, as was the fact of my presence there being in some sense to elude the demands of Governor Wise, who, having learned that I was not in Michigan, but was on a British steamer bound for England, publicly declared that "could he overtake that vessel he would take me from her deck at any cost."

I should have now gratified a long-cherished desire to visit France had not news reached me from home of the death of my beloved daughter. Annie, the light and life of my house. Deeply distressed by this bereavement, and acting upon the impulse of the moment, regardless of the peril, I at once resolved to return home, and took the first outgoing steamer for Portland, Maine. After a rough passage of seventeen days I reached home by way of Canada, and remained in my house nearly a month before the knowledge got abroad that I was again in this country. Great changes had now taken place in the public mind touching the John Brown raid. Virginia had satisfied her thirst for blood. She had executed all the raiders who had fallen into her hands. She had not given Captain Brown the benefit of a reasonable doubt, but hurried him to the scaffold in panic-stricken haste. She had made herself ridiculous by her fright and despicable by her fury. Emerson's prediction that Brown's gallows would become like the cross was already being fulfilled.

At any rate the country was soon engaged in the heat and turmoil of a presidential canvass—a canvass which had no parallel, involving as it did the question of peace or war, the integrity or the dismemberment of

An 1840s steamer, traveling between New York and Liverpool.

the Republic, and, I may add, the maintenance or destruction of slavery. In some of the Southern States the people were already organizing and arming to be ready for an apprehended contest, and with this work on their hands they had no time to spare to those they had wished to convict as instigators of the raid, however desirous they might have been to do so under other circumstances, for they had parted with none of their hate.

Though disappointed in my tour on the Continent, and called home by one of the saddest events that can afflict the domestic circle, my presence here was fortunate, since it enabled me to participate in the most important and memorable presidential canvass ever witnessed in the United States, and to labor for the election of a man who in the order of events was destined to do a greater service to his country and to mankind than any man who had gone before him in the presidential office. It is something to couple one's name with great occasions, and it was a great thing to me to be permitted to bear some humble part in this, the greatest that had thus far come to the American people. It was a great thing to achieve American independence when we numbered three millions, but it was a greater thing to save this country from dismemberment and ruin when it numbered thirty millions. He alone of all our Presidents was to have the opportunity to destroy slavery, and to lift into manhood millions of his countrymen hitherto held as chattels and numbered with the beasts of the field.

The presidential canvass of 1860 was three-sided, and each side had its distinctive doctrine as to the question of slavery and slavery extension. We had three candidates in the field. Stephen A. Douglas was the standard-bearer of what may be called the western faction of the old divided democratic party, and John C. Breckenridge was the standard-bearer of the southern or slaveholding faction of that party. Abraham Lincoln represented the then young, growing, and united republican party. The lines between these parties and candidates were about as distinctly and clearly drawn as political lines are capable of being

The interior of the engine house where John Harper holed up after the Harper's Ferry insurrection, just before the marines broke through the gate.

drawn. Against both Douglas and Breckenridge Abraham Lincoln proposed his grand historic doctrine of the power and duty of the National Government to prevent the spread and perpetuity of slavery. Into this contest I threw myself, with firmer faith and more ardent hope than ever before, and what I could do by pen or voice was done with a will. The most remarkable and memorable feature of this canvass was, that it was prosecuted under the portentous shadow of a threat: leading public men of the South had, with the vehemence of fiery purpose, given it out in advance that in case of their failure to elect their candidate (Mr. John C. Breckenridge) they would proceed to take the slaveholding States out of the Union, and that, in no event whatever, would they submit to the rule of Abraham Lincoln. To many of the peace-loving friends of the Union, this was a fearful announcement, and it doubtless cost the Republican candidates many votes. To many others, however, it was deemed a mere bravado—sound and fury signifying nothing. With a third class its effect was very different. They were tired of the rule-or-ruin intimidation adopted by the South, and felt then, if never before, that they had quailed before it too often and too long. This southern threat lost many votes, but it gained more than would cover the lost. It frightened the timid, but stimulated the brave; and the result was—the triumphant election of Abraham Lincoln.

Then came the question. What will the South do about it? Will she eat her bold words, and submit to the verdict of the people, or proceed to the execution of the programme she had marked out for herself prior to the election? The inquiry was an anxious one, and the blood of the North stood still, waiting for the response. It had not to wait long, for the trumpet of war was soon sounded, and the tramp of armed men was heard in that region. During all the winter of 1860 notes of preparation for a tremendous conflict came to us from that quarter on every wind. Still the warning was not taken. Few of the North could really believe that this insolent display of arms would end in anything more substantial than dust and smoke.

The shameful and shocking course of President Buchanan and his cabinet towards this rising rebellion against the government which each and all of them had solemnly sworn to "support, defend and maintain"—the facts that the treasury was emptied; that the army was scattered; that our ships of war were sent out of the way; that our forts and arsenals in the South were weakened and crippled—purposely left an easy prey to the prospective insurgents—that one after another the States were allowed to secede; that these rebel measures were largely

encouraged by the doctrine of Mr. Buchanan, that he found no power in the Constitution to coerce a State, are all matters of history, and need only the briefest mention here.

The reaction from the glorious assertion of freedom and independence on the part of the North in the triumphant election of Abraham Lincoln, was a painful and humiliating development of its weakness. It seemed as if all that had been gained in the canvass was about to be surrendered to the vanquished, and that the South, though beaten at the polls, was to be victorious and have everything its own way in the final result. During all the intervening months, from November to the ensuing March, the drift of Northern sentiment was towards compromise. The feeling everywhere seemed to be that something must be done to convince the South that the election of Mr. Lincoln meant no harm to slavery or the slave power, and that the North was sound on the question of the right of the master to hold and hunt his slave as long as he pleased, and that even the right to hold slaves in the Territories should be submitted to the supreme court, which would probably decide in favor of the most extravagant demands of the slave States.

Happily for the cause of human freedom, and for the final unity of the American nation, the South was mad, and would listen to no concessions. It would neither accept the terms offered, nor offer others to be accepted. It had made up its mind that under a given contingency it would secede from the Union and thus dismember the Republic. That contingency had happened, and it should execute its threat. This haughty and unreasonable and unreasoning attitude of the imperious South saved the slave and saved the nation. Had the South accepted our concessions and remained in the Union, the slave power would in all probability have continued to rule; the North would have become utterly demoralized; the hands on the dial-plate of American civilization would have been reversed, and the slave would have been dragging his hateful chains to-day wherever the American flag floats to the breeze. Those who may wish to see to what depths of humility and self-abasement a noble people can be brought under the sentiment of fear, will find no chapter of history more instructive than that which treats of the events in official circles in Washington during the space between the months of November, 1859, and March, 1860.

A campaign button for Abraham Lincoln, the Republican candidate for the 1860 presidential election.

CHAPTER XI

SECESSION AND WAR

The cowardly and disgraceful reaction from a courageous and manly assertion of right principles, as described in the foregoing pages, continued surprisingly long after secession and war were commenced. The patience and forbearance of the loyal people of the North were amazing. Speaking of this feature of the situation in Corinthian Hall, Rochester, at the time, I said:

"We (the people of the North) are a charitable people, and, in the excess of this feeling, we were disposed to put the very best construction upon the strange behavior of our southern brethren. We hoped that all would yet go well. We thought that South Carolina might secede. It was entirely like her to do so. She had talked extravagantly about going out of the Union, and it was natural that she should do something extravagant and startling, if for nothing else, to make a show of consistency. Georgia, too, we thought might possibly secede. But, strangely enough, we thought and felt quite sure that these twin rebellious States would stand alone and unsupported in their infamy and their impotency, that they would soon tire of their isolation, repent of their folly, and come back to their places in the Union. Traitors withdrew from the Cabinet, from the House of Representatives, and from the Senate, and hastened to their several States to 'fire the Southern heart,' and to fan the hot flames of treason at home . . .

"But this confidence, patience, and forbearance could not last forever. These blissful illusions of hope were, in a measure, dispelled when the batteries of Charleston harbor were opened upon the starving garrison at Fort Sumter. For the moment the northern lamb was transformed into a lion, and his roar was terrible. But he only showed his teeth, and clearly had no wish to use them. We preferred to fight with dollars, and not daggers. 'The fewer battles the better,' was the hopeful motto at Washington. 'Peace in sixty days' was held out by the astute Secretary of State. In fact, there was at the North no disposition to fight, no spirit of hate, no comprehension of the stupendous character and dimensions of the rebellion, and no proper appreciation of its inherent wickedness. . . . It was in such a condition of

An unidentified African American soldier in a Union uniform.

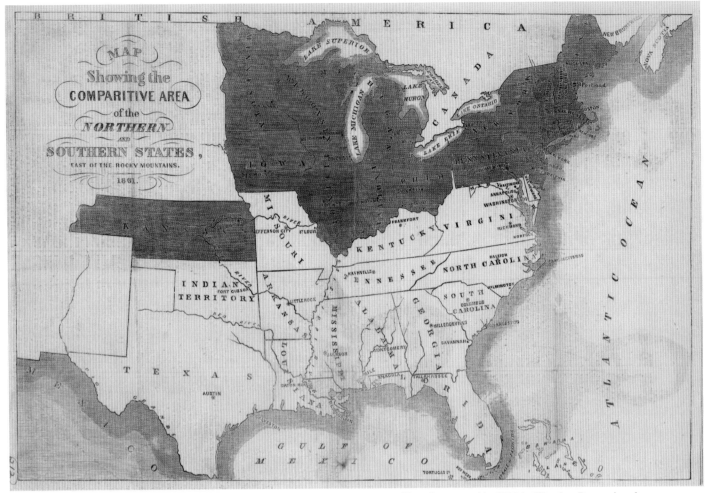

MAP
Showing the
COMPARITIVE AREA
of the
NORTHERN
AND
SOUTHERN STATES,
EAST OF THE ROCKY MOUNTAINS.
1861.

Above: A map showing the North-South divide in 1861. Opposite: This statue of Douglass, erected in 1899 by Theodore Roosevelt, who was then governor of New York state, stands in Rochester. It was the first memorial statue for an African American to be erected in the country.

things as this that Abraham Lincoln (compelled from fear of assassination to enter the capital in disguise) was inaugurated and issued his proclamation for the 'repossession of the forts, places, and property which had been seized from the Union,' and his call upon the militia of the several States to the number of 75,000 men—a paper which showed how little even he comprehended the work then before the loyal nation. It was perhaps better for the country and for mankind that the good man could not know the end from the beginning. Had he foreseen the thousands who must sink into bloody graves, the mountains of debt to be laid on the breast of the nation, the terrible hardships and sufferings involved in the contest, and his own death by an assassin's hand, he too might have adopted the weak sentiment of those who said 'Erring sisters, depart in peace.'"

From the first, I, for one, saw in this war the end of slavery; and truth requires me to say that my interest in the success of the North was largely due to this belief. . . . When General McClellan and General Butler warned the slaves in advance that, "if any attempt was made by them to gain their freedom it would be suppressed with an iron hand"—when

the government persistently refused to employ colored troops—when the emancipation proclamation of General John C. Fremont, in Missouri, was withdrawn—when slaves were being returned from our lines to their masters—when Union soldiers were stationed about the farm-houses of Virginia to guard and protect the master in holding his slaves—when Union soldiers made themselves more active in kicking colored men out of their camps than in shooting rebels—when even Mr. Lincoln could tell the poor negro that "he was the cause of the war," I still believed, and spoke as I believed, all over the North, that the mission of the war was the liberation of the slave, as well as the salvation of the Union; and hence from the first I reproached the North that they fought the rebels with only one hand, when they might strike effectually with two—that they fought with their soft white hand, while they kept their black iron hand chained and helpless behind them—that they fought the effect, while they protected the cause, and that the Union cause would never prosper till the war assumed an anti-slavery attitude, and the negro was enlisted on the loyal side. It is surprising how long and bitterly the government resisted and rejected this view of the situation. Bull Run, Ball's

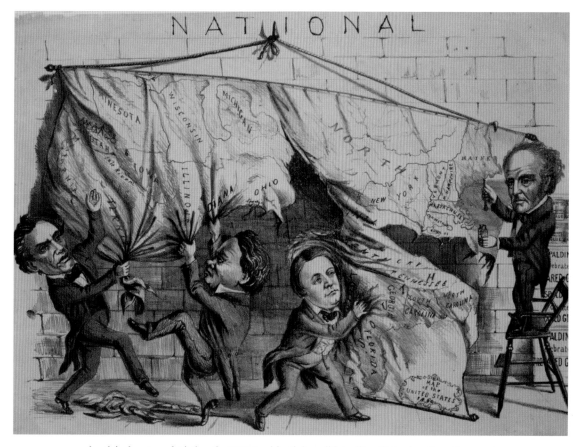

A satirical cartoon depicting the 1860 presidential candidates literally tearing the nation apart.

Bluff, Big Bethel, Fredericksburg, and the Peninsula disasters were the only teachers whose authority was of sufficient importance to excite the attention or respect of our rulers, and they were even slow in being taught by these. An important point was gained, however, when General B. F. Butler, at Fortress Monroe, announced the policy of treating the slaves as "contrabands," to be made useful to the Union cause, and was sustained therein at Washington.

When at last the truth began to dawn upon the administration that the negro might be made useful to loyalty, as well as to treason, to the Union as well as to the Confederacy, it began to consider in what way it could employ him which would the least shock and offend the popular prejudice against him. He was already in the army as a waiter, and in that capacity there was no objection to him; and so it was thought that as this was the case, the feeling which tolerated him as a waiter would not seriously object if he should be admitted to the army as a laborer, especially as no one under a southern sun cared to have a monopoly of digging and toiling in trenches. This was the first step in employing negroes in the United States service. The second step was to give them a peculiar costume which should distinguish them from soldiers, and yet mark them as a part of the loyal force. As the eyes of the loyal administration still

Opposite: The Bombardment of Fort Sumter.

further opened, it was proposed to give these laborers something better than spades and shovels with which to defend themselves in cases of emergency. Still later it was proposed to make them soldiers, but soldiers without the blue uniform, soldiers with a mark upon them to show that they were inferior to other soldiers; soldiers with a badge of degradation upon them. However, once in the army as a laborer, once there with a red shirt on his back and a pistol in his belt, the negro was not long in appearing on the field as a soldier. But still, he was not to be a soldier in the sense, and on an equal footing, with white soldiers. It was given out that he was not to be employed in the open field with white troops, under the inspiration of doing battle and winning victories for the Union cause, and in the face and teeth of his old masters, but that he should be made to garrison forts in yellow-fever and otherwise unhealthy localities of the South, to save the health of white soldiers; and, in order to keep up the distinction further, the black soldiers were to have only half the wages of the white soldiers, and were to be commanded entirely by white commissioned officers. While of course I was deeply pained and saddened by the estimate thus put upon my race, and grieved at the slowness of heart which marked the conduct of the loyal government, I was not discouraged, and urged every man who could, to enlist; to get an eagle on his button, a musket on his shoulder, and the star-spangled banner over his head. Hence, as soon as Governor Andrew of Massachusetts

The inauguration of Lincoln at the Capitol in 1861.

received permission from Mr. Lincoln to raise two colored regiments, the 54th and 55th, I made the following address to the colored citizens of the North through my paper, then being published in Rochester, which was copied in the leading journals:

"MEN OF COLOR, TO ARMS!

"When first the rebel cannon shattered the walls of Sumter and drove away its starving garrison, I predicted that the war then and there inaugurated would not be fought out entirely by white men. Every month's experience during these dreary years has confirmed that opinion. A war undertaken and brazenly carried on for the perpetual enslavement of colored men, calls logically and loudly for colored men to help suppress it. Only a moderate share of sagacity was needed to see that the arm of the slave was the best defense against the arm of the slaveholder. Hence, with every reverse to the national arms, with every exulting shout of victory raised by the slaveholding rebels, I have implored the imperiled nation to unchain against her foes her powerful black hand. There is no time to delay. The tide is at its flood that leads on to fortune. From East to West, from North to South, the sky is written all over, 'Now OR NEVER.'

"Massachusetts now welcomes you to arms as soldiers. She has but a small colored population from which to recruit. She has full leave of the general government to send one regiment to the war, and she has undertaken to do it. Go quickly and help fill up the first colored regiment from the North. I am authorized to assure you that you will

Left: Charles Douglass (1844–1920). Right: Lewis Douglass (1840–1908) and his wife, Amelia.

receive the same wages, the same rations, the same equipments, the same protection, the same treatment, and the same bounty, secured to white soldiers. You will be led by able and skillful officers, men who will take especial pride in your efficiency and success. They will be quick to accord to you all the honor you shall merit by your valor, and to see that your rights and feelings are respected by other soldiers. I have assured myself on these points, and can speak with authority. . . .

"ROCHESTER, March 2, 1863."

The raising of these two regiments—the 54th and 55th—and their splendid behavior in South and North Carolina, was the beginning of great things for the colored people of the whole country; and not the least satisfaction I now have in contemplating my humble part in raising them, is the fact that my two sons, Charles and Lewis, were the first two in the State of New York to enlist in them. The 54th was not long in the field before it proved itself gallant and strong, worthy to rank with the most courageous of its white companions in arms. Its assault upon Fort Wagner, in which it was so fearfully cut to pieces, and lost nearly half its officers, including its beloved and trusted commander, Col. Shaw, at once gave it a name and a fame throughout the country. In that terrible battle, under the wing of night, more cavils in respect of the quality of

negro manhood were set at rest than could have been during a century of ordinary life and observation.

After the 54th and 55th Massachusetts colored regiments were placed in the field, and one of them had distinguished itself with so much credit in the hour of trial, the desire to send more such troops to the front became pretty general. Pennsylvania proposed to raise ten regiments. I was again called by my friend Mr. Stearns to assist in raising these regiments, and I set about the work with full purpose of heart, using every argument of which I was capable, to persuade every colored man able to bear arms to rally around the flag and help to save the country and the race. It was during this time that the attitude of the government at Washington caused me deep sadness and discouragement, and forced me in a measure to suspend my efforts in that direction. I had assured colored men that, once in the Union army, they would be put upon an equal footing with other soldiers; that they would be paid, promoted, and exchanged as prisoners of war, Jeff Davis's threat that they would be treated as felons, to the contrary notwithstanding. But thus far, the government had not kept its promise, or the promise made for it.

I was induced to go to Washington and lay the complaints of my people before President Lincoln and the Secretary of War and to urge

The 54th Massachusetts regiment at the Second Battle of Fort Wagner, July 18, 1863.

The White House, sometimes referred to as the executive mansion throughout history, pictured in the 1860s.

upon them such action as should secure to the colored troops then fighting for the country a reasonable degree of fair play. I need not say that at the time I undertook this mission it required much more nerve than a similar one would require now. The distance then between the black man and the white American citizen was immeasurable. I was an ex-slave, identified with a despised race, and yet I was to meet the most exalted person in this great republic. It was altogether an unwelcome duty, and one from which I would gladly have been excused. I shall never forget my first interview with this great man. I was accompanied to the executive mansion and introduced to President Lincoln by Senator Pomeroy. The room in which he received visitors was the one now used by the President's secretaries. I entered it with a moderate estimate of my own consequence, and yet there I was to talk with, and even to advise, the head man of a great nation. Happily for me, there was no vain pomp and ceremony about him. I was never more quickly or more completely put at ease in the presence of a great man than in that of Abraham Lincoln. He was seated, when I entered, in a low armchair with his feet extended on the floor, surrounded by a large number of documents and several busy secretaries. The room bore the marks of business, and the persons in it, the President included, appeared to

be much over-worked and tired. Long lines of care were already deeply written on Mr. Lincoln's brow, and his strong face, full of earnestness, lighted up as soon as my name was mentioned. As I approached and was introduced to him he arose and extended his hand, and bade me welcome. I at once felt myself in the presence of an honest man— one whom I could love, honor, and trust without reserve or doubt. Proceeding to tell him who I was and what I was doing, he promptly, but kindly, stopped me, saying: "I know who you are, Mr. Douglass; Mr. Seward has told me all about you. Sit down. I am glad to see you." I then told him the object of my visit: that I was assisting to raise colored troops; that several months before I had been very successful in getting men to enlist, but that now it was not easy to induce the colored men to enter the service, because there was a feeling among them that the government did not, in several respects, deal fairly with them. Mr. Lincoln asked me to state particulars. I replied that there were three particulars which I wished to bring to his attention. First, that colored soldiers ought to receive the same wages as those paid to white soldiers. Second, that colored soldiers ought to receive the same protection when taken prisoners, and be exchanged as readily and on the same terms as any other prisoners, and if Jefferson Davis should shoot or hang colored

This 1862 photograph, colorized at that time, shows "contrabands," which was a term used during the Civil War to describe people who escaped slavery to the Union lines and affiliated themselves with the Northern cause. The Union used many as laborers in the war effort. They were paid wages, and the army helped to support and educate them.

soldiers in cold blood the United States government should, without delay, retaliate in kind and degree upon Confederate prisoners in its hands. Third, when colored soldiers, seeking "the bubble reputation at the cannon's mouth," performed great and uncommon service on the battle-field, they should be rewarded by distinction and promotion precisely as white soldiers are rewarded for like services.

Mr. Lincoln listened with patience and silence to all I had to say.

He began by saying that the employment of colored troops at all was a great gain to the colored people; that the measure could not have been successfully adopted at the beginning of the war; that the wisdom of making colored men soldiers was still doubted; that their enlistment was a serious offense to popular prejudice; that they had larger motives for being soldiers than white men; that they ought to be willing to enter the service upon any condition; that the fact that they were not to receive the same pay as white soldiers seemed a necessary concession to smooth the way to their employment at all as soldiers, but that ultimately they would receive the same. On the second point, in respect to equal protection, he said the case was more difficult. Retaliation was a terrible

remedy, and one which it was very difficult to apply; that, if once begun, there was no telling where it would end; that if he could get hold of the Confederate soldiers who had been guilty of treating colored soldiers as felons he could easily retaliate, but the thought of hanging men for a crime perpetrated by others was revolting to his feelings. He thought that the rebels themselves would stop such barbarous warfare; that less evil would be done if retaliation were not resorted to and that he had already received information that colored soldiers were being treated as prisoners of war. In all this I saw the tender heart of the man rather than the stern warrior and commander-in-chief of the American army and navy, and, while I could not agree with him, I could but respect his humane spirit.

On the third point he appeared to have less difficulty, though he did not absolutely commit himself. He simply said that he would sign any commission to colored soldiers whom his Secretary of War should commend to him. Though I was not entirely satisfied with his views, I was so well satisfied with the man and with the educating tendency of the conflict that I determined to go on with the recruiting.

CHAPTER XII

HOPE FOR THE NATION

Proclamation of emancipation—Its reception in Boston—Objections brought against it—Its effect on the country—Interview with President Lincoln—New York riots—Re-election of Mr. Lincoln—His inauguration, and inaugural—Vice-President Johnson—Presidential reception—The fall of Richmond—The assassination—Condolence.

The first of January, 1863, was a memorable day in the progress of American liberty and civilization. It was the turning-point in the conflict between freedom and slavery. A death-blow was given to the slaveholding rebellion. On this day of January 1st, 1863, the formal and solemn announcement was made that thereafter the government would be found on the side of emancipation. This proclamation changed everything. It gave a new direction to the councils of the Cabinet, and to the conduct of the national arms. I shall leave to the statesman, the philosopher and the historian, the more comprehensive discussion of this document, and only tell how it touched me, and those in like condition with me at the time. I was in Boston, and its reception there may indicate the importance attached to it elsewhere. An immense assembly convened in Tremont Temple to await the first flash of the electric wires announcing the "new departure." Two years of war, prosecuted in the interests of slavery, had made free speech possible in Boston, and we were now met together to receive and celebrate the first utterance of the long-hoped-for proclamation, if it came,

and, if it did not come, to speak our minds freely; for, in view of the past, it was by no means certain that it would come. The occasion, therefore, was one of both hope and fear.

Eight, nine, ten o'clock came and went, and still no word. A visible shadow seemed falling on the expecting throng, which the confident utterances of the speakers sought in vain to dispel. At last, when patience was well-nigh exhausted, and suspense was becoming agony, a man (I think it was Judge Russell) with hasty step advanced through the crowd, and with a face fairly illumined with the news he bore, exclaimed in tones that thrilled all hearts, "It is coming!" "It is on the wires!!" The effect of this announcement was startling beyond description, and the scene was wild and grand. Joy and gladness exhausted all forms of expression, from shouts of praise to sobs and tears.

About twelve o'clock, seeing there was no disposition to retire from the hall, which must be vacated, my friend Grimes (of blessed memory), rose and moved that the meeting adjourn to the Twelfth Baptist church, of which he was pastor, and soon that church was packed from doors to pulpit, and

This image personifies African American emancipation as a goddess, "Columbia."

People gathered on New Year's Eve, 1862, waiting for the Emancipation Proclamation.

this meeting did not break up till near the dawn of day. It was one of the most affecting and thrilling occasions I ever witnessed, and a worthy celebration of the first step on the part of the nation in its departure from the thraldom of ages.

There was evidently no disposition on the part of this meeting to criticise the proclamation; nor was there with any one at first. At the moment we saw only its antislavery side. But further and more critical examination showed it to be extremely defective. It was not a proclamation of "liberty throughout all the land, unto all the inhabitants thereof," such as we had hoped it would be, but was one marked by discriminations and reservations. Its operation was confined within certain geographical and military lines. It only abolished slavery where it did not exist, and left it intact where it did exist. It was a measure apparently inspired by the low motive of military necessity, and by so far as it was so, it would become inoperative and useless when military necessity should cease. For my own part, I took the proclamation, first and last, for a little more than it purported, and saw in its spirit a life and power far beyond its letter. Its meaning to me was the entire abolition of slavery, wherever the evil could be reached by the Federal arm, and I saw that its moral power would extend much further. It was, in my estimation, an immense gain to have the war for the Union committed to the extinction of slavery, even from a military necessity. It is not a bad thing to have individuals or nations do right, though they do so from selfish motives.

The old cry was raised by the copperhead organs of "an abolition war," and a pretext was thus found for an excuse for refusing to enlist, and for marshaling all the negro prejudice of the North on the rebel side. Men could say they were willing to fight for the Union, but that they were not willing to fight for the freedom of the negroes; and thus it was made difficult to procure enlistments or to enforce the draft. This was especially true of New York. The attempt to enforce the draft in that city was met by mobs, riot, and bloodshed. There is perhaps no darker chapter in the whole history of the war than this cowardly and bloody uprising in July, 1863. For three days and nights New York was in the hands of a ferocious mob, and there was not sufficient power in the government of the country or of the city itself to stay the hand of violence and the effusion of blood. Though this mob was nominally against the draft which had been ordered, it poured out its fiercest wrath upon the colored people and their friends. It spared neither age nor sex; it hanged negroes simply because they were negroes; it murdered women in their homes, and burnt their homes over their heads; it dashed out the brains of young children against the lamp-posts; it burned the colored orphan

Copy of PRESIDENTIAL OATH
RANDOLPH
CALHOUN
LORD LYONS
LIBBY
A PROCLAMATION
JANY 1st. 1863.
HOLY BIBLE
BORDER STATES
AT RICHMOND
BUILT BY NEGROES
WEBSTER ON THE CONSTITUTION
MAP OF REBEL STATES

WITHOUT SLAVERY THE WAR WOULD NOT EX
AND WITHOUT SLAVERY
IT WOULD NOT BE CONTINUED.

MAP of EUROPE

CALL

PETITION

PROTEST

PLYMOUTH CHURCH

FROM J.B. FLOYD
Asking to be EXCHANGED

MEMORIAL
from the
U.P.
CHURCH

PROTECTION
from
RAIDS

MEMORIAL
from the
QUAKERS

DEMOCRATIC
RESOLUTION

CONSTITUT

UNCLE TOM

PROTEST
FROM ARMY OF
POTOMAC
AGAINST
QUARDING
PROPERTY
OF
TRAITOR

This 1864 print of the David Gilmour Blythe painting President
Lincoln, Writing the Proclamation of Freedom *is an artistic
interpretation of Lincoln drafting the Emancipation Proclamation.*

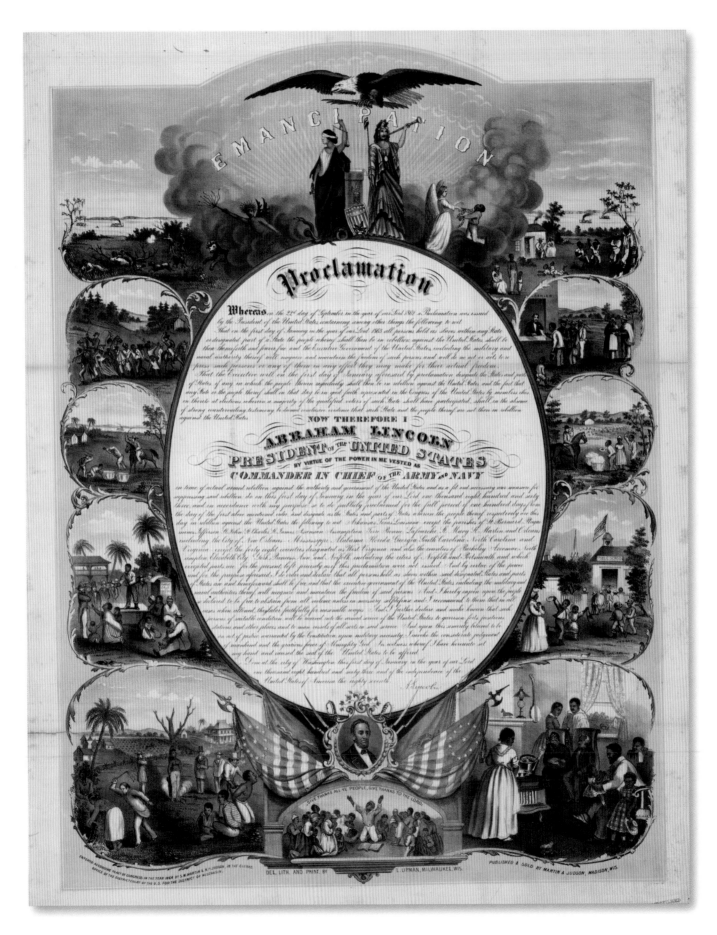

asylum, a noble charity on the corner of Fifth avenue, and, scarce allowing time for the helpless two hundred children to make good their escape, plundered the building of every valuable piece of furniture; and forced colored men, women and children to seek concealment in cellars or garrets or wheresoever else it could be found, until this high carnival of crime and reign of terror should pass away.

My interviews with President Lincoln and his able Secretary, before narrated, greatly increased my confidence in the anti-slavery integrity of the government. I, however, faithfully believed, and loudly proclaimed my belief, that the rebellion would be suppressed, the Union preserved, the slaves emancipated and that the colored soldiers would in the end have justice done them. This confidence was immeasurably strengthened when I saw Gen. George B. McClellan relieved from the command of the army of the Potomac and Gen. U. S. Grant placed at its head, and in command of all the armies of the United States. My confidence in Gen. Grant was not entirely due to his brilliant military successes, but there was a moral as well as military basis for my faith in him. He had shown his single-mindedness and superiority to popular prejudice by his prompt cooperation with President Lincoln in his policy of employing colored troops and by his order commanding his soldiers to treat such troops with due respect.

It was when General Grant was fighting his way through the Wilderness to Richmond, on the "line" he meant to pursue "if it took all summer," and every reverse to his arms was made the occasion for a fresh demand for peace without emancipation, that President Lincoln did me the honor to invite me to the Executive Mansion for a conference on the situation. I need not say I went most gladly. The main subject on which he wished to confer with me was as to the means most desirable to be employed outside the army to induce the slaves in the rebel States to come within the Federal lines. He spoke with great earnestness and much solicitude, and seemed troubled by the growing impatience at the war that was being manifested throughout the North. He said he was being accused of protracting the war beyond its legitimate object and of failing to make peace when he might have done so to advantage. He was afraid of what might come of all these complaints, but was persuaded that no solid and lasting peace could come short of absolute submission on the part of the rebels, and he was not for giving them rest by futile conferences with unauthorized persons, at Niagara Falls, or elsewhere. He saw the danger of premature peace, and, like a thoughtful and sagacious man as he was, wished to provide means of rendering such consummation as harmless as possible.

With this condition of national affairs came the summer of 1864, and with it the revived Democratic party with the story in its mouth

A man reads a headline about the Proclamation by candlelight.

that the war was a failure, and with it Gen. George B. McClellan, the greatest failure of the war, as its candidate for the presidency. It is needless to say that the success of such a party, on such a platform, with such a candidate, at such a time, would have been a fatal calamity. It was said that this Democratic party, which under Mr. Buchanan had betrayed the government into the hands of secession and treason, was the only party which could restore the country to peace and union. No doubt it would have "patched up" a peace, but it would have been a peace more to be dreaded than war. Regarding, as I did, the continuance of the war to the complete suppression of the rebellion and the retention in office of President Lincoln as essential to the total destruction of slavery, I certainly exerted myself to the uttermost in my small way to secure his reelection. This most important object was not attained, however, by speeches, letters, or other electioneering appliances. The staggering blows dealt upon the rebellion that year by the armies under Grant and Sherman, and his own great character, ground all opposition to dust and made his election sure even before the question reached the polls. It was my good fortune to be present at his inauguration in March, and to hear on that occasion his remarkable inaugural address.

The inauguration, like the election, was a most important event. Four years before, after Mr. Lincoln's first election, the pro-slavery spirit determined against his inauguration, and it no doubt would have accomplished its purpose had he attempted to pass openly and recognized

Opposite: An 1864 color lithograph of the Emancipation Proclamation, surrounded by scenes depicting the horrors of slavery on the left juxtaposed with reimagined scenes of African American life on the right.

DOUGLASS AND LINCOLN

From *The Radical and the Republican* by James Oakes

Douglass sensed immediately the greatness of Lincoln's second inaugural address. In the months and years to come he often quoted "these solemn words of our martyred President." But on that day he decided to break all precedent by going to the inaugural reception at the White House, though no African American had ever dared such a thing. That evening he joined the procession heading toward the executive mansion, only to be stopped at the door by guards claiming they had been instructed "to admit no persons of color." Douglass did not believe them.

"No such order could have emanated from President Lincoln," Douglass believed. If Lincoln knew Douglass was there, he told the guards, Lincoln would certainly wish to see him. They then resorted to trickery, escorting Douglass through the door only to steer him toward the exit.

"You have deceived me," Douglass declared, "I shall not go out of this building till I see President Lincoln." Douglass then noticed someone he knew and asked him to convey a message. "Be so kind as to say to Mr. Lincoln that Frederick Douglass is detained by officers at the door." Within moments Douglass entered the East Room.

Lincoln, visible above all his guests, quickly spotted Douglass moving toward him. "Here comes my friend Douglass," he exclaimed to the crowded room. Lincoln took Douglass by the hand. "I am glad to see you," he said. "I saw you in the crowd today, listening to my inaugural address; how did you like it?"

"Mr. Lincoln," Douglass replied, "I must not detain you with my poor opinion, when there are thousands waiting to shake hands with you."

"No, no," Lincoln said. "You must stop a little[,] Douglass; there is no man in the country whose opinion I value more than yours. I want to know what you think of it."

"Mr. Lincoln," Douglass answered, "that was a sacred effort."

"I am glad you liked it!"

Douglass wrote later that anybody no matter how distinguished, would "regard himself honored by such expressions from such a man." He went home to Rochester, honored.

Six weeks later, on April 15, 1865, a crowd of citizens called upon Douglass to deliver a spontaneous eulogy for Abraham Lincoln. The President had died early that morning, having been shot by John Wilkes Booth the previous evening at a theater in Washington, D.C. Douglass was stunned. "I have scarcely been able to say a word to any of those friends who have taken my hand and looked sadly in my eyes to-day." Daniel Moore, the mayor of Rochester, called a memorial service for three o'clock that afternoon in City Hall. So many people showed up that large numbers were turned away. But Douglass managed to get in and found a seat at the rear. The mayor spoke first, followed by several others, including a judge, the rector of St. Luke's Episcopal Church, and the president of the Rochester Theological Seminary. Douglass himself had not been invited to speak, but once he was noticed "his name burst upon the air from every side, and filled the house." Pressed by the crowd, Douglass rose to speak, and although he began his remarks by claiming that he found it "almost impossible to respond" to the invitation, by the time he had finished he had delivered a eulogy that was among the most heartfelt and moving speeches of his life.

"A dreadful disaster has befallen the nation," Douglass said. "It is a day for silence and meditation; for grief and tears." No doubt the people of Rochester were shaken by the death of their President "and feel in it a stab at Republican institutions." There was some consolation in the fact that "though Abraham Lincoln dies, the Republic lives; though that great and good man, one of the noblest men [to] trod God's earth, is struck down by the hand of the assassin, yet I know that the nation is saved and liberty is established forever." It was natural on such occasions, Douglass added, to struggle through "tears and anguish, to catch some gleam of hope—some good that may be born of the tremendous evil." For Douglass this desperate search through "the blinding mists that rise from this yawning gulf" gave him a glimpse of the great promise of freedom and "hope for all" that Lincoln had given them.

He then evoked Lincoln's second inaugural address to make a more salient point. He noted with dismay the recent impulse to lionize Robert E. Lee and to forget the crimes

Douglass appealing to Lincoln to enlist African Americans for the Union's cause.

of "treason and slavery" for which Lee fought. He warned against rushing to reconcile with our southern foes while forgetting our southern friends, the freed people "who had so recently proved their loyalty to the Union cause." Douglass suggested that Lincoln's martyrdom might serve to reawaken the nation to its true mission. "It may be in the inscrutable wisdom of Him who controls the destinies of Nations," Douglass said, "that this drawing of the Nation's most precious heart's blood was necessary to bring us back to that equilibrium which we must maintain if the Republic was to be permanently redeemed." He then quoted from memory the already familiar passage from the Second Inaugural in which Lincoln, though praying for a speedy end to the war, yet promised if need be to fight on until the blood shed by generations of slaves was at last repaid by the blood of thousands of soldiers in battle. "If it teaches us this lesson, it may be that the blood of our beloved martyred President will be the salvation of our country."

Draft rioters in New York burning the orphanage for black children.

through Baltimore. There was murder in the air then, and there was murder in the air now. His first inauguration arrested the fall of the Republic, and the second was to restore it to enduring foundations.

Reaching the Capitol, I took my place in the crowd where I could see the presidential procession as it came upon the east portico, and where I could hear and see all that took place. The whole proceeding was wonderfully quiet, earnest, and solemn. From the oath as administered by Chief Justice Chase, to the brief but weighty address delivered by Mr. Lincoln, there was a leaden stillness about the crowd. The address sounded more like a sermon than like a state paper. In the fewest words possible he referred to the condition of the country four years before on his first accession to the presidency, to the causes of the war, and the reasons on both sides for which it had been waged "With malice toward none, with charity for all, with firmness in the right as God gives us to see the right, let us strive to finish the work we are in, to bind up the nation's wounds, to care for him who shall have borne the battle, and for his widow and his orphans, to do all which may achieve and cherish a just and lasting peace among ourselves and with all nations."

On this inauguration day, while waiting for the opening of the ceremonies, I made a discovery in regard to the Vice President, Andrew Johnson. I was standing in the crowd by the side of Mrs. Thomas J.

Dorsey, when Mr. Lincoln touched Mr. Johnson and pointed me out to him. The first expression which came to his face, and which I think was the true index of his heart, was one of bitter contempt and aversion. Seeing that I observed him, he tried to assume a more friendly appearance, but it was too late. I turned to Mrs. Dorsey and said, "Whatever Andrew Johnson may be, he certainly is no friend of our race." The fact was, though it was yet early in the day, Mr. Johnson was drunk.

In the evening of the day of the inauguration, another new experience awaited me. The usual reception was given at the executive mansion, and though no colored persons had ever ventured to present themselves on such occasions, it seemed, now that freedom had become the law of the republic, and colored men were on the battle-field mingling their blood with that of white men in one common effort to save the country, that it was not too great an assumption for a colored man to offer his congratulations to the President with those of other citizens. I had for some time looked upon myself as a man, but now in this multitude of the élite of the land, I felt myself a man among men. I regret to be obliged to say, however, that this comfortable assurance was not of long duration, for on reaching the door, two policemen stationed there

Opposite: Lincoln's second inauguration.

*General William Tecumseh Sherman's
march to the sea.*

Top: The Battle of the Wilderness was fought on May 5–7, 1864.
Bottom: A lithograph depicting the assassination of President Lincoln.

took me rudely by the arm and ordered me to stand back, for their directions were to admit no persons of my color. The reader need not be told that this was a disagreeable set-back. At this moment a gentleman who was passing in recognized me, and I said to him: "Be so kind as to say to Mr. Lincoln that Frederick Douglass is detained by officers at the door." It was not long before I walked into the spacious East Room, amid a scene of elegance such as in this country I had never before witnessed. Like a mountain pine high above all others, Mr. Lincoln stood, in his grand simplicity, and home-like beauty. Recognizing me, even before I reached him, he exclaimed, so that all around could hear him, "Here comes my friend Douglass." Taking me by the hand, he said, "I am glad to see you. I saw you in the crowd to-day, listening to my inaugural address; how did you like it?" I said, "Mr. Lincoln, I must not detain you with my poor opinion, when there are thousands waiting to shake hands with you." "No, no," he said, "you must stop a little, Douglass; there is no man in the country whose opinion I value more than yours. I want to know what you think of it?" I replied, "Mr. Lincoln, that was a sacred effort." "I am glad you liked it!" he said; and I passed on, feeling

that any man, however distinguished, might well regard himself honored by such expressions, from such a man.

A series of important events followed soon after the second inauguration of Mr. Lincoln, conspicuous amongst which was the fall of Richmond. The strongest endeavor, and the best generalship of the Rebellion, was employed to hold that place, and when it fell, the pride, prestige, and power of the rebellion fell with it, never to rise again. The news of this great event found me again in Boston. The enthusiasm of that loyal city cannot be easily described. After the fall of Richmond the collapse of the rebellion was not long delayed, though it did not perish without adding to its long list of atrocities one which sent a thrill of horror throughout the civilized world, in the assassination of Abraham Lincoln; a man so amiable, so kind, humane, and honest, that one is at a loss to know how he could have had an enemy on earth.

Mr. Lincoln had reason to look forward to a peaceful and happy term of office. To all appearance, we were on the eve of a restoration of the union and of a solid and lasting peace. He had served one term as President of the Disunited States, he was now for the first time to be President of the United States. Heavy had been his burden, hard had been his toil, bitter had been his trials, and terrible had been his anxiety; but the future seemed now bright and full of hope. Richmond had fallen, Grant had General Lee and the army of Virginia firmly in his clutch; Sherman had fought and found his way from the banks of the great river to the shores of the sea, leaving the two ends of the rebellion squirming and twisting in agony, like the severed parts of a serpent, doomed to inevitable death; and now there was but a little time longer for the good President to bear his burden, and be the target of reproach. His accusers, in whose opinion he was always too fast or too slow, too weak or too strong, too conciliatory or too aggressive, would soon become his admirers; it was soon to be seen that he had conducted the affairs of the nation with singular wisdom, and with absolute fidelity to the great trust confided in him.

I was in Rochester, N. Y., where I then resided, when news of the death of Mr. Lincoln was received. Our citizens, not knowing what else to do in the agony of the hour, betook themselves to the city hall. Though all hearts ached for utterance, few felt like speaking. We were stunned and overwhelmed by a crime and calamity hitherto unknown to our country and our government. The hour was hardly one for speech, for no speech could rise to the level of feeling. Doctor Robinson, then of Rochester University, but now of Brown University, Providence, R. I., was prevailed upon to take the stand, and made one of the most touching and eloquent speeches I ever heard. At the close of his address, I was called upon, and spoke out of the fullness of my heart, and, happily, gave expression to so much of the soul of the people present that my voice was several times utterly silenced by the sympathetic tumult of the great audience.

CHAPTER XIII

VAST CHANGES

SATISFACTION AND ANXIETY—NEW FIELDS OF LABOR OPENING—LYCEUMS AND COLLEGES SOLICITING ADDRESSES—PECUNIARY GAIN—STILL PLEADING FOR HUMAN RIGHTS—PRESIDENT ANDY JOHNSON—COLORED DELEGATION—THEIR REPLY TO HIM—NATIONAL LOYALIST CONVENTION, 1866, AND ITS PROCESSION—MEETING WITH AN OLD FRIEND—ENFRANCHISEMENT DISCUSSED—ITS ACCOMPLISHMENT—THE NEGRO A CITIZEN.

When the war for the Union was substantially ended, and peace had dawned upon the land, as was the case almost immediately after the tragic death of President Lincoln; when the gigantic system of American slavery which had defied the march of time and resisted all the appeals and arguments of the abolitionists and the humane testimonies of good men of every generation during two hundred and fifty years, was finally abolished and forever prohibited by the organic law of the land, a strange and, perhaps, perverse feeling came over me. My great and exceeding joy over these stupendous achievements, especially over the abolition of slavery (which had been the deepest desire and the great labor of my life), was slightly tinged with a feeling of sadness.

I felt that I had reached the end of the noblest and best part of my life; my school was broken up, my church disbanded, and the beloved congregation dispersed, never to come together again. The anti-slavery platform had performed its work, and my voice was no longer needed. Outside the question of slavery my thoughts had not been much directed, and I could hardly hope to make myself useful in any other cause than that to which I had given the best twenty-five years of my life. A man in the situation in which I found myself has not only to divest himself of the old, which is never easily done, but to adjust himself to the new, which is still more difficult. This question, however, was soon decided for me. I had after all acquired (a very unusual thing) a little more knowledge and aptitude fitting me for the new condition of things than I knew, and had a deeper hold upon public attention than I had supposed. Invitations began to pour in upon me from colleges, lyceums, and literary societies, offering me one hundred, and even two hundred dollars for a single lecture.

I had been invited by one of the literary societies of Western Reserve College (then at Hudson, but recently removed to Cleveland, Ohio), to address it on Commencement day; and never having spoken on such an occasion, never, indeed, having been myself inside of a school-house for the purpose of an education, I hesitated about accepting

James Cowles Prichard (1786–1848), author of Researches into the Physical History of Mankind.

the invitation, and finally called upon Prof. Henry Wayland, son of the great Doctor Wayland of Brown University, and on Doctor Anderson, and asked their advice whether I ought to accept. Both gentlemen advised me to do so. But the puzzling question now was, what shall I say if I do go there? It won't do to give them an old-fashioned anti-slavery discourse. But what shall I talk about? became the difficult question. I had read, with great interest, when in England a few years before, parts of Doctor Prichard's "Natural History of Man," a large volume marvelously calm and philosophical in its discussion of the science of the origin of the races, and was thus in the line of my then convictions. For many days and nights I toiled, and succeeded at last in getting something together in due form. Written orations had not been in my line. I had usually depended upon my unsystematized knowledge and the inspiration of the hour and the occasion, but I had now got the "scholar bee in my bonnet," and supposed that inasmuch as I was to speak to college professors and students I must at least make a show of some familiarity with letters.

My lecture on "The Races of Men" was seldom called for, but that on "Self-made Men" was in great demand, especially through the West. I found that the success of a lecturer depends more upon the quality of his stock in store than the amount. I adhered pretty closely to my old lecture on "Self-made Men," retouching and shading it a little from time to time as occasion seemed to require.

Here, then, was a new vocation before me, full of advantages mentally and pecuniarily. When in the employment of the American Anti-Slavery Society my salary was about four hundred and fifty dollars a year, and I felt I was well paid for my services; but I could now make from fifty to a hundred dollars a night, and have the satisfaction, too, that I was in some small measure helping to lift my race into consideration, for no man who lives at all lives unto himself—he either helps or hinders all who are in any wise connected with him.

From the first I saw no chance of bettering the condition of the freedman until he should cease to be merely a freedman and should become a citizen. I insisted that there was no safety for him or for anybody else in America outside the American government; that to guard, protect, and maintain his liberty the freedman should have the ballot; that the liberties of the American people were dependent upon the ballot-box, the jury-box, and the cartridge-box; that without these no class of people could live and flourish in this country; and this was now the word for the hour with me, and the word to which the people of the North willingly listened when I spoke. I set myself to work with whatever force and energy I possessed to secure this power for the recently-emancipated millions.

The enfranchisement of the freedmen was resisted on many grounds, but mainly on these two: first, the tendency of the measure to bring the freedmen into conflict with the old master-class and the white people of the South generally; secondly, their unfitness, by reason of

their ignorance, servility and degradation, to exercise over the destinies of this great nation so great a power as the ballot.

Unlike the movement for the abolition of slavery, the success of the effort for the enfranchisement of the freedmen was not long delayed. It is another illustration of how any advance in pursuance of a right principle prepares and makes easy the way to another. In this achievement, an interview with President Andrew Johnson, on the 7th of February, 1866, by a delegation consisting of George T. Downing, Lewis H. Douglass, Wm. E. Matthews, John Jones, John F. Cook, Joseph E. Otis, A. W. Ross, William Whipper, John M. Brown, Alexander Dunlop, and myself, will take its place in history as one of the first steps. What was said on that occasion brought the whole question virtually before the American people. From this time onward the question of suffrage for the freedmen was not allowed to rest. The rapidity with which it gained strength was something quite marvelous and surprising even to its advocates. A committee of the Senate had reported a proposition giving to the States lately in rebellion, in so many words, complete option as to the enfranchisement of their colored citizens; only coupling with that proposition the condition that, to such States as chose to enfranchise such citizens, the basis of their representation in Congress should be proportionately increased; or, in other words, that only three-fifths of the colored citizens should be counted in the basis of representation in States where colored citizens were not allowed to vote, while in the States granting suffrage to colored citizens, the entire colored people should be counted in the basis of representation.

In defeating the option proposed to be given to the States to extend or deny suffrage to their colored population, much credit is due to the delegation already named as visiting President Johnson. That delegation made it their business to personally see and urge upon leading republican statesmen the wisdom and duty of impartial suffrage.

The second marked step in effecting the enfranchisement of the negro was made at the "National Loyalist's Convention," held at Philadelphia, in September, 1866. This body was composed of delegates from the South, North, and West. Its object was to diffuse clear views of the situation of affairs at the South and to indicate the principles by it deemed advisable to be observed in the reconstruction of society in the Southern States.

I was at the time residing in Rochester and was duly elected as a delegate from that city to attend this convention. The honor was a surprise and a gratification to me. It was unprecedented for a city of over sixty thousand white citizens and only about two hundred colored residents, to elect a colored man to represent them in a national political convention, and the announcement of it gave a shock of no

Opposite: A campaign banner promoting Lincoln for president and Andrew Johnson for vice president, but Johnson would take on the role of commander in chief after Lincoln's assassination.

TEMPLE OF LIBERTY.

ABRAHAM LINCOLN.

ANDREW JOHNSON.

John Minor Botts (1802–1869).

a high and influential position—the editor of a weekly journal having the largest circulation of any weekly paper in the city or State of New York—and that man was Mr. Theodore Tilton. He came to me in my isolation, seized me by the hand in a most brotherly way, and proposed to walk with me in the procession.

Well! what came of all these dark forebodings of timid men? How was my presence regarded by the populace? and what effect did it produce? I will tell you. The fears of the loyal governors who wished me excluded to propitiate the favor of the crowd, met with a signal reproof. Their apprehensions were shown to be groundless, and they were compelled, as many of them confessed to me afterwards, to own themselves entirely mistaken. The people were more enlightened and had made more progress than their leaders had supposed.

During the passage of the procession, as we were marching through Chestnut street, an incident occurred which excited some interest in the crowd, and was noticed by the press at the time, and may perhaps be properly related here as a part of the story of my eventful life. It was my meeting Mrs. Amanda Sears, the daughter of my old mistress, Miss Lucretia Auld, the same Lucretia to whom I was indebted for so many acts of kindness when under the rough treatment of Aunt Katy, at the "old plantation home" of Col. Edward Lloyd. Mrs. Sears now resided in Baltimore, and as I saw her on the corner of Ninth and Chestnut streets, I hastily ran to her, and expressed my surprise and joy at meeting her. "But what brought you to Philadelphia at this time?" I asked. She replied, with animated voice and countenance, "I heard you were to be here, and I came to see you walk in this procession." The dear lady, with her two children, had been following us for hours. Mrs. Sears died three years ago in Baltimore, but she did not depart without calling me to her bedside, that I might tell her as much as I could about her mother, whom she was firm in the faith that she should meet in another and better world.

But I must now return from this digression and further relate my experience in the loyalist national convention, and how, from that time, there was an impetus given to the enfranchisement of the freedmen which culminated in the fifteenth amendment to the Constitution of the United States. From the first the members of the convention were divided in their views of the proper measures of reconstruction, and this division was in some sense sectional. The men from the far South, strangely enough, were quite radical, while those from the border States were mostly conservative, and unhappily, these last had from the first the control of the convention. A Kentucky gentleman was made president. Its other officers were for the most part Kentuckians and all were in sentiment opposed to colored suffrage. The result was that the convention was broken square in two. The Kentucky president declared it adjourned, and left the chair, against the earnest protests of the friends of manhood suffrage.

But the friends of this measure were not to be out-generaled and suppressed in this way, and instantly reorganized, elected Hon. John

inconsiderable violence to the country. On the previous night I had been warned that I should not be allowed to walk through the city in the procession; fears had been expressed that my presence in it would so shock the prejudices of the people of Philadelphia, as to cause the procession to be mobbed.

The members of the convention were to walk two abreast, and as I was the only colored member of the convention, the question was, as to who of my brother members would consent to walk with me? The answer was not long in coming. There was one man present who was broad enough to take in the whole situation, and brave enough to meet the duty of the hour; one who was neither afraid nor ashamed to own me as a man and a brother; one man of the purest Caucasian type, a poet and a scholar, brilliant as a writer, eloquent as a speaker, and holding

African American students gathered in a school in Richmond, Virginia, during the Reconstruction era, 1866.

M. Botts of Virginia president, discussed and passed resolutions in favor of enfranchising the freedmen, and thus placed the question before the country in such a manner that it could not be ignored. The delegates from the Southern States were quite in earnest, and bore themselves grandly in support of the measure; but the chief speakers and advocates of suffrage on that occasion were Mr. Theodore Tilton and Miss Anna E. Dickinson. Of course, on such a question, I could not be expected to be silent. I was called forward and responded with all the energy of my soul, for I looked upon suffrage to the Negro as the only measure which could prevent him from being thrust back into slavery.

As it was, the question was speedily taken out of the hands of colored delegations and mere individual efforts and became a part of the policy of the Republican party, and President U. S. Grant, with his characteristic nerve and clear perception of justice, promptly recommended the great amendment to the Constitution by which colored men are to-day invested with complete citizenship—the right to vote and to be voted for in the American Republic.

CHAPTER XIV

LIVING AND LEARNING

Inducements to a political career—Objections—A newspaper enterprise—The *New National Era*—Its abandonment—The Freedmen's Savings and Trust Company—Sad experience—Vindication.

The adoption of the fourteenth and fifteenth amendments and their incorporation into the Constitution of the United States opened a very tempting field to my ambition, and one to which I should probably have yielded had I been a younger man. I was earnestly urged by many of my respected fellow-citizens, both colored and white, and from all sections of the country, to take up my abode in some one of the many districts of the South where there was a large colored vote and get myself elected, as they were sure I easily could do, to a seat in Congress—possibly in the Senate. That I did not yield to this temptation was not entirely due to my age, for the idea did not square well with my better judgment and sense of propriety. The thought of going to live among a people in order to gain their votes and acquire official honors was repugnant to my self-respect, and I had not lived long enough in the political atmosphere of Washington to have this sentiment sufficiently blunted to make me indifferent to its suggestions.

I was not, however, to remain long in my retired home in Rochester, where I had planted my trees and was reposing under their shadows. An effort was being made about this time to establish a large weekly newspaper in the city of Washington, which should be devoted to the defence and enlightenment of the newly-emancipated and enfranchised people; and I was urged by such men as George T. Downing, J. H. Hawes, J. Sella Martin, and others, to become its editor-in-chief. My sixteen years' experience as editor and publisher of my own paper, and the knowledge of the toil and anxiety which such a relation to a public journal must impose, caused me much reluctance and hesitation; nevertheless, I yielded to the wishes of my friends and counsellors, went to Washington, threw myself into the work, hoping to be able to lift up a standard at the national capital for my people which should cheer and strengthen them in the work of their own improvement and elevation.

I was not long connected with this enterprise before I discovered my mistake. The cooperation so liberally promised, and the support which had been assured, were not very largely realized. By a series of circumstances, a little bewildering as I now look back upon them, I found myself alone, under the mental and pecuniary burden involved in the prosecution of the enterprise. I was unwilling to have it prove a failure, and had allowed it to become in debt to me, both for money loaned and for services, and at last it seemed wise that I should purchase the whole concern,

Senator John Sherman (1823–1900).

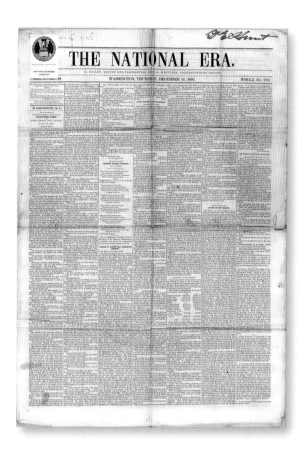

Left: An 1851 edition of the National Era. *Right: Senator John Scott (1824–1869).*

which I did, and turned it over to my sons Lewis and Frederic, who were practical printers, and who, after a few years, were compelled to discontinue its publication. This paper was the *New National Era*, to the columns of which the colored people are indebted for some of the best things ever uttered in behalf of their cause; for, aside from its editorials and selections, many of the ablest colored men of the country made it the medium through which to convey their thoughts to the public. A misadventure though it was, which cost me from nine to ten thousand dollars, over it I have no tears to shed. The journal was valuable while it lasted, and the experiment was to me full of instruction, which has to some extent been heeded, for I have kept well out of newspaper undertakings since.

Some one has said that "experience is the best teacher." Unfortunately the wisdom acquired in one experience seems not to serve for another and new one; at any rate, my first lesson at the national capital, bought rather dearly as it was, did not preclude the necessity of a second whetstone to sharpen my wits in this, my new

home and new surroundings. It is not altogether without a feeling of humiliation that I must narrate my connection with the "Freedmen's Savings and Trust Company."

This was an institution designed to furnish a place of security and profit for the hard earnings of the colored people, especially at the South. Though its title was "The Freedmen's Savings and Trust Company," it is known generally as the "Freedmen's Bank." Branches were established in all the Southern States, and as a result, money to the amount of millions flowed into its vaults.

After settling myself down in Washington in the office of the *New Era*, I could and did occasionally attend the meetings of the Board of Trustees, and had the pleasure of listening to the rapid reports of the condition of the institution, which were generally of a most encouraging character. My confidence in the integrity and wisdom of the management was such that at one time I had entrusted to its vaults about twelve thousand dollars. About four months before this splendid institution was compelled to close its doors in the starved and deluded faces of its

A print showing vignettes of black life and a parade celebrating the Fifteenth Amendment, which granted African American men the right to vote.

to our liabilities, we could not in all likelihoods of the case pay seventy-two cents on the dollar.

Not to make too long a story, I was, in six weeks after my election as president of this bank, convinced that it was no longer a safe custodian of the hard earnings of my confiding people. This conclusion once reached, I could not hesitate as to my duty in the premises, and this was, to save as much as possible of the assets held by the bank for the benefit of the depositors; and to prevent their being further squandered in keeping up appearances, and in paying the salaries of myself and other officers in the bank. Fortunately, Congress, from which we held our charter, was then in session, and its committees on finance were in daily session. I felt it my duty to make known as speedily as possible to Hon. John Sherman, Chairman of the Senate Committee on Finance, and to Senator Scott of Pennsylvania, also of the same committee, that I regarded the institution as insolvent and irrecoverable, and that I could no longer ask my people to deposit their money in it. The finance committee substantially agreed with me and in a few weeks so legislated, by appointing three commissioners to take charge of its affairs, as to bring this imposing banking business to a close.

When I became connected with the bank I had a tolerably fair name for honest dealing; I had expended in the publication of my paper in Rochester thousands of dollars annually, and had often to depend upon my credit to bridge over immediate wants, but no man there or elsewhere can say I ever wronged him out of a cent.

depositors, and while I was assured by its President and by its Actuary of its sound condition, I was solicited by some of its trustees to allow them to use my name in the board as a candidate for its presidency. So I waked up one morning to find myself seated in a comfortable arm chair, with gold spectacles on my nose, and to hear myself addressed as President of the Freedmen's Bank. Gradually I discovered that the bank had, through dishonest agents, sustained heavy losses at the South; that there was a discrepancy on the books of forty thousand dollars for which no account could be given, and that, instead of our assets being equal

A check from the Freedman's Savings and Trust Company for sixteen cents.

CHAPTER XV

WEIGHED IN THE BALANCE

DECORATION DAY AT ARLINGTON, 1871—SPEECH DELIVERED THERE—NATIONAL COLORED CONVENTION AT NEW ORLEANS, 1872—ELECTOR AT LARGE FOR THE STATE OF NEW YORK.

I have thus far told my story without copious quotations from my letters, speeches, or other writings, and shall not depart from this rule in what remains to be told, except to insert here my speech, delivered at Arlington, near the monument to the "Unknown Loyal Dead," on Decoration Day, 1871. It was delivered under impressive circumstances, in presence of President Grant, his Cabinet, and a great multitude of distinguished people, and expresses, as I think, the true view which should be taken of the great conflict between slavery and freedom to which it refers.

"Friends and Fellow Citizens: Tarry here for a moment. My words shall be few and simple. The solemn rites of this hour and place call for no lengthened speech. There is, in the very air of this resting ground of the unknown dead a silent, subtle and all-pervading eloquence, far more touching, impressive, and thrilling than living lips have ever uttered. Into the measureless depths of every loyal soul it is now whispering lessons of all that is precious, priceless, holiest, and most enduring in human existence. . . .

"Those unknown heroes whose whitened bones have been piously gathered here, and whose green graves we now strew with sweet and beautiful flowers choice emblems alike of pure hearts and brave spirits, reached, in their glorious career that last highest point of nobleness beyond which human power cannot go. They died for their country.

"No loftier tribute can be paid to the most illustrious of all the benefactors of mankind than we pay to these unrecognized soldiers when we write above their graves this shining epitaph.

"When the dark and vengeful spirit of slavery, always ambitious, preferring to rule in hell than to serve in heaven, fired the Southern heart and stirred all the malign elements of discord, when our great Republic, the hope of freedom and self-government throughout the world, had reached the point of supreme peril, when the Union of these States was torn and rent asunder at the center, and the armies of a gigantic rebellion came forth with broad blades and bloody hands to destroy the very foundation of American society, the unknown braves who flung themselves into the yawning chasm, where cannon roared and bullets whistled, fought and fell. They died for their country. . . .

"If we ought to forget a war which has filled our land with widows and orphans; which has made stumps of men of the very flower of our youth; which has sent them on the journey of life armless, legless, maimed and

Parker Pillsbury (1809–1898).

A celebration of the first official Decoration Day (today known as Memorial Day) at Arlington Cemetery.

mutilated; which has piled up a debt heavier than a mountain of gold, swept uncounted thousands of men into bloody graves and planted agony at a million hearthstones—I say, if this war is to be forgotten, I ask, in the name of all things sacred, what shall men remember?

"The essence and significance of our devotions here to-day are not to be found in the fact that the men whose remains fill these graves were brave in battle. If we met simply to show our sense of bravery, we should find enough on both sides to kindle admiration. In the raging storm of fire and blood, in the fierce torrent of shot and shell, of sword and bayonet, whether on foot or on horse, unflinching courage marked the rebel not less than the loyal soldier. "But we are not here to applaud manly courage, save as it has been displayed in a noble cause. We must never forget that victory to the rebellion meant death to the republic. We must never forget that the loyal soldiers who rest beneath this sod flung themselves between the nation and the nation's destroyers. If to-day we have a country not boiling in an agony of blood, like France, if now we have a united country, no longer cursed by the hell-black system of human bondage, if the American name is no longer a by-word and a hissing to a mocking earth, if the star-spangled banner floats only over free American citizens in every quarter of the land, and our country has before it a long and glorious career of justice, liberty, and civilization, we are indebted to the unselfish devotion of the noble army who rest in these honored graves all around us."

In the month of April, 1872, I had the honor to attend and preside over a national convention of colored citizens held in New Orleans. It was a critical period in the history of the Republican party, as well as in

that of the country. Eminent men who had hitherto been looked upon as the pillars of republicanism had become dissatisfied with President Grant's administration, and determined to defeat his nomination for a second term. The division in the Republican ranks seemed to be growing deeper and broader every day. The colored people of the country were much affected by the threatened disruption, and their leaders were much divided as to the side upon which they should give their voice and their votes. The names of Greeley and Sumner, on account of their long and earnest advocacy of justice and liberty to the blacks, had powerful attractions for the newly-enfranchised class, and there was in this convention at New Orleans naturally enough a strong disposition to fraternize with the new party and follow the lead of their old friends. Against this policy I exerted whatever influence I possessed, and, I think, succeeded in holding back that convention from what I felt sure then would have been a fatal political blunder.

From this convention onward, until the nomination and election of Grant and Wilson, I was actively engaged on the stump. Since 1872 I have been regularly what my old friend Parker Pillsbury would call a "field hand" in every important political campaign, and at each national convention have sided with what has been called the stalwart element of the Republican party. It was in the Grant presidential campaign that New York took an advanced step in the renunciation of a timid policy. The Republicans of that State, not having the fear of popular prejudice before their eyes, placed my name as an elector at large at the head of their presidential ticket. The result proved not only the justice and generosity of the measure, but its wisdom. The Republicans carried the State by a majority of fifty thousand over the heads of the Liberal-Republican and Democratic parties combined.

Equally significant of the turn now taken in the political sentiment of the country was the action of the Republican electoral college at its meeting in Albany, when it committed to my custody the sealed-up electoral vote of the great State of New York and commissioned me to bring that vote to the national capital. Only a few years before this any colored man was forbidden by law to carry a United States mail bag from one post-office to another.

My appointment as United States Marshal of the District of Columbia, was in keeping with the rest of my life, as a freeman. It was an innovation upon long established usage, and opposed to the general current of sentiment in the community. It came upon the people of the District as a gross surprise, and almost a punishment; and provoked something like a scream—I will not say a yell—of popular displeasure. As soon as I was named by President Hayes for the place, efforts were made by members of the bar to defeat my confirmation before the Senate. All sorts of reasons against my appointment, but the true one, were given, and that was withheld more from a sense of shame, than from a sense of justice. The apprehension doubtless was, that if appointed marshal, I would surround myself with colored deputies, colored bailiffs

Frederick Douglass moved to this house in Washington, D.C., in 1878 after he became the United States Marshal of the District of Columbia.

and colored messengers and pack the jury-box with colored jurors; in a word, Africanize the courts. But the most dreadful thing threatened, was a colored man at the Executive Mansion in white kid gloves, sparrow-tailed coat, patent-leather boots, and alabaster cravat, performing the ceremony—a very empty one—of introducing the aristocratic citizens of the republic to the President of the United States. This was something entirely too much to be borne; and men asked themselves in view of it. To what is the world coming? and where will these things stop? Dreadful! Dreadful!

The effort to prevent my confirmation having failed, nothing could be done but to wait for some overt act to justify my removal; and for this my unfriends had not long to wait. In the course of one or two months I was invited by a number of citizens of Baltimore to deliver a lecture in that city, in Douglass Hall—a building named in honor of myself, and devoted to educational purposes. With this invitation I complied, giving the same lecture which I had two years before delivered in the

city of Washington, and which was at the time published in full in the newspapers, and very highly commended by them. The subject of the lecture was, "Our National Capital" and in it I said many complimentary things of the city, which were as true as they were complimentary. I spoke of what it had been in the past, what it was at that time, and what I thought it destined to become in the future; giving it all credit for its good points, and calling attention to some of its ridiculous features. For this I got myself pretty roughly handled. The newspapers worked themselves up to a frenzy of passion, and committees were appointed to procure names to a petition to President Hayes demanding my removal.

This violent hostility kindled against me was singularly evanescent. It came like a whirlwind, and like a whirlwind departed. I soon saw nothing of it, either in the courts among the lawyers, or on the streets among the people; for it was discovered that there was really in my speech at Baltimore nothing which made me "worthy of stripes or of bonds." I can say of my experience in the office of

Left: "A war . . . which has made stumps of men of the very flower of our youth; which has sent them on the journey of life armless, legless, maimed and mutilated." Veterans John J. Long, Walter H. French, E. P. Robinson, and an unidentified companion all sacrificed a leg to the Civil War. Right: President Rutherford B. Hayes (1822–1893).

United States Marshal of the District of Columbia that it was every way agreeable.

In all my forty years of thought and labor to promote the freedom and welfare of my race, I never found myself more widely and painfully at variance with leading colored men of the country than when I opposed the effort to set in motion a wholesale exodus of colored people of the South to the Northern States; and yet I never took a position in which I felt myself better fortified by reason and necessity. It was said of me, that I had deserted to the old master class, and that I was a traitor to my race; that I had run away from slavery myself, and yet I was opposing others in doing the same. When my opponents condescended to argue, they took the ground that the colored people of the South needed to be brought into contact with the freedom and civilization of the North; that no emancipated and persecuted people ever had or ever could rise in the presence of the people by whom they had been enslaved, and that the true remedy for the ills which the freedmen were suffering, was to initiate the Isrealitish departure from our modern Egypt to a land abounding, if not in "milk and honey," certainly in pork and hominy.

Influenced, no doubt, by the dazzling prospects held out to them by the advocates of the exodus movement, thousands of poor, hungry, naked and destitute colored people were induced to quit the South amid the frosts and snows of a dreadful winter in search of a better country. I regret to say that there was something sinister in this so-called exodus, for it transpired that some of the agents most active in promoting it had an understanding with certain railroad companies, by which they were to receive one dollar per head upon all such passengers. Thousands of these poor people, traveling only so far as they had money to bear their expenses, were dropped in the extremest destitution on the levees of St. Louis, and their tales of woe were such as to move a heart much less sensitive to human suffering than mine. But while I felt for these poor deluded people, and did what I could to put a stop to their ill-advised and ill-arranged stampede, I also did what I could to assist such of them as were within my reach, who were on their way to this land of promise. Hundreds of these people came to Washington, and at one time there were from two to three hundred lodges here unable to get further for the want of money. I lost no time in appealing to my friends for the means of assisting them.

CHAPTER XVI

"TIME MAKES ALL THINGS EVEN"

RETURN TO THE "OLD MASTER"—A LAST INTERVIEW—CAPTAIN AULD'S ADMISSION, "HAD I BEEN IN YOUR PLACE I SHOULD HAVE DONE AS YOU DID"—SPEECH AT EASTON—THE OLD JAIL THERE—VISIT TO THE OLD PLANTATION—HOME OF COLONEL LLOYD—KIND RECEPTION AND ATTENTIONS—FAMILIAR SCENES—OLD MEMORIES—SPEECH AT HARPER'S FERRY, DECORATION DAY, 1881—STORER COLLEGE.

The leading incidents to which it is my purpose to call attention and make prominent in the present chapter will, I think, address the imagination of the reader with peculiar and poetic force, and might well enough be dramatized for the stage. They certainly afford another striking illustration of the trite saying that "truth is stranger than fiction."

The first of these events occurred four years ago, when, after a period of more than forty years, I visited and had an interview with Captain Thomas Auld at St. Michaels, Talbot county, Maryland. It will be remembered by those who have followed the thread of my story that St. Michaels was at one time the place of my home and the scene of some of my saddest experiences of slave life, and that I left there, or rather was compelled to leave there, because it was believed that I had written passes for several slaves to enable them to escape from slavery, and that prominent slaveholders in that neighborhood had, for this alleged offense, threatened to shoot me on sight, and to prevent the execution of this threat my master had sent me to Baltimore. My return, therefore, in peace, to this place and among the same people, was strange enough in itself; but that I should, when there, be formally invited by Captain Thomas Auld, then over eighty years old, to come to the side of his dying bed, evidently with a view to a friendly talk over our past relations, was a fact still more strange, and one which, until its occurrence, I could never have thought possible. I had by my writings made his name and his deeds familiar to the world in four different languages, yet here we were, after four decades, once more face to face—he on his bed, aged and tremulous, drawing near the sunset of life, and I, his former slave, United States Marshal of the District of Columbia, holding his hand and in friendly conversation with him in a sort of final settlement of past differences preparatory to his stepping into his grave, where all distinctions are at an end, and where the great and the small, the slave and his master, are reduced to the same level. The conditions were favorable

A circa 1870 bust portrait of Douglass by famed photographer of the day Mathew Brady.

Today, the Talbot County Courthouse's lawn boasts
a statue of Douglass giving a speech.

for remembrance of all his good deeds, and generous extenuation of all his evil ones. He was to me no longer a slaveholder either in fact or in spirit, and I regarded him as I did myself, a victim of the circumstances of birth, education, law, and custom.

Though broken by age and palsy, the mind of Capt. Auld was remarkably clear and strong. After he had become composed I asked him what he thought of my conduct in running away and going to the north. He hesitated a moment as if to properly formulate his reply, and said: "Frederick, I always knew you were too smart to be a slave, and had I been in your place, I should have done as you did." I said, "Capt. Auld, I am glad to hear you say this. I did not run away from you, but from slavery; it was not that I loved Caesar less, but Rome more." I told him that I had made a mistake in my narrative, a copy of which I had sent him, in attributing to him ungrateful and cruel treatment of my grandmother; that I had done so on the supposition that in the division of the property of my old master, Mr. Aaron Anthony, my grandmother had fallen to him, and that he had left her in her old age, when she could be no longer of service to him, to pick up her living in solitude with none to help her, or, in other words, had turned her out to die like an old horse. "Ah!" he said, "that was a mistake, I never owned your grandmother; she in the division of the slaves was awarded to my brother-in-law, Andrew Anthony; but," he added quickly, "I brought her down here and took care of her as long as she lived." The fact is, that, after writing my narrative describing the condition of my grandmother, Capt. Auld's attention being thus called to it, he rescued her from her destitution. I told him that this mistake of mine was corrected as soon as I discovered

it, and that I had at no time any wish to do him injustice; that I regarded both of us as victims of a system. "Oh, I never liked slavery," he said, "and I meant to emancipate all of my slaves when they reached the age of twenty-five years." I told him I had always been curious to know how old I was and that it had been a serious trouble to me, not to know when was my birthday. He said he could not tell me that, but he thought I was born in February, 1818. This date made me one year younger than I had supposed myself from what was told me by Mistress Lucretia, Captain Auld's former wife, when I left Lloyd's for Baltimore in the Spring of 1825; she having then said that I was eight, going on nine.

It may not, perhaps, be quite artistic to speak in this connection of another incident of something of the same nature as that which I have just narrated, and yet it quite naturally finds place here; and that is, my visit to the town of Easton, county seat of Talbot County, two years later, to deliver an address in the Court House, for the benefit of some association in that place. The visit was made interesting to me, by the fact that forty-five years before I had, in company with Henry and John Harris, been dragged behind horses to Easton, with my hands tied, put in jail and offered for sale, for the offense of intending to run away from slavery.

It may easily be seen that this visit, after this lapse of time, brought with it feelings and reflections such as only unusual circumstances can awaken. There stood the old jail, with its white-washed walls and iron gratings, as when in my youth I heard its heavy locks and bolts clank behind me. Strange too, Mr. Joseph Graham, who was then sheriff of the County, and who locked me in this gloomy place, was still living, though verging towards eighty, and was one of the gentlemen who now gave me a warm and friendly welcome, and was among my hearers when I delivered my address at the Court House.

When one has advanced far in the journey of life, when he has seen and traveled over much of this great world, and has had many and strange experiences of shadow and sunshine, when long distances of time and space have come between him and his point of departure, it is natural that his thoughts should return to the place of his beginning, and that he should be seized with a strong desire to revisit the scenes of his early recollection, and live over in memory the incidents of his childhood. At least such for several years had been my thoughts and feeling in respect of Col. Lloyd's plantation on Wye River, Talbot County, Maryland; for I had never been there since I left it, when eight years old, in 1825.

The opportunity for the trip however did not occur till the 12th of June, and on that day, in company with Messrs. Thomas, Thompson, and Chamberlain, on board the cutter, we started for the contemplated visit. In four hours after leaving Baltimore we were anchored in the river off the Lloyd estate, and from the deck of our vessel I saw once more the stately chimneys of the grand old mansion which I had last seen from the deck of the *Sallie Lloyd* when a boy. I left there as a slave, and returned as a freeman; I left there unknown to the outside world, and returned well known; I left there on a freight boat, and returned on a revenue cutter; I left on a vessel belonging to Col. Edward Lloyd, and returned on one belonging to the United States.

As soon as we had come to anchor, Mr. Thomas dispatched a note to Col. Edward Lloyd, announcing my presence on board his cutter, and inviting him to meet me, informing him it was my desire, if agreeable to him, to revisit my old home. In response to this note, Mr. Howard Lloyd, a son of Col. Lloyd, a young gentleman of very pleasant address, came on board the cutter, and was introduced to the several gentlemen and myself.

He told us that his father had gone to Easton on business, expressed his regret at his absence, hoped he would return before we should leave, and in the meantime received us cordially, and invited us ashore, escorted us over the grounds, and gave us as hearty a welcome as we could have wished. I hope I shall be pardoned for speaking with much complacency of this incident. It was one which could happen to but few men, and only once in the life time of any. The span of human life is too short for the repetition of events which occur at the distance of fifty years. That I was deeply moved and greatly affected by it can be easily imagined.

There was the long quarter, the quarter on the hill, the dwelling-house of my old master Aaron Anthony, and the overseer's house, once occupied by William Sevier, Austin Gore, James Hopkins, and other overseers. In connection with my old master's house was the kitchen where Aunt Katy presided, and where my head had received many a thump from her unfriendly hand. I looked into this kitchen with peculiar interest, and remembered that it was there I last saw my mother. I went round to the window at which Miss Lucretia used to sit with her sewing, and at which I used to sing when hungry, a signal which she well understood, and to which she readily responded with bread. The little closet in which I slept in a bag had been taken into the room; the dirt floor, too, had disappeared under plank. But upon the whole the house is very much as it was in the old time.

Leaving the Great House we bade good-bye to Mr. Howard Lloyd, with many thanks for his kind attentions, and steamed away to St. Michael's, a place of which I have already spoken.

The next, and last noteworthy incident in my experience, and one which further and strikingly illustrates the idea with which this chapter sets out, is my visit to Harper's Ferry on the 30th of May, of this year, and my address on John Brown, delivered in that place before Storer College, an Institution established for the education of the children of those whom John Brown endeavored to liberate. It is only a little more than twenty years ago when the subject of my discourse (as will be seen elsewhere in this volume) made a raid upon Harper's Ferry; when its people, and we may say the whole nation were filled with astonishment, horror, and indignation at the mention of his name. I was, after two decades, allowed to deliver an address,

An illustration from an original edition of Narrative of the Life of Frederick Douglass, an American Slave.

not merely defending John Brown, but extolling him as a hero and martyr to the cause of liberty, and doing it with scarcely a murmur of disapprobation. I confess that as I looked out upon the scene before me and the towering heights around me, and remembered the bloody drama there enacted; as I saw the log-house in the distance where John Brown collected his men and saw the little engine-house where the brave old Puritan fortified himself against a dozen companies of Virginia Militia, and the place where he was finally captured by the United States troops under Col. Robert E. Lee, I was a little shocked at my own boldness in attempting to deliver in such presence an address of the character advertised in advance of my coming. But there was no cause of apprehension. The people of Harper's Ferry have made wondrous progress in their ideas of freedom, of thought and speech. Upon the whole, taking the visit to Capt. Auld, to Easton with its old jail, to the home of my old master at Col. Lloyd's, and this visit to Harper's Ferry, with all their associations, they fulfill the expectation created at the beginning of this chapter.

CHAPTER XVII

INCIDENTS AND EVENTS

EXPERIENCES AT HOTELS AND ON STEAMBOATS AND OTHER MODES
OF TRAVEL—HON. MOSES NORRIS—REFLECTIONS AND CONCLUSIONS.

In escaping from the South, the reader will have observed that I did not escape from its widespread influence in the North. That influence met me almost everywhere outside of pronounced antislavery circles, and sometimes even within them. It was in the air, and men breathed it and were permeated by it often when they were quite unconscious of its presence.

I might recount many occasions when I have encountered this feeling, some painful and melancholy, some ridiculous and amusing. It has been a part of my mission to expose the absurdity of this spirit of caste and in some measure help to emancipate men from its control.

Many years ago, on my way from Cleveland to Buffalo on one of the lake steamers, the gong sounded for supper. There was a rough element on board, such as at that time might be found anywhere between Buffalo and Chicago. It was not to be trifled with, especially when hungry. At the first sound of the gong there was a furious rush for the table. From prudence, more than from lack of appetite, I waited for the second table, as did several others. At this second table I took a seat far apart from the few gentlemen scattered along its side, but directly opposite a well-dressed, fine-featured man of the fairest complexion, high forehead, golden hair, and light beard. His whole appearance told me he was somebody.

I had been seated but a minute or two when the steward came to me and roughly ordered me away. I paid no attention to him, but proceeded to take my supper, determined not to leave unless compelled to do so by superior force, and, being young and strong, I was not entirely unwilling to risk the consequences of such a contest. A few moments passed, when on each side of my chair there appeared a stalwart of my own race. I glanced at the gentleman opposite. His brow was knit, his color changed from white to scarlet, and his eyes were full of fire. I saw the lightning flash, but I could not tell where it would strike. Before my sable brethren could execute their captain's order, and just as they were about to lay violent hands upon me, a voice from that man of golden hair and fiery eyes resounded like a clap of summer thunder. "Let the gentleman alone! I am not ashamed to take my tea with Mr. Douglass." His was a voice to be obeyed, and my right to my seat and my supper was no more disputed.

I bowed my acknowledgment to the gentleman and thanked him for his chivalrous interference, and, as modestly as I could, asked him his name. "I am Edward Marshall of Kentucky, now of California," he said. "Sir, I am very glad to know you; I have just been reading your speech in Congress," I said. Supper over, we passed several hours in conversation with each other,

William Lloyd Garrison, portrait by Nathaniel Jocelyn (1796–1881) in 1833.

An advertisement for the steamer that traveled from Buffalo to Cleveland.

during which he told me of his political career in California, of his election to Congress, and that he was a Democrat, but had no prejudice against color. He was then just coming from Kentucky, where he had been in part to see his black mammy, for, said he, "I nursed at the breasts of a colored mother."

In 1842 I was sent by the Massachusetts Anti-Slavery Society to hold a Sunday meeting in Pittsfield, N. H., and was given the name of Mr. Hilles, a subscriber to the *Liberator*. It was supposed that any man who had the courage to take and read the *Liberator*, edited by William Lloyd Garrison, or the *Herald of Freedom*, edited by Nathaniel P. Rodgers, would gladly receive and give food and shelter to any colored brother laboring in the cause of the slave. As a general rule this was very true.

Arriving at Pittsfield, I was asked by the driver where I would stop. I gave him the name of my subscriber to the *Liberator*. "That is two miles beyond," he said. So, after landing his other passengers, he took me on to the house of Mr. Hilles.

I confess I did not seem a very desirable visitor. The day had been warm and the road dusty. I was covered with dust, and then I

was not of the color fashionable in that neighborhood, for colored people were scarce in that part of the old Granite State. I saw in an instant that, though the weather was warm, I was to have a cool reception; but, cool or warm, there was no alternative left me but to stay and take what I could get.

Mr. Hilles scarcely spoke to me, and, from the moment he saw me jump down from the top of the stage, carpet-bag in hand, his face wore a troubled look. His good wife took the matter more philosophically, and evidently thought my presence there for a day or two could do the family no especial harm; but her manner was restrained, silent, and formal, wholly unlike that of anti-slavery ladies I had met in Massachusetts and Rhode Island.

Sunday morning came, and in due season the hour for meeting. I had arranged a good supply of work for the day. I was to speak four times: at ten o'clock A. M., at one P. M., at five, and again at half-past seven in the evening.

When meeting-time came, Mr. Hilles brought his fine phaeton to the door, assisted his wife in, and, although there were two vacant seats in his carriage, there was no room in it for me. On driving off

Sibley Hall, Rochester, New York.

from his door, he merely said, addressing me, "You can find your way to the town hall, I suppose?" "I suppose I can," I replied, and started along behind his carriage on the dusty road toward the village. I found the hall, and was very glad to see in my small audience the face of good Mrs. Hilles. Her husband was not there, but had gone to his church. There was no one to introduce me, and I proceeded with my discourse without introduction. I held my audience till twelve o'clock—noon—and then took the usual recess of Sunday meetings in country towns, to allow the people to take their lunch. No one invited me to lunch, so I remained in the town hall till the audience assembled again, when I spoke till nearly three o'clock, when the people again dispersed, and left me as before. By this time I began to

be hungry, and, seeing a small hotel near, I went into it and offered to buy a meal; but I was told "they did not entertain niggers there." I went back to the old town hall hungry and cold, for an infant "New England northeaster" was beginning to chill the air, and a drizzling rain to fall. I was approached rather hesitatingly by a gentleman, who inquired my name. "My name is Douglass," I replied. "You do not seem to have any place to stay while in town." I told him I had not. "Well," said he, "I am no abolitionist, but if you will go with me I will take care of you." I thanked him, and turned with him toward his fine residence. On the way I asked him his name. "Moses Norris," he said. "What! Hon. Moses Norris?" I asked. "Yes," he answered. I did not, for a moment, know what to do, for I had read that this

I have never felt myself isolated since I entered the field to plead the cause of the slave, and demand equal rights for all.

same man had literally dragged the Reverend George Storrs from the pulpit, for preaching abolitionism. I, however, walked along with him, and was invited into his house, when I heard the children running and screaming, "Mother, mother, there is a nigger in the house! There's a nigger in the house!" I spoke again in the evening, and at the close of the meeting there was quite a contest between Mrs. Norris and Mrs. Hilles as to which one I should see home. I considered Mrs. Hilles' kindness to me, though her manner had been formal. I knew the cause, and I thought, especially as my carpet-bag was there, I would go with her. So giving Mr. and Mrs. Norris many thanks, I bade them good-bye, and went home with Mr. and Mrs. Hilles, where I found the atmosphere wondrously and most agreeably changed. Next day, Mr. Hilles took me, in the same carriage in which I did not ride on Sunday, to my next appointment, and on the way told me he felt more honored by having me in it than he would be if he had the President of the United States.

When on my way, in 1852, to attend at Pittsburg the great Free Soil Convention which nominated John P. Hale for President and George W. Julian for Vice-President, the train stopped for dinner at Alliance, Ohio, and I attempted to enter the hotel with the other delegates, but was rudely repulsed, when many of them, learning of it, rose from the table, denounced the outrage and refused to finish their dinners.

In anticipation of our return, at the close of the convention, Mr. Sam. Beck, the proprietor of the hotel, prepared dinner for three hundred guests, but when the train arrived not one of the large company went into his place, and his dinner was left to spoil.

It may possibly be inferred from what I have said of the prevalence of prejudice, and the practice of proscription, that I have had a very miserable sort of life, or that I must be remarkably insensible to public aversion. Neither inference is true. I have neither been miserable because of the ill-feeling of those about me, nor indifferent to popular approval; and I think, upon the whole, I have passed a tolerably cheerful and even joyful life. I have never felt myself isolated

This "negro" Southern Hotel was reportedly part of the American Negro exhibit at the Paris Exposition, 1900.

since I entered the field to plead the cause of the slave, and demand equal rights for all. In every town and city where it has been my lot to speak, there have been raised up for me friends of both colors to cheer and strengthen me in my work. I have always felt, too, that I had on my side all the invisible forces of the moral government of the universe. Happily for me I have had the wit to distinguish between what is merely artificial and transient and what is fundamental and permanent; and resting on the latter, I could cheerfully encounter the former. During a quarter of a century I resided in the city of Rochester, N. Y. When I removed from there, my friends caused a marble bust to be made from me, and have since honored it with a place in Sibley Hall, of Rochester University.

CHAPTER XVIII

"HONOR TO WHOM HONOR"

GRATEFUL RECOGNITION—LUCRETIA MOTT—LYDIA MARIA CHILD—ABBY KELLEY—H. BEECHER STOWE—OTHER FRIENDS—WOMAN SUFFRAGE.

ratitude to benefactors is a well recognized virtue, and to express it in some form or other, however imperfectly, is a duty to ourselves as well as to those who have helped us. Never reluctant or tardy, I trust, in the discharge of this duty, I have seldom been satisfied with the manner of its performance. When I have made my best effort in this line, my words have done small justice to my feelings. And now, in mentioning my obligations to my special friends, and acknowledging the help I received from them in the days of my need, I can hope to do no better than give a faint hint of my sense of the value of their friendship and assistance. It was my good fortune to get out of slavery at the right time, and to be speedily brought into contact with that circle of highly cultivated men and women, banded together for the overthrow of slavery, of which Wm. Lloyd Garrison was the acknowledged leader. To these friends, earnest, courageous, inflexible, ready to own me as a man and brother, against all the scorn, contempt, and derision of a slavery-polluted atmosphere, I owe my success in life. The story is simple, and the truth plain. They thought that I possessed qualities that might be made useful to my race, and through them I was brought to the notice of the world, and

gained a hold upon the attention of the American people, which I hope remains unbroken to this day.

Nor were my influential friends all of the Caucasian race. While many of my own people thought me unwise and somewhat fanatical in announcing myself a fugitive slave, and in practically asserting the rights of my people, on all occasions, in season and out of season, there were brave and intelligent men of color all over the United States who gave me their cordial sympathy and support. Among these, and foremost, I place the name of Doctor James McCune Smith; educated in Scotland, and breathing the free air of that country, he came back to his native land with ideas of liberty which placed him in advance of most of his fellow citizens of African descent.

It is also due to myself, to make some more emphatic mention than I have yet done, of the honorable women, who have not only assisted me, but who according to their opportunity and ability, have generously contributed to the abolition of slavery, and the recognition of the equal manhood of the colored race. When the true history of the anti-slavery cause shall be written, women will occupy a large space in its pages; for the cause of the slave has been peculiarly woman's cause. I shall never forget the first time I ever saw and heard Lucretia

Lucretia Mott (1793–1880).

Left: "When lovely women stoops to lobby—a capital picture" promoting an idea that pretty women had an easier time lobbying.
Right: A cartoon of "an emancipated women's club" where a messenger tells a mother her husband wishes to inform her their baby
has cut their first tooth—one in a long line of messages trying to undercut women's suffrage.

Mott. It was in the town of Lynn, Massachusetts. Kindred in spirit with Mrs. Mott was Lydia Maria Child. For solid, persistent, indefatigable work for the slave Abby Kelley was without a rival. And what can be said of the gifted authoress of "Uncle Tom's Cabin," Harriet Beecher Stowe? Happy woman must she be that to her was given the power in such unstinted measure to touch and move the popular heart! More than to reason or religion are we indebted to the influence which this wonderful delineation of American chattel slavery produced on the public mind.

Observing woman's agency, devotion, and efficiency in pleading the cause of the slave, gratitude for this high service early moved me to give favorable attention to the subject of what is called "woman's rights" and caused me to be denominated a woman's-rights man. I am glad to say that I have never been ashamed to be thus designated. Recognizing not sex nor physical strength, but moral intelligence and the ability to discern right from wrong, good from evil, and the power to choose between them, as the true basis of republican government, to which all are alike subject and all bound alike to obey, I was not long in reaching the conclusion that there was no foundation in reason or justice for woman's exclusion from the right of choice in the selection of the persons who should frame the laws, and thus shape the destiny of all the people, irrespective of sex.

Elizabeth Cady Stanton
(1815–1902).

In a conversation with Mrs. Elizabeth Cady Stanton when she was yet a young lady and an earnest abolitionist, she was at the pains of setting before me in a very strong light the wrong and injustice of this exclusion. I could not meet her arguments except with the shallow plea of "custom," "natural division of duties," "indelicacy of woman's taking part in politics," the common talk of "woman's sphere," and the like, all of which that able woman, who was then no less logical than now, brushed away by those arguments which she has so often and effectively used since, and which no man has yet successfully refuted. If intelligence is the only true and rational basis of government, it follows that that is the best government which draws its life and power from the largest sources of wisdom, energy, and goodness at its command. The force of this reasoning would be easily comprehended and readily assented to in any case involving the employment of physical strength.

I would give woman a vote, give her a motive to qualify herself to vote, precisely as I insisted upon giving the colored man the right to vote; in order that she shall have the same motives for making herself a useful citizen as those in force in the case of other citizens. In a word, I have never yet been able to find one consideration, one argument, or suggestion in favor of man's right to participate in civil government which did not equally apply to the right of woman.

CHAPTER XIX

RETROSPECTION

On the day of the interment of the late James A. Garfield, at Lake View cemetery, Cleveland, Ohio, a day of gloom long to be remembered as the closing scene in one of the most tragic and startling dramas ever witnessed in this or in any other country, the colored people of the District of Columbia assembled in the Fifteenth street Presbyterian church, and expressed by appropriate addresses and resolutions their respect for the character and memory of the illustrious deceased. On that occasion I was called on to preside, and by way of introducing the subsequent proceedings (leaving to others the grateful office of delivering eulogies), made the following brief reference to the solemn and touching event:

"Friends and fellow citizens:

To-day our common mother Earth has closed over the mortal remains of James A. Garfield, at Cleveland, Ohio. The light of no day in our national history has brought to the American people a more intense bereavement, a deeper sorrow, or a more profound sense of humiliation. It seems only as yesterday, that in my quality as United States Marshal of the District of Columbia, it was made my duty and privilege to walk at the head of the column in advance of this our President-elect, from the crowded Senate Chamber of the national capitol, through the long corridors and the grand rotunda, beneath the majestic dome, to the platform on the portico, where, amid a sea of transcendent pomp and glory, he who is now dead was hailed with tumultuous applause from uncounted thousands of his fellow citizens, and was inaugurated Chief Magistrate of the United States. The scene was one never to be forgotten by those who beheld it. It was a great day for the nation, glad and proud to do honor to their chosen ruler. It was a glad day for James A. Garfield. It was a glad day for me, that I—one of the proscribed race—was permitted to bear so prominent a part in its august ceremonies. Mr. Garfield was then in the midst of his years, in the fulness and vigor of his manhood, covered with honors beyond the reach of princes, entering upon a career more abundant in promise than ever before invited president or potentate. . . .

Fellow citizens, we are here to take suitable notice of the sad and appalling event of the hour. We are here, not merely as American citizens, but as colored American citizens. Although our hearts have gone along with those of the nation at large, in every expression, in every token and demonstration of honor to the dead, of sympathy with the living, and abhorrence for the horrible deed which has at last done its final work; though we have watched with beating

Frederick Douglass, circa 1875.

The Garfield Memorial at Lake View Cemetery, Cleveland, Ohio.

hearts the long and heroic struggle for life, and endured all the agony of suspense and fear; we have felt that something more, something more specific and distinctive, was due from us."

Conclusion: As far as this volume can reach that point I have now brought my readers to the end of my story. What may remain of life to me, through what experiences I may pass, what heights I may attain, into what depths I may fall, what good or ill may come to me, or proceed from me in this breathing world where all is change and uncertainty and largely at the mercy of powers over which the individual man has no absolute control; all this, if thought worthy and useful, will probably be told by others when I have passed

from the busy stage of life. I am not looking for any great changes in my fortunes or achievements in the future. The most of the space of life is behind me and the sun of my day is nearing the horizon. Notwithstanding all that is contained in this book my day has been a pleasant one. My joys have far exceeded my sorrows and my friends have brought me far more than my enemies have taken from me. I have written out my experience here, not in order to exhibit my wounds and bruises and to awaken and attract sympathy to myself personally, but as a part of the history of a profoundly interesting period in American life and progress.

I have aimed to assure that knowledge can be obtained under difficulties; that poverty may give place to competency; that obscurity

Forty years of my life have been given to the cause of my people, and if I had forty years more they should all be sacredly given to the same great cause.

President James A. Garfield (1831–1881).

is not an absolute bar to distinction, and that a way is open to welfare and happiness to all who will resolutely and wisely pursue that way; that neither slavery, stripes, imprisonment nor proscription need extinguish self-respect, crush manly ambition, or paralyze effort; that no power outside of himself can prevent a man from sustaining an honorable character and a useful relation to his day and generation; that neither institutions nor friends can make a race to stand unless it has strength in its own legs; that there is no power in the world which can be relied upon to help the weak against the strong or the simple against the wise; that races, like individuals, must stand or fall by their own merits; that all the prayers of Christendom cannot stop the force of a single bullet, divest arsenic of poison, or suspend any law of nature. Schooled as I have been among the abolitionists of New England, I recognize that the universe is governed by laws which are unchangeable and eternal, that what men sow they will reap, and that there is no way to dodge or circumvent the consequences of any act or deed. My views at this point receive but limited endorsement among my people. They, for the most part, think they have means of procuring special favor and help from the Almighty; and, as their "faith is the substance of things hoped for and the evidence of things not seen," they find much in this expression which is true to faith, but utterly false to fact. But I meant here only to say a word in conclusion. Forty years of my life have been given to the cause of my people, and if I had forty years more they should all be sacredly given to the same great cause. If I have done something for that cause, I am, after all, more a debtor to it than it is debtor to me.

APPENDIX

ORATION BY FREDERICK DOUGLASS, DELIVERED ON THE OCCASION OF THE UNVEILING OF THE FREEDMEN'S MONUMENT, IN MEMORY OF ABRAHAM LINCOLN, IN THE LINCOLN PARK, WASHINGTON, D. C., APRIL 14, 1876.

Friends and Fellow Citizens:

I warmly congratulate you upon the highly interesting object which has caused you to assemble in such numbers and spirit as you have to-day. This occasion is, in some respects, remarkable. Wise and thoughtful men of our race who shall come after us and study the lesson of our history in the United States, who shall survey the long and dreary spaces over which we have traveled and who shall count the links in the great chain of events by which we have reached our present position, will make a note of this occasion. They will think of it and speak of it with a sense of manly pride and complacency. . . .

For the first time in the history of our people, and in the history of the whole American people, we join in this high worship, and march conspicuously in the line of this time-honored custom. First things are always interesting, and this is one of our first things. It is the first time that, in this form and manner, we have sought to do honor to an American great man, however deserving and illustrious. I commend the fact to notice. Let it be told in every part of the Republic. Let men of all parties and opinions hear it. Let those who despise us, not less than those who respect us, know it and that now and here, in the spirit of liberty, loyalty and gratitude, we unite in this act of reverent homage. Let it be known every where, and by everybody who takes an interest in human progress and in the amelioration of the condition of mankind, that, in the presence and with the approval of the members of the American House of Representatives, reflecting the general sentiment of the country: that in the presence of that august body, the American Senate, representing the highest intelligence and the calmest judgment in the country; in the presence of the Supreme Court and Chief-Justice of the United States, to whose decisions we all patriotically bow; in the presence and under the steady eye of the honored and trusted President of the United States, with the members of his wise and patriotic Cabinet, we, the colored people, newly emancipated and rejoicing in our blood-bought freedom, near the close of the first century in the life of this Republic, have now and here unveiled, set apart, and dedicated a monument of enduring granite and bronze, in every line, feature, and figure of which the men of this generation may read, and those of after-coming generations may read, something of the exalted character and great works of Abraham Lincoln, the first martyr President of the United States. . . .

President Abraham Lincoln (1809–1865).

The Emancipation Memorial monument was erected in 1876. Though it was said to have been paid for exclusively by donations from people formerly subjected to slavery, its depiction of an African American shackled at the feet of the president is seen as highly controversial.

Fellow citizens, ours is no new-born zeal and devotion—merely a thing of this moment. The name of Abraham Lincoln was near and dear to our hearts in the darkest and most perilous hours of the Republic. We were no more ashamed of him when shrouded in clouds of darkness, of doubt, and defeat than when we saw him crowned with victory, honor, and glory. Our faith in him was often taxed and strained to the uttermost, but it never failed. . . . We saw him, measured him, and estimated him; not by stray utterances to injudicious and tedious delegations, who often tried his patience; not by isolated facts torn from their connection; not by any partial and imperfect glimpses, caught at inopportune moments; but by a broad survey, in the light of the stern logic of great events, and in view of that "divinity which shapes our ends, rough hew them how we will." We came to the conclusion that the hour and the man of our redemption had somehow met in the person of Abraham Lincoln. It mattered little to us what language he might employ on special occasions; it mattered little to us, when we fully knew him, whether he was swift or slow in his movements; it was enough for us that Abraham Lincoln was at the head of a great movement, and was in living and earnest sympathy with that movement, which, in the nature of things, must go on until slavery should be utterly and forever abolished in the United States.

Can any colored man, or any white man friendly to the freedom of all men, ever forget the night which followed the first day of January, 1863, when the world was to see if Abraham Lincoln would prove to be as good as his word? I shall never forget that memorable night, when at a public meeting, in a distant city, with three thousand others not less anxious than myself, I waited and watched for the word of deliverance which we have heard read today. Nor shall I ever forget the outburst of joy and thanksgiving that rent the air when the lightning brought to us the emancipation proclamation. In that happy hour we forgot all delay and forgot all tardiness; forgot that the President, by a promise to withhold the bolt which would smite the slave system with destruction, had bribed the rebels to lay down their arms; and we were thenceforward willing to allow the President all the latitude of time, phraseology and every honorable device that statesmanship might require for the achievement of a great and beneficent measure of liberty and progress. . . .

But now behold the change: the judgment of the present hour is, that, taking him for all in all; measuring the tremendous magnitude of the work before him; considering the necessary means to ends, and surveying the end from the beginning, infinite wisdom has seldom sent any man into the world better fitted for his mission than was Abraham Lincoln. . . .

Upon his inauguration as President of the United States, an office fitted to tax and strain the largest abilities, even when it is assumed under the most favorable conditions, Abraham Lincoln was met by a tremendous crisis. He was called upon not merely to administer the government, but to decide in the face of terrible odds the fate of the republic.

A formidable rebellion rose in his path before him. The Union was practically dissolved. His country was torn and rent asunder at the center. Hostile armies, armed with the munitions of war which the republic had provided for its own defense, were already organized against the republic.

Happily for the country, happily for you and for me, the judgment of James Buchanan, the patrician, was not the judgment of Abraham Lincoln, the plebeian. He brought his strong common sense, sharpened in the school of adversity, to bear upon the question. He did not hesitate, he did not doubt, he did not falter; but at once resolved that, at whatever peril, at whatever cost, the union of the States should be preserved. A patriot himself, his faith was strong and unwavering in the patriotism of his countrymen. . . . The trust which Abraham Lincoln had in himself and in the people was surprising and grand, but it was also enlightened and well founded. He knew the American people better than they knew themselves and his truth was based upon this knowledge.

A patriot himself, his faith was strong and unwavering in the patriotism of his countrymen.

Fellow-citizens, the fourteenth day of April, 1866, of which this is the eleventh anniversary, is now and will ever remain a memorable day in the annals of this republic. It was on the evening of this day, while a fierce and sanguinary rebellion was in the last stages of its desolating power, while its armies were broken and scattered before the invincible armies of Grant and Sherman, while a great nation, torn and rent by war, was already beginning to raise to the skies loud anthems of joy at the dawn of peace, that it was startled, amazed, and overwhelmed by the crowning crime of slavery—the assassination of Abraham Lincoln. . . . Dying as he did die, by the red hand of violence, killed, assassinated, taken off without warning, not because of personal hate—for no man who knew Abraham Lincoln could hate him—but because of his fidelity to union and liberty, he is doubly dear to us, and his memory will be precious forever.

Fellow-citizens, I end as I began, with congratulations. We have done a good work for our race to-day. In doing honor to the memory of our friend and liberator we have been doing highest honors to ourselves and to those who come after us. We have been attaching to ourselves a name and fame imperishable and immortal; we have also been defending ourselves from a blighting scandal. When now it shall be said that the colored man is soulless, that he has no appreciation of benefits or benefactors; when the foul reproach of ingratitude is hurled at us, and it is attempted to scourge us beyond the range of human brotherhood, we may calmly point to the monument we have this day erected to the memory of Abraham Lincoln.

EX-SENATOR BRUCE

HON. FREDERICK

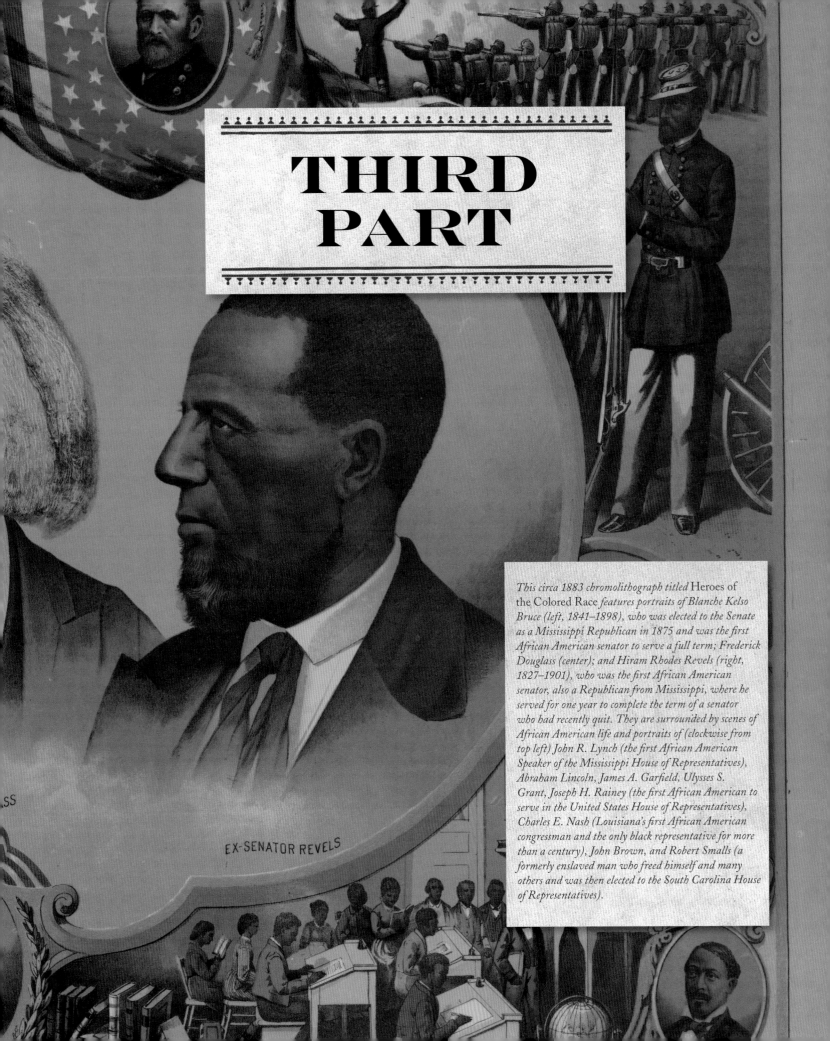

THIRD PART

EX-SENATOR REVELS

This circa 1883 chromolithograph titled Heroes of the Colored Race *features portraits of Blanche Kelso Bruce (left, 1841–1898), who was elected to the Senate as a Mississippi Republican in 1875 and was the first African American senator to serve a full term; Frederick Douglass (center); and Hiram Rhodes Revels (right, 1827–1901), who was the first African American senator, also a Republican from Mississippi, where he served for one year to complete the term of a senator who had recently quit. They are surrounded by scenes of African American life and portraits of (clockwise from top left) John R. Lynch (the first African American Speaker of the Mississippi House of Representatives), Abraham Lincoln, James A. Garfield, Ulysses S. Grant, Joseph H. Rainey (the first African American to serve in the United States House of Representatives), Charles E. Nash (Louisiana's first African American congressman and the only black representative for more than a century), John Brown, and Robert Smalls (a formerly enslaved man who freed himself and many others and was then elected to the South Carolina House of Representatives).*

CHAPTER I

LATER LIFE

AGAIN SUMMONED TO THE DEFENCE OF HIS PEOPLE—THE DIFFICULTIES OF THE TASK—THE RACE PROBLEM—HIS LIFE WORK—THE ANTI-SLAVERY MOVEMENT.

Ten years ago when the preceding chapters of this book were written, having then reached in the journey of life the middle of the decade beginning at sixty and ending at seventy, and naturally reminded that I was no longer young, I laid aside my pen with some such sense of relief as might be felt by a weary and over-burdened traveler when arrived at the desired end of a long journey, or as an honest debtor wishing to be square with all the world might feel when the last dollar of an old debt was paid off. I have, too, been embarrassed by the thought of writing so much about myself when there was so much else of which to write. It is far easier to write about others than about one's self. I write freely of myself, not from choice, but because I have, by my cause, been morally forced into thus writing. Time and events have summoned me to stand forth both as a witness and an advocate for a people long dumb, not allowed to speak for themselves, yet much misunderstood and deeply wronged.

Fifty years have passed since I entered upon that work, and now that it is ended, I find myself summoned again by the popular voice and by what is called the negro problem, to come a second time upon the witness stand and give evidence upon disputed points concerning myself and my emancipated brothers and sisters who, though free, are yet oppressed and are in as much need of an advocate as before they were set free. There is no disguising the fact that the American people are much interested and mystified about the mere matter of color as connected with manhood. It seems to them that color has some moral or immoral qualities and especially the latter. They do not feel quite reconciled to the idea that a man of different color from themselves should have all the human rights claimed by themselves. How is the race problem to be solved in this country? Will the negro go back to Africa or remain here? Under this shower of purely American questions, more or less personal, I have endeavored to possess my soul in patience and get as much good out of life as was possible with so much to occupy my time; and, though often perplexed, seldom losing my temper, or abating heart or hope for the future of my people.

Many things touched me and employed my thoughts and activities between the years 1881 and 1891. I am willing to speak of them. Like most men who give the world their autobiographies I wish my story to be told as favorably

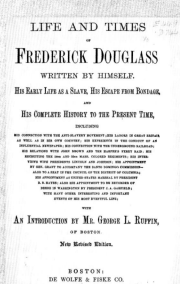

The title page from Douglass's final autobiography.

Though freed, many African Americans lived in terribly impoverished conditions and were segregated from more prosperous white communities. Shown here is the "negro quarter" in Savannah, Georgia, circa 1886.

towards myself as it can be with a due regard to truth. I do not wish it to be imagined by any that I am insensible to the singularity of my career, or to the peculiar relation I sustain to the history of my time and country. I know and feel that it is something to have lived at all in this Republic during the latter part of this eventful century, but I know it is more to have had some small share in the great events which have distinguished it from the experience of all other centuries. The anti-slavery movement, that truly great moral conflict which rocked the land during thirty years, and the part taken by the men and women engaged in it, are not quite far enough removed from us in point of time to admit at present of an impartial history. Some of the sects and parties that took part in it still linger with us and are zealous for distinction, for priority and superiority. There is also the disposition to unduly magnify the importance of some men and to diminish the importance of others. As one of those whose bonds have been broken, I cannot see without pain any attempt to disparage and undervalue any man's work in this cause.

CHAPTER II

A GRAND OCCASION

INAUGURATION OF PRESIDENT GARFIELD—A VALUABLE PRECEDENT—AN AFFECTING SCENE—THE GREED OF THE OFFICE-SEEKERS—CONFERENCE WITH PRESIDENT GARFIELD—DISTRUST OF THE VICE-PRESIDENT.

In the first part of this remarkable decade of American life and history, we had the election and grand inauguration of James A. Garfield as President of the United States, and in a few months thereafter we had his tragic death by the hand of a desperate assassin. On the 4th of March in that year, I happened to be United States Marshal of the District of Columbia, having been appointed to that office four years previous to that date by President Rutherford B. Hayes. This official position placed me in touch with both the outgoing President and the President elect. By the unwritten law of long-established usage, the United States Marshal of the District of Columbia is accorded a conspicuous position on the occasion of the inauguration of a new President of the United States. He has the honor of escorting both the outgoing and the incoming President, from the imposing ceremonies in the U. S. Senate Chamber to the east front of the Capitol, where, on a capacious platform erected for the purpose, before uncounted thousands and in the presence of grave Senators, Members of Congress and representatives of all the civilized nations of the world, the presidential oath is solemnly administered to the President elect, who proceeds to deliver his inaugural address, a copy of which has already been given to the press. In the procession from the Senate I had the honor, in the presence of all the many thousands of the dignitaries there assembled, of holding the right and marching close by the side of both Presidents. The grandeur and solemnity of the occasion appeared to me no less great and uncommon because of the honorable and responsible position I that day held. I was a part of a great national event and one which would pass into American history, but at the moment I had no intimation or foreshadowing of how dark, dreadful and bloody would be the contents of the chapter. But I knew that my elevation was temporary; that it was brilliant but not lasting; and that like many others tossed by the late war to the surface, I should soon be reduced to the ranks of my common people. However, I deemed the event highly important as a new circumstance in my career, as a new recognition of my class, and as a new step in the progress of the nation.

The inauguration of President Garfield was exceptional in its surroundings. The coronation of a king could hardly have been characterized by more display of joy and satisfaction. The delight and enthusiasm of the President's friends knew no bounds. The pageant was to the last degree brilliant and memorable, and the scene became sublime when, after his grand inaugural address, the soldier, the orator, the statesman, the President elect of this great nation, stepped aside, bowed his splendid form, and, in sight of all the people, kissed his mother. It was a reminder to the dear mother that, though her son

Above: President Garfield's assassin, Charles J. Guiteau (1841–1882), who was hanged for his crime. Opposite: The scene of the assassination of President Garfield.

An illustration from an original edition of Life and Times of Frederick Douglass.

cleave the air, and cannon pour out their thunders. Only the common people, animated by patriotism, and without hope of reward, know on such occasions the thrill of a pure enthusiasm. To the office-seeker the whole is gone through with as a mere hollow, dumb show. The madness of Guiteau was but the exaggerated madness of other men.

Only a few weeks before his tragic death, he invited me to the executive mansion to talk over matters pertaining to the cause of my people, and here came up the subject of his foreign appointments.

Few men in the country felt more than I the shock caused by the assassination of President Garfield, and few men had better reason for thus feeling. I not only shared with the nation its great common sorrow because a good man had been cruelly and madly slain in the midst of his years and in the morning of his highest honors and usefulness, but because of the loss which I thought his death had entailed upon the colored people of the country. Only a few weeks before his tragic death, he invited me to the executive mansion to talk over matters pertaining to the cause of my people, and here came up the subject of his foreign appointments. In this conversation he referred to the fact that his Republican predecessors in office had never sent colored men to any of the white nations. He said that he meant to depart from this usage; that he had made up his mind to send some colored men abroad to some of the white nationalities, and he wanted to know of me if such persons would be acceptable to some such nations. The hopes awakened by the kind-hearted President had no support in my knowledge of the character of the self-indulgent man who was elected, in the contingency of death, to succeed him. The announcement, at the Chicago Convention, of this man's name as that of the candidate for the Vice-Presidency, strangely enough brought over me a shudder such as one might feel in coming upon an armed murderer or a poisonous reptile. For some occult and mysterious cause, I know not what, I felt the hand of death upon me. I do not say or intimate that Mr. Arthur had anything to do with the taking off of the President. I might have had the same shudder had any other man been named, but I state the simple fact precisely as it was.

was President of the United States, he was still her son, and that none of the honors he that day received could make him forget for a moment the debt of love due to that mother whose hand had guided his infancy. On that day of glory, and amid demonstrations so sublime, no thought of the tragic death that awaited the illustrious object of this grand ovation could have intruded itself. It is not to be supposed that, even in the mind of the mad assassin Guiteau, the thought of murdering the President had yet dawned. I heard at his trial this demon-possessed man talk, and came to the conclusion that this deed was the result of madness for office, and that this madness carried the assassin beyond the limit to which the same madness sometimes carries other men.

No doubt there were many present at this inauguration who, like the assassin, thought that in the bestowment of patronage, the new President would not forget them. It is painful to think that to this selfish feeling we may rightfully ascribe much of the display and seeming enthusiasm on such occasions; that because of it, banners wave, men march, rockets

CHAPTER III

DOUBTS AS TO GARFIELD'S COURSE

GARFIELD NOT A STALWART—HOPE IN PROMISES OF A NEW DEPARTURE—THE SORROW STRICKEN NATION.

Whether President Garfield would have confirmed or disappointed my hopes had his life been spared by the assassin's bullet can, of course, never be known. Mr. Garfield, though a good man, was not my man for the Presidency. For that place I wanted a man of sterner stuff. I was for General Grant, and for him with all the embarrassment and burden of a "third term" attaching to his candidacy. I held that even defeat with Grant was better than success with a temporizer. I knew both men personally and valued the qualities of both. Under the disguise of meekly accepting the results and decisions of the war, the rebels had come back to Congress more with the pride of conquerors than with the repentant humility of defeated traitors. Their heads were high in the air. It was not they but the loyal men who were at fault. Under the fair-seeming name of local self-government, they were shooting to death just as many of the newly made citizens of the South as was necessary to put the individual States of the Union entirely into their power. The object which through violence and bloodshed they had accomplished in the several States, they were already aiming to accomplish in the United States by address and political strategy. They had captured the individual States and meant now to capture the United States. The moral difference between those who fought for the Union and liberty, and those who had fought for slavery and the dismemberment of the Union, was fast fading away. The language of a sickly conciliation, inherited from the administration of President Hayes, was abroad. Insolency born of slave mastery had begun to exhibit itself in the House and Senate of the nation. The recent amendments of the Constitution, adopted to secure the results of the war for the Union, were beginning to be despised and scouted, and the ship of state seemed fast returning to her ancient moorings. It was therefore no blind partiality that led me to prefer General Grant to General Garfield. In nature exuberant, readily responsive in sympathy, shrinking from conflict with his immediate surroundings, abounding in love of approbation, Mr. Garfield himself admitted that he had made promises that he could not fulfill. His amiable disposition to make himself agreeable to those with whom he came in contact made him weak and led him to create false hopes in those who approached him for favors. This was shown in a case to which I was a party. Prior to his inauguration he solemnly promised Senator Roscoe Conkling that he would appoint

This political cartoon shows President Garfield attempting to bond Senators Roscoe Conkling and James Blaine together in friendship through their mutual patronage of the president.

CORNEL WEST ON FREDERICK DOUGLASS

An excerpt from an interview in *Black Prophetic Fire:*
In Dialogue with and Edited by Christa Buschendorf

CORNEL WEST: Frederick Douglass is a very complicated, complex man. I think that Douglass is, on the one hand, the towering Black freedom fighter of the nineteenth century; on the other hand, he is very much a child of his age, which is not to say that he does not have things to teach those of us in the twenty-first century, but he both transcends context and yet he is very much a part of his context at the same time. I think that's part of the complexity in our initial perception of his influence on America, on Black America, on Du Bois and subsequent freedom fighters.

CHRISTA BUSCHENDORF: What are the factors we should consider, when you call him a child of his age, and would you say that these factors contribute to reducing his status in a sense?

CW: I think that his freedom fighting is very much tied to the ugly and vicious institution of white supremacist slavery. Those of us in the post-slavery era experienced Jim Crow and other forms of barbarism, but that's still different from white supremacist slavery, and we learn from Douglass's courage, his vision, his willingness to stand up, the unbelievable genius of his oratory and his language. And yet there is a sense in which with the ending of slavery, there was a certain ending of his high moment. He undoubtedly remained for thirty years a very important and towering figure, but for someone like myself, he peaks. It's almost like Stevie Wonder, who peaks, you know, with *Songs in the Key of Life, The Secret Life of Plants*, despite his later great moments. There are moments when people peak, and that peak is just sublime; it's an unbelievable peak. I don't think any freedom fighter in America peaks in the way Douglass peaks. And that's true even for Martin Luther King in a certain sense. And yet Douglass lives on another thirty years; that's a long time. Martin peaked and was shot and killed. Malcolm peaked and was shot and killed. But what if Martin had died in 1998 saying, "Well, what am I? Well, I'm a professor at Union Theological Seminary teaching Christian ethics." There are different stages and phases of their lives. So it's not a matter to reduce Douglass, but to contextualize him, to historicize him. And any time you historicize and contextualize, you pluralize; you see a variety of different moments, a variety of different voices. His voice in the 1880s is very different than his voice on July 4, 1852, July 5, 1852.

CHB: Yes, when he gave his famous speech "What to the Slave Is the Fourth of July?" But while you love the militant Douglass—as did Angela Davis, for example, when she referred to him in the late 1960s—others seem to appreciate him for his later development, for his integrationist policies. And often Douglass the "race man" is juxtaposed to Douglass the "Republican party man." Did he become too pragmatic a politician? Was he in his later years out of touch with the ongoing suffering of African Americans? Had he adopted a bourgeois mentality? Did his second marriage to Helen Pitts play a role in his development, as some critics claim?

CW: I think that the old distinction between the freedom fighter against slavery early on and then the Republican Party man later on might be a bit crude, but it makes some sense, because Douglass in his second stage, the later stages of his life, certainly is significant and never entirely loses sight of trying to fight for the rights of Black people and, by extension, the rights of women and rights of others. But the relevance for us is that he is less international, he is less global in those later years. You see, when he spends time with the Chartist Movement in Britain in the late 1840s—when he is pushed out of the country twice, after publication of the first autobiography, and then following John Brown's raid on Harper's Ferry—he makes his connections in Europe, makes the connection between the planetizing, globalizing of the struggle for freedom; whereas in the later phase of his life, Douglass became such a nationalist and a patriot and so US centered. He is so tied in to the machinations of the Republican Party and willing to make vulgar compromises, and he is relatively silent against Jim Crow, and his refusal to speak out boldly, openly, publicly, courageously against barbarism in the South is troubling.

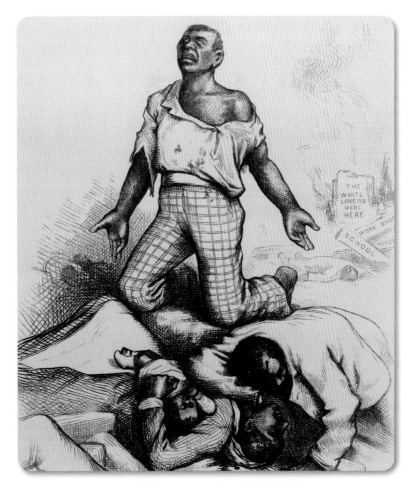

The caption for this 1876 illustration of a man kneeling before the murdered bodies of fellow African Americans reads, "Is this a republican form of government? Is this protecting life, liberty, or property? Is this the equal protection of the laws?" A piece of rubble in the background reads, "The White Liners Were Here." The White Liners were a terrorist group in the South, like the Ku Klux Klan, and men with these beliefs were responsible for the Hamburg Riots in South Carolina that year in which six black men were murdered.

CHB: But what about his speech against lynching?

CW: Yes, but it was a somewhat isolated thing. For example, at the great Freedman's Memorial ceremony in 1876, when they unveiled Lincoln's grand statue, Douglass hardly makes any reference to what was happening in the South at that time. He says Lincoln is the white man's president, you are his children, Black people are his step-children, seemingly beginning with a critique. But the twenty thousand Black folk who were there waited for him to say something about the present: nothing, nothing. And then, you see, to allow himself to be used and manipulated by Rutherford B. Hayes, so that at the final withdrawal of American troops he is right away appointed to the honorable position of US Marshal of the District of Columbia, as if that were a kind of symbolic exchange, you see.

You say: "Oh Frederick, Frederick, oh my God! How could you allow that to take place, given who you are, given the tremendous respect that is so well earned that people have for you, especially Black people but all freedom-loving people, and the degree to which once you get caught in the machinations of any political party in the United States as a freedom fighter you are going to be asked to make tremendous concessions, compromises." The shift from prudence to opportunism looms large. And I think you can see this also in terms of his role in the American imperial apparatus: as he became the minister to Haiti and so on. It's just hard to be that kind of bold, free-thinking, free-speaking, freedom fighter we witness in the early Douglass when you are caught within the political system.

James G. Blaine (1830–1890).

me United States Marshal for the District of Columbia. He not only promised, but did so with emphasis. He slapped the table with his hand when he made the promise. When I apologized to Mr. Conkling for the failure of Mr. Garfield to fulfill his promise, that gentleman silenced me by repeating with increasing emphasis, "But he told me he would appoint you United States marshal of the District of Columbia." To all I could say in defense of Mr. Garfield, Mr. Conkling repeated this promise with increasing solemnity till it seemed to reproach me not less than Mr. Garfield; he for failing to keep his word and I for defending him. It need not be said to those who knew the character and composition of Senator Conkling that it was impossible for him to tolerate or excuse a broken promise. No man more than he considered a man's word his bond. The difference between the two men is the difference between one guided by principle and one controlled by sentiment.

Although Mr. Garfield had given me this cause to doubt his word, I still had faith in his promised new departure. I believed in it all the more because Mr. Blaine, then Secretary of State and known to have great influence with the President, was with him in this new measure. Mr. Blaine went so far as to ask me to give him the names of several colored men who could fill such places with credit to the Government and to themselves. All this was ended by the accursed bullet of the assassin. I therefore not only shared the general sorrow of the woe-smitten nation, but lamented the loss of a great benefactor. Nothing could be more sad and pathetic than the death of this lovable man.

Opposite: Douglass used this small house on the back of his property in Washington, D.C., as a place to get away.

CHAPTER IV

RECORDER OF DEEDS

ACTIVITY IN BEHALF OF HIS PEOPLE—INCOME OF THE RECORDER OF DEEDS—FALSE IMPRESSIONS AS TO HIS WEALTH—APPEALS FOR ASSISTANCE—PERSISTENT BEGGARS.

Although I was not reappointed to the office of Marshal of the District of Columbia as I had reason to expect and to believe that I should be, not only because under me the office had been conducted blamelessly, but because President Garfield had solemnly promised Senator Conkling that I should be so appointed, I was given the office of Recorder of Deeds for the District of Columbia. This office was, in many respects, more congenial to my feelings than was that of United States Marshal of the District which made me the daily witness in the criminal court of a side of the District life to me most painful and repulsive. The duties of Recorder, though specific, exacting, and imperative, are easily performed. The office is one that imposes no social duties whatever, and therefore neither fettered my pen nor silenced my voice in the cause of my people. I wrote much and spoke often, and perhaps because of this activity gave to envious tongues a pretext against me. My cause first, midst, last, and always, whether in office or out of office, was and is that of the black man; not because he is black, but because he is a man, and a man subjected in this country to peculiar wrongs and hardships.

In my experience in public life I have learned that there are many ways by which confidence in public men may be undermined and destroyed, and against which they are comparatively helpless. One of the most successful methods is to start the rumor that a man has made a large fortune out of the Government and is rich. I have, for instance, seen myself described, in some of our Afro-American newspapers, as a man of large fortune, worth half a million of dollars, and the impression was given by the writer that I had made this large fortune out of the Government. The rumors of my wealth are not only not true, but in the nature of my work and history could not be true. A half a million indeed! The fact is, I never was worth one-fifth of that sum and never expect to be.

Numerous pressing and pathetic appeals for assistance, written under the delusion of my great wealth, have come to me from colored people from all parts of the country, with heart-rending tales of destitution and misery, such as I would gladly relieve did my circumstances admit of it. This confidence in my benevolent disposition has been flattering enough and gratefully appreciated by me, but I have found it difficult to make the applicants believe that I have no power to justify it. Though I could not exactly see how or why I should be called upon to pay the debt of emancipation for the whole four millions of liberated people, I have always tried to do my part as opportunity has offered. At the same time it has seemed to me incomprehensible that they did not see that the real debtors in this woeful account are themselves, and that the absurdity of their posing as creditors did not occur to them.

Above: This statue of Douglass was unveiled in Emancipation Hall in the United States Capitol Visitor Center on June 19, 2013. Opposite: The living room in Douglass's Washington, D.C., home.

CHAPTER V

PRESIDENT CLEVELAND'S ADMINISTRATION

CIRCUMSTANCES OF CLEVELAND'S ELECTION—ESTIMATE OF CLEVELAND'S CHARACTER—RESPECT FOR MR. CLEVELAND—DECLINE OF STRENGTH IN THE REPUBLICAN PARTY—TIME OF GLOOM FOR THE COLORED PEOPLE.

The last year of my service in the comfortable office of Recorder of Deeds for the District of Columbia, to which aspirants have never been few in number or wanting in zeal, was under the early part of the remarkable administration of President Grover Cleveland. It was thought by some of my friends, and especially by my Afro-American critics, that I ought instantly to have resigned this office upon the incoming of the new administration. I do not know how much the desirableness of the office influenced my opinion in an opposite direc-tion, for the human heart is very deceitful, but I took a different view in this respect from my colored critics. The office of Recorder, like that of the Register of Wills, is a purely local office, though held at the pleasure of the President, and it is in no sense a federal or political office. The Federal Government provides no salary for it. It is supported solely by fees paid for work actually done by its employees for the cit-izens of the District of Columbia. Then, too, President Cleveland did not appear to be in haste or to desire my

resignation half as much as some of my Afro-American brethren desired me to make room for them. Besides, he owed his election to a peculiar combination of cir-cumstances favorable to my remaining where I was. He had been supported by Republican votes as well as by Democratic votes. He had been the candidate of civil-service reformers, the fundamen-tal idea of whom is that there should be no removal from an office the duties of which have been fully and faithfully performed by the incumbent. Being elected by the votes of civil-service reformers, there was an implied political obli-gation imposed upon Mr. Cleveland to respect the idea represented by the votes of these reformers. During the first part of his administration, the time in which I held office under him, the disposition on the part of the President to ful-fil that obligation was quite manifest, and the feeling at the time was that we were entering upon a new era of American politics, in which there would be no removals from office on the ground of party politics. It seemed that for better or for worse we had reversed the practice of both

Douglass and his new wife, Helen Pitts, on their honeymoon in Niagara Falls.

Left: President Chester A. Arthur (1829–1886). Right: First Lady Frances Folsom Cleveland Preston (1864–1947).

parties in our political history, and that the old formula, "To the victor belong the spoils," was no longer to be the approved rule in politics.

For these reasons I rested securely in the Recorder's office until the President, whether intentionally or not, had excited the admiration of the civil-service reformers by whom he was elected, after which he vigorously endeavored to conform his policy to the opposing ideas of the Democratic party. Having received all possible applause from the reformers, and thus made it difficult for them to contradict their approval and return to the Republican party, he went to work in earnest at the removal from office of all those whom he regarded as offensive partisans, myself among the number. Seldom has a political device worked better.

In parting with President Grover Cleveland, it is due to state that, personally, I have no cause of complaint against him. On the contrary, there is much for which I have reason to commend him. I found him a robust, manly man, one having the courage to act upon his convictions, and to bear with equanimity the reproaches of those who differed from him. When President Cleveland came to Washington, I was under a considerable cloud not altogether free from angry lightning. I had married a wife. People who had remained silent over the unlawful relations of the white slave masters with their colored slave women loudly condemned me for marrying a wife a few shades lighter than myself. They would have had no objection to my

HARMONY AND ENVY.

This Puck *magazine illustration titled* Harmony and Envy *shows President Cleveland in a band of merry revelers that represent the North, the South, and the African American community. The band of dour monks that precedes them are politicians bested by Cleveland in elections.*

marrying a person much darker in complexion than myself, but to marry one much lighter, and of the complexion of my father rather than of that of my mother, was, in the popular eye, a shocking offense, and one for which I was to be ostracized by white and black alike. Mr. Cleveland found me covered with these unjust, inconsistent, and foolish reproaches, and instead of joining in with them or acting in accordance with them, or in anywise giving them countenance as a cowardly and political trickster might and probably would have done, he, in the face of all vulgar criticism, paid me all the social consideration due to the office of Recorder of Deeds of the District of Columbia. He never failed, while I held office under him, to invite myself and wife to his grand receptions, and we never failed to attend them. Surrounded by distinguished men and women from all parts of the country and by diplomatic representatives from all parts of the world, and under the gaze of the late slaveholders, there was nothing in the bearing of Mr. and Mrs. Cleveland toward Mrs. Douglass and myself less cordial and courteous than that extended to the other ladies and gentlemen present.

During the administration of Chester A. Arthur, as also during that of Rutherford B. Hayes, the spirit of slavery and rebellion increased in power and advanced towards ascendency. At the same time, the spirit which had abolished slavery and saved the Union steadily and proportionately declined, and with it the strength and unity of the Republican party also declined. The dawn of this deplorable action became visible when the Republican Speaker of the House of Representatives defeated the bill to protect colored citizens of the South from rapine and murder. Under President Hayes it took organic, chronic form, and rapidly grew in bulk and force. The whole four years of this administration were, to the loyal colored citizen, full of darkness and dismal terror. The death of Mr. Garfield placed in the Presidential chair Chester A. Arthur, who did nothing to correct the errors of President Hayes, or to arrest the decline and fall of the Republican party, but, on the contrary, by his self-indulgence, indifference and neglect of opportunity, allowed the country to drift (like an oarless boat in the rapids) towards the howling chasm of the slaveholding Democracy.

CHAPTER VI

THE SUPREME COURT DECISION

ACTION OF THE SUPREME COURT—ITS EFFECT ON THE COLORED PEOPLE.

In further illustration of the reactionary tendencies of public opinion against the black man and of the increasing decline, since the war for the Union, in the power of resistance to the onward march of the rebel States to their former control and ascendency in the councils of the nation, the decision of the United States Supreme Court, declaring the Civil Rights law of 1875 unconstitutional, is striking and convincing. The strength and activities of the malign elements of the country against equal rights and equality before the law seem to increase in proportion to the increasing distance between that time and the time of the war. From the hour that the loyal North began to fraternize with the disloyal and slaveholding South; from the hour that they began to "shake hands over the bloody chasm"; from that hour the cause of justice to the black man began to decline and lose its hold upon the public mind, and it has lost ground ever since.

The future historian will turn to the year 1883 to find the most flagrant example of this national deterioration. Here he will find the Supreme Court of the nation reversing the action of the Government, defeating the manifest purpose of the Constitution, nullifying the Fourteenth Amendment, and placing itself on the side of prejudice, proscription, and persecution.

Whatever this Supreme Court may have been in the past, or may by the Constitution have been intended to be, it has, since the days of the Dred Scott decision, been wholly under the influence of the slave power, and its decisions have been dictated by that power rather than by what seemed to be sound and established rules of legal interpretation.

Although we had, in other days, seen this court bend and twist the law to the will and interest of the slave power, it was supposed that by the late war and the great fact that slavery was abolished, and the further fact that the members of the bench were now appointed by a Republican administration, the spirit as well as the body had been exorcised. Hence the decision in question came to the black man as a painful and bewildering surprise. It was a blow from an unsuspected quarter. The surrender of the national capital to Jefferson Davis in time of the war could hardly have caused a greater shock. For the moment the colored citizen felt as if the earth was opened beneath him. He was wounded in the house of his friends. He felt

Lincoln Hall, a grand auditorium in Washington, D.C., was destroyed by a fire in 1886.

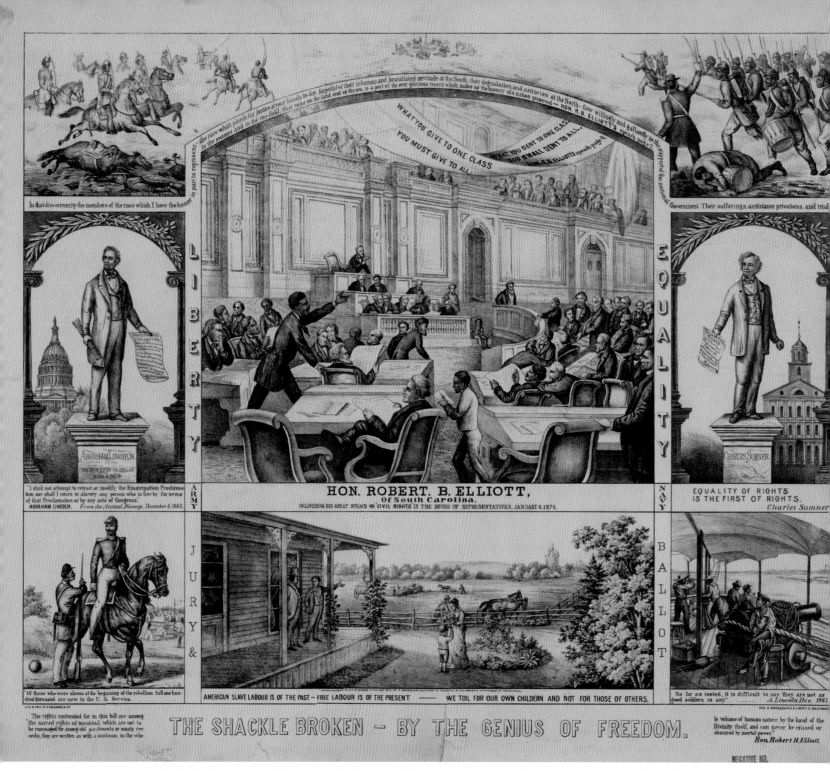

South Carolina representative Robert B. Elliott giving his famous speech (January 6, 1874) in favor of the Civil Rights Act.

that this decision drove him from the doors of the great temple of American Justice. The nation that he had served against its enemies had thus turned him over naked to those enemies. His trouble was without any immediate remedy. The decision must stand until the gates of death could prevail against it.

The colored men in the capital of the nation where the deed was done were quick to perceive its disastrous significance, and in the helpless horror of the moment they called upon myself and others to express their grief and indignation. In obedience to that call a meeting was assembled in Lincoln Hall, the largest hall in the city, which was packed by an audience of all colors, to hear what might be said to this new and startling event. Though we were powerless to arrest the wrong or modify the consequences of this extraordinary decision, we could, at least, cry out against its absurdity and injustice.

CHAPTER VII

DEFEAT OF JAMES G. BLAINE

CAUSES OF THE REPUBLICAN DEFEAT—TARIFF AND FREE TRADE—NO CONFIDENCE IN THE DEMOCRATIC PARTY.

The next event worthy of remark after the decision of the Supreme Court against the validity of the Civil Rights Law, and one which strikingly illustrated the reaction of public sentiment and the steady march of the slave power toward national supremacy since the agonies of the war, was the defeat in 1884 of Mr. James G. Blaine, the Republican candidate for the presidency, and the election of Mr. Grover Cleveland, the Democratic candidate for that office. This result, in view of the men and the parties represented, was a marked surprise. Mr. Blaine was supposed to be the most popular statesman in the country, while his opponent was little known outside of his own State. Besides, the attitude and behavior of the Democratic party during the war had been such as to induce belief that many years must elapse before it could again be trusted with the reins of the National Government. Events show that little dependence can be wisely placed upon the political stability of the masses. Popularity to-day is, with them, no guaranty of

popularity to-morrow. Offenses and services are alike easily and speedily forgotten by them. They change front at the command of the moment. Yet it is never difficult to account for a change after that change has taken place.

The defeat of the Republican party in 1884 was due rather to its own folly than to the wisdom of the Democratic party. It despised and rejected the hand that had raised it to power, and it paid the penalty of its own folly. The life of the Republican party lay in its devotion to justice, liberty and humanity. When it abandoned or slighted these great moral ideas and devoted itself to materialistic measures, it no longer appealed to the heart of the nation, but to its pocket. It became a Samson shorn of its locks.

This degeneracy in the Republican party began to manifest itself when the voices of Sumner, Wade, Morton, Conkling, Stevens, and Logan were no longer controlling in its councils; when Morton was laughed at for "waving the bloody shirt" and for exposing the bloody

A portrait of Charles Sumner (1866–1873) from Douglass's Washington, D.C., house.

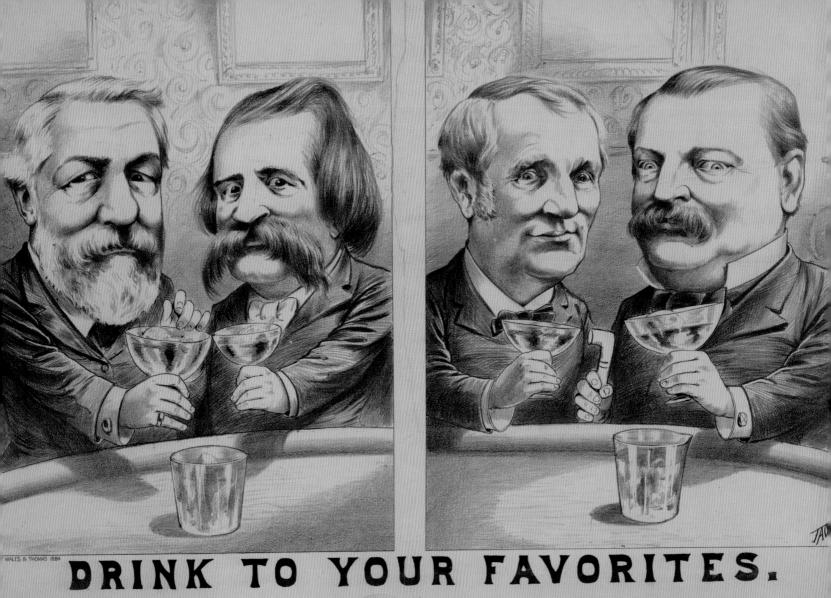

WALES & THOMAS 1884

DRINK TO YOUR FAVORITES.

"Drink to your favorites." A poster for the 1884 presidential election in which James G. Blaine and John A. Logan ran against Grover Cleveland and Thomas A. Hendricks.

crimes and outrages against the Republican voters of the South; when the talk of unloading the negro waxed louder and louder; when Southern men pretended to be aching for a favorable moment for deserting the Democratic party and joining the Republican party, and when it was thought that the white vote of the South could be secured if the black vote was abandoned. Then came along the old issues of tariff and free trade, and kindred questions of material interests, to the exclusion of the more vital principles for which the Republican party stood in the days of its purity and power. But the expected accessions to its ranks from the white voters of the South did not take place. If anything, the South became, with every concession made by the Republicans to win its white vote, more solidly Democratic. There never was yet, and there never will be, an instance of permanent success where a party abandons its righteous principles to win favor of the opposing party. Mankind abhors the idea of abandoning friends in order to win the support of enemies. Considering that the Republican

party had fallen away from the grand ideas of liberty, progress, and national unity in which it had originated, and no longer felt that it should protect the rights it had recognized in the Constitution, some of its foremost men lost their interest in its success, and others deserted outright, claiming that as there was now, on the Southern question, no difference between the two parties, there was therefore no choice.

Mankind abhors the idea of abandoning friends in order to win the support of enemies.

CHAPTER VIII

EUROPEAN TOUR

September, 1886, was quite a milestone in my experience and journey of life. I had long desired to make a brief tour through several countries in Europe and especially to revisit England, Ireland and Scotland, and to meet once more the friends I met with in those countries more than forty years before. I had twice visited England, but I had never been on the continent of Europe, and this time I was accompanied by my wife.

I shall attempt here no ample description of our travels abroad. For this more space would be required than the limits of this volume will permit. Besides, with such details the bookshelves are already crowded. To revisit places, scenes, and friends after forty years is not a very common occurrence in the lives of men; and while the desire to do so may be intense, the realization has to it a sad side as well as a cheerful one. The old people first met there have passed away, the middle-aged have grown old, and the young have only heard their fathers and mothers speak of you. The places are there, but the people are gone. I felt this when looking upon the members of the House of Commons. When I was

there forty-five years before, I saw many of England's great men; men whom I had much desired to see and hear and was much gratified by being able to see and hear. There were Sir Robert Peel, Daniel O'Connell, Richard Cobden, John Bright, Lord John Russell, Sir James Graham, Benjamin Disraeli, Lord Morpeth, and others, but except Mr. Gladstone, not one who was there then is there now. In the House of Lords, where, five and forty years before, I saw and heard Lord Brougham, all were gone, and he with the rest. He was the most remarkable speaker I ever heard.

While in England during this last visit I had the good fortune to see and hear Mr. William E. Gladstone, the great Liberal leader, and, since Sir Robert Peel, the acknowledged prince of parliamentary debaters. He was said by those who had often heard him to be on this occasion in one of his happiest speaking moods, and he made one of his best speeches. Expectation had been raised by the announcement in advance that Mr. Gladstone would that day move for the indefinite postponement of the Irish Force Bill, the measure of all others to which the Government was

This racist cartoon mocks Douglass's marriage to the Caucasian Helen Pitts. Young boys taunt that Douglass is taking sulphur bitters "for his complexion" as a dog growls at the couple.

There seemed neither in members nor spectators any desire to hear another voice after hearing Mr. Gladstone's, and I shared this feeling with the rest.

committed as a remedy for the ills of Ireland. His argument against the bill was based upon statistics which he handled with marvelous facility. He showed that the amount of crimes in Ireland for which the Force Bill was claimed as a remedy by the Government was not greater than the great class of crimes in England; and that therefore there was no reason for a Force Bill in one country more than in the other. After marshaling his facts and figures to this point, in a masterly and convincing manner, raising his voice and pointing his finger directly at Mr. Balfour, he exclaimed, in a tone almost menacing and tragic, "What are you fighting for?" The effect was thrilling. His peroration was a splendid appeal to English love of liberty. When he sat down the House was instantly thinned out. There seemed neither in members nor spectators any desire to hear another voice after hearing Mr. Gladstone's, and I shared this feeling with the rest. A few words were said in reply by Mr. Balfour, who, though an able debater, was no match for the aged Liberal leader.

I missed the presence of George Thompson, one of the most eloquent men who ever advocated the cause of the colored man, either in England or America. Joseph Sturge and most of his family had also passed away. But I will pursue this melancholy enumeration no further, except to say that, in meeting with the descendants of anti-slavery friends in England, Ireland and Scotland, it was good to have confirmed the scriptural saying, "Train up a child in the way he should go and when he is old he will not depart from it."

Left: The Palace of Westminster, 1850, where the House of Commons and Parliament meet.
Right: Douglass with his wife Helen (seated) and her sister, Eva.

CHAPTER IX

CONTINUATION OF EUROPEAN TOUR

Through France—The palace of the Popes—The Amphitheater at Arles—Visits Nice—Pisa and its leaning tower—The Pantheon—Modern Rome—Rome of the past—Vesuvius and Naples—Through the Suez Canal—Life in the East—The Nile—At the graves of Theodore Parker and Mrs. Browning.

Aside from the great cities of London and Paris, with their varied and brilliant attractions, the American tourist will find no part of a European tour more interesting than the country lying between Paris and Rome. Here was the cradle in which the civilization of Western Europe and our own country was rocked and developed. The whole journey between these two great cities is deeply interesting and thought-suggesting. It was the battle-ground and the scene of heroic endeavor, where every inch of the field was sternly disputed; where the helmet, shield, and spear of Eastern civilization met the sling and arrow and desperate courage of determined barbarism. Nor was the tide of battle always in one direction. Indications of the sternness and duration of the conflict are still visible all along the line. These are seen in walled and fortified towns, in grim and solemn convents, in old monasteries and castles, in massive walls and gates, in huge iron

bolts and heavily barred windows, and fortifications built after the wisdom of the wary eagle on lofty crags and clefts of rocks and mountain fastnesses, hard to assault and easy to defend.

As the traveler moves eastward and southward between those two great cities, he will observe an increase of black hair, black eyes, full lips, and dark complexions. He will observe a Southern and Eastern style of dress; gay colors, startling jewelry, and an outdoor free-and-easy movement of the people.

Leaving Paris and passing the famous grounds of Fontainebleau, one is reminded that they are no longer, as of yore, the proud abode of royalty. Like all else of imperial and monarchical possessions, the palace here has, under the Republic, passed from the hands of princes to the possession of the people. It is still kept in excellent condition. Its grounds conform in the strictest sense to French taste and skill, the main feature of which is perfect uniformity.

Helen Pitts (1838–1903) was a graduate of Mount Holyoke Female Seminary (today Mount Holyoke College), a suffragist, and teacher. Douglass hired her as a clerk in his office of the Recorder of Deeds in 1882 and they were married in 1884. Their families largely did not approve. In 1886, they left for their yearlong trip across Europe and into Egypt.

The royal French Château Fontainebleau, circa 1905.

Dijon, so closely associated with the names of Bossuet and St. Bernard, the center, also, of the finest vineyards and the finest wines in France, and the ancient seat of the great dukes of Burgundy, traces of whose wealth and power are still visible in what remains of the ducal palace and the ancient castle, whose walls when a prison inclosed the restless Mirabeau, takes a deep hold upon the interest of the traveler.

Avignon, more than seventy years the home of the popes and the scene of pontifical magnificence, powerfully impresses the mind. Five ecclesiastical dignitaries at the least, according to history, were here consecrated to the service of the church. The object of chief interest in Avignon, its palace of the popes, is certainly a very striking feature. Situated on an eminence proudly overlooking the city and its surroundings, the grounds large and beautiful, the popes who resided there no doubt found it a very pleasant abode.

One of the oldest and most fascinating old towns met with in a trip from Paris to Marseilles is that of Arles. Its streets are the narrowest, queerest and crookedest of any yet seen in our journey. It speaks of

Greek as well as of Roman civilization. The bits of marble picked up in the streets show that they have been under the skillful hands either of the Greek or Roman workmen. The old Amphitheater, a miniature Coliseum, where men fought with wild beasts amid the applauding shouts of ladies and gentlemen of the period, though used no longer for its old-time purposes, is in good condition and may yet stand for a thousand years.

An hour or two after leaving this quaint and sinuous old town, we were confronted at Marseilles by the blue and tideless waters of the Mediterranean, a sea charming in itself and made more charming by the poetry and eloquence it has inspired. Its deep blue waters sparkling under a summer sun and a half tropical sky, fanned by balmy breezes from Afric's golden sand, was in fine contrast with the snow-covered mountains and plains we had just left behind us. Only a few hours before reaching Marseilles we were in mid-winter; but now all at once we were greeted with the lemon and the orange, the olive and the oleander, all flourishing under the open sky. The transition was so sudden and so agreeable and

The Arles, France, amphitheater that charmed Douglass.

so completely in contrast, that it seemed more like magic than reality. Not only was the climate different, but the people and everything else seemed different. There was a visible blending of the orient with the occident. We, however, cared less for all this than for Château D'If, the old prison anchored in the sea and around which the genius of Alexander Dumas has woven such a network of enchantment that a desire to visit it is irresistible; hence, the first morning after our arrival Mrs. Douglass and myself hired one of the numerous boats in the harbor and employed an old man to row us out to the enchanted scene.

On our way along the far-famed Riviera to Genoa, once the city of sea-kings and merchant princes, we, like most travelers, tarried awhile at Nice, that favorite resort of health and pleasure and one beautiful for situation. The outlook from it on the sea is enchanting, but no one should visit Nice with a lean purse, and a man with a full one will be wise not to tarry long. It was the most expensive place we found abroad.

Genoa, the birthplace of Christopher Columbus, the man who saw by an eye of faith the things hoped for and the evidence of things not

seen, is a grand old city with its multitude of churches, numerous narrow streets, many-colored buildings, and splendid palaces. Like most Italian cities, Genoa upholds the reputation of its country in respect of art. The old masters in painting and sculpture—and their name is legion—are still largely represented in the palaces of the merchant princes of this city. One of its singular features is the abundance of fresco work seen on both the inside and the outside of buildings. One feels emphatically the presence and power of the Roman Catholic Church in the multitude of shrines seen everywhere and containing pictures of apostles or saints, or the Virgin Mother and the infant Jesus. But of all the interesting objects collected in the Museum of Genoa, the one that touched me most was the violin that had belonged to and been played upon by Paganini, the greatest musical genius of his time. This violin is treasured in a glass case and beyond the touch of careless fingers, a thing to be seen and not handled.

Never to be forgotten by one who has enjoyed it is a morning at Pisa, the city of the leaning tower; a city renowned in Italian history.

The Columbus Monument, Genoa, Italy.

Though still possessing many imposing buildings, like many other once famous places its glory has departed. Its grand old cathedral, baptistery, and leaning tower are the features that most attract the attention of the tourist. The baptistery is especially interesting for its acoustic properties. The human voice heard here has imparted to it the richest notes of the organ, and goes on repeating and prolonging itself, increasing in volume and ranging higher and higher in ascent till lost in whispers almost divine at the very top of the dome.

But no American sensitive and responsive to what is old, grand and historic, with his face towards the East and the city of Rome only a few hours away, will tarry long even in this fine old city of Pisa. Like the mysterious loadstone to steel, he is attracted by an invisible power, and the attraction increases with every step of his approach. All that one has ever read, heard, felt, thought, or imagined concerning Rome comes thronging upon mind and heart and makes one eager and impatient to be there. The privilege of daylight was denied us on our arrival, and our first glimpse of Rome was by the light of moon and stars. With the light of day, the Eternal City, seated on its throne of seven hills, fully gave us all it had promised, banished every feeling of disappointment, and filled our minds with ever-increasing wonder and amazement. In all directions were disclosed those indications of her ancient greatness for which we were looking, and of her fitness to be the seat of the most powerful empire that man had ever seen—truly the mistress of the known world and for a thousand years the recognized metropolis of the Christian faith and the head still of the largest organized church in the world. Here can be seen together the symbols of both Christian and pagan Rome; the temples of discarded gods and those of the accepted Saviour of the world, the Son of the Virgin Mary. Empires, principalities, powers, and dominions have perished; altars and their gods have mingled with the dust; a religion which made men virtuous in peace and invincible in war has perished or been supplanted, yet the Eternal City itself remains. It speaks from the spacious Forum, yet studded with graceful but time-worn columns, and from the Pantheon, built twenty-seven years before the songs of the angels were heard on the plains of Bethlehem.

Though two thousand years have rolled over it, and though the beautiful marble which once adorned and protected its exterior has been torn off and made to serve other and inferior purposes, there, speaking to us of ages past, it stands, erect and strong, and may stand yet a thousand years longer. Its walls, twenty feet thick, give few signs of decay.

Château d'If, seen from the seashore, Marseilles, France.

The Leaning Tower of Pisa.

The Trevi Fountain in Rome.

More than any building I saw in Rome, it tells of the thoroughness of the Romans in everything they thought it worth their while to undertake to be or to do.

The streets of Rome, except in the newest part, are generally very narrow, and the houses on either side of them being very high, there is much more shade than sunshine in them, and hence the remarkably chilly atmosphere of which strangers complain. Yet the city is not without redeeming and compensating features. It has many fine open spaces and public squares, supplied with large flowing fountains, and adorned with various attractive devices, where the people have abundant pure water, fresh air, and bright, health-giving sunlight.

Of street life in Rome I must not speak except to mention one feature of it which overtops all others, and that is the part taken both consciously and unconsciously by members of various bodies of the church. All that we see and hear impresses us with the gigantic,

all-pervading, complicated, accumulated and mysterious power of this great religious and political organization. Wherever else the Roman Church may question its own strength and practice a modest reserve, here she is open, free, self-asserting and bold in her largest assumptions.

The two best points from which to view the exterior of Rome are the Pincian Hill and the Janiculum. Of the seven hills these are not the least interesting, and from their summits can be taken in its full magnificence a general view of the Eternal City. Once seen from these points it will never be forgotten, but will dwell in the mind forever.

The ride from Rome to Naples in winter is delightful. A beautiful valley diversified on either side by mountain peaks capped with snow, is a perpetual entertainment to the eye of the traveler. Only a few hours' ride and behold a scene of startling sublimity! It is a broad column of white vapor from the summit of Vesuvius, slowly and majestically rising against the blue Italian sky and before gentle northern and land breezes

The Bay of Naples with Mount Vesuvius in the background.

grandly moving off to sea, a thing of wonder. Naples is a great city, and its bay is all that its fame has taught us to expect. Its beautiful surroundings rich with historical associations would easily keep one lingering for months.

When once an American tourist has quitted Rome and has felt the balmy breezes of the Mediterranean; has seen the beautiful Bay of Naples; reveled in the wonders of its neighborhood; stood at the base of Vesuvius; surveyed the narrow streets, the majestic halls, and the luxurious houses of long-buried Pompeii; stood upon the spot where the great apostle Paul first landed at Puteoli after his eventful and perilous voyage on his way to Rome—he is generally seized with an ardent desire to wander still farther eastward and southward. Sicily will tempt him, and once there, and his face turned towards the rising sun, he will want to see Egypt, the Suez Canal, the Libyan desert, the wondrous Nile—land of obelisks and hieroglyphs which men are so well learning to read;

land of sphinxes and mummies many thousand years old, of great pyramids and colossal ruins that speak to us of a civilization which extends back into the misty shadows of the past, far beyond the reach and grasp of authentic history. The more he has seen of modern civilization in England, France and Italy, the more he will want to see the traces of that civilization which existed when these countries of Europe were inhabited by barbarians. When once so near to this more renowned and ancient abode of civilization, the scene of so many Bible events and wonders, the desire to see it becomes almost irresistible.

I confess, however, that my desire to visit Egypt did not rest entirely upon the basis thus foreshadowed. I had a motive far less enthusiastic and sentimental; an ethnological purpose in the pursuit of which I hoped to turn my visit to some account in combating American prejudice against the darker colored races of mankind, and at the same time to raise colored people somewhat in their own estimation and thus

The entrance to the Suez Canal at Port Said.

stimulate them to higher endeavors. I had a theory for which I wanted the support of facts in the range of my own knowledge.

We pass through the straits of Messina, leave behind us the smoke and vapor of Mount Etna, and in three days are safely anchored in front of Port Said, the west end of the Suez Canal, that stupendous work which has brought the occident face to face with the orient and changed the route taken by the commerce of the world.

At Port Said, where we entered the Suez Canal, the vessels of all nations halt. The few houses that make up the town look white, new and temporary, reminding one of some of the hastily built wooden towns of the American frontier, where there is much space outside and little within. Here our good ship, the *Ormuz*, the largest vessel that had then ever floated through the Suez Canal, stopped to take in a large supply of coal prior to proceeding on her long voyage to Australia. It was something to see these men of the desert at work. As I looked at them and listened to their fun and frolic while bearing their heavy burdens, I said to myself: "You fellows are, at least in your disposition, half

brothers to the negro." The negro works best and hardest when it is no longer work, but becomes play with joyous singing. These children of the desert performed their task in like manner, amid shouts of laughter and tricks of fun, as if their hard work were the veriest sport.

Slowly and carefully moving through the canal an impressive scene was presented to the eye. Nothing in my American experience ever gave me such a deep sense of unearthly silence, such a sense of vast, profound, unbroken sameness and solitude, as did this passage through the Suez Canal, moving smoothly and noiselessly between two spade-built banks of yellow sand, watched over by the jealous care of England and France, two rival powers each jealous of the other. We find here, too, the motive and mainspring of English Egyptian occupation and of English policy.

After more than a day and a night on this weird, silent, and dreamy canal, under a cloudless sky, almost unconscious of motion, yet moving on and on without pause and without haste, through a noiseless, treeless, houseless, and seemingly endless wilderness of sand, where not even the crowing of a cock or the barking of a dog is heard, we were transferred to

A tributary to the Suez Canal at Ismailia.

a smart little French steamer and landed at Ismailia, where, since leaving the new and shambling town of Port Said, we see the first sign of civilization and begin to realize that we are entering the land of the Pharaohs.

Here the Khedive has one of his many palaces, and here and there are a few moderately comfortable dwellings with two or three hotels and a railroad station. Here we first caught sight of the living locomotive of the East, that marvelous embodiment of strength, docility, and obedience, of patient endurance of hunger and thirst—the camel. I have large sympathy with all burden-bearers, whether they be men or beasts, and having read of the gentle submission of the camel to hardships and abuse, of how he will kneel to receive his heavy burden and groan to have it made lighter, I was glad right here in the edge of Egypt to have a visible illustration of these qualities of the animal. I saw him kneel and saw the heavy load of sand put on his back; I saw him try to rise under its weight and heard his sad moan. I had at the moment much the same feeling as when I first saw a gang of slaves chained together and shipped to a foreign market.

Cairo, circa 1846.

A long line of camels attended by three or four Arabs came slowly moving over the desert. This spectacle, more than the language or customs of the people, gave me a vivid impression of Eastern life; a picture of it as it was in the days of Abraham and Moses. It was from the vastness and silence of the desert that Mahomet learned his religion, and once he thought he had discovered man's true relation to the Infinite he proclaimed himself a prophet and began to preach with that sort of authority and power which never failed to make converts. Such speculations were for me ended by the startling whistle of the locomotive and the sound of the rushing train.

Cairo with its towers, minarets and mosques presents a strangely fascinating scene, especially from the citadel, where away off in the distance, rising between the yellow desert and the soft blue cloudless sky, we discern the unmistakable forms of those mysterious piles of masonry, the Pyramids. According to one theory they were built for sepulchral purposes; and according to another they were built for a standard of measurement, but neither theory has perhaps entirely set aside the other, and both may be wrong. There they stand, however, grandly, in sight of Cairo, just in the edge of the Libyan desert and overlooking the valley of the Nile, as they have stood during more than three thousand years and are likely to stand as many thousand years longer, for nothing grows old here but time, and that lives on forever.

I went, with seventy years on my head, to the top of the highest Pyramid, but nothing in the world would tempt me to try the experiment again.

One of the first exploits a tourist is tempted to perform here is to ascend to the top of the highest Pyramid. The task is by no means an easy one, nor is it entirely free from danger. It is clearly dangerous if undertaken without the assistance of two or more guides. You need them not only to show you where to put your feet, but to lift you over the huge blocks of stone of which the Pyramids are built, for some of these stones are from three to four feet in thickness and height. Neither in ascending nor descending is it safe to look down. One misstep and

The sphinx with the pyramids of Giza in the background, pictured in the late 1800s.

The railroad into Florence, Italy.

all is over. I went, with seventy years on my head, to the top of the highest Pyramid, but nothing in the world would tempt me to try the experiment again. Taking the view altogether—the character of the surroundings, the great unexplained and inexplicable Sphinx, the Pyramids and other wonders of Sakkara, the winding river of the valley of the Nile, the silent, solemn and measureless desert, the seats of ancient Memphis and Heliopolis, the distant mosques, minarets, and stately palaces, the ages and events that have swept over the scene and the millions on millions that lived, wrought and died there—there are stirred in the one who beholds it for the first time thoughts and feelings never thought and felt before. While nothing could tempt me to climb the rugged jagged, steep and perilous sides of the Great Pyramid again, yet I am very glad to have had the experience once, and once is enough for a lifetime.

Touching at Naples, we returned to Rome, where the longer one stays the longer one wants to stay. Next to Rome, in point of interest to me, is the classic city of Florence, and thither we went from the Eternal City. One might never tire of what is here to be seen. The first thing Mrs. Douglass and I did, on our arrival in Florence, was to visit the grave of Theodore Parker and at the same time that of Elizabeth Barrett Browning. The preacher and the poet lie near each other. The soul of each was devoted to liberty. The brave stand taken by Theodore Parker during the anti-slavery conflict endeared him to my heart, and naturally enough the spot made sacred by his ashes was the first to draw me to its side. He had a voice for the slave when nearly all the pulpits of the land were dumb.

Its ducal palaces, its grand Duomo, its fine galleries of art, its beautiful Arno, its charming environs, and its many associations of great historical personages, especially of Michel Angelo, Dante and Savonarola, give it a controlling power over mind and heart. I have traveled over no equal space between any two cities in Italy where the scenery was more delightful than that between Florence and Venice. I enjoyed it with the ardor of a boy to whom all the world is new. The railway between Florence and Venice is over some of the oldest and best cultivated parts of Italy. The land is rich and fruitful. I could tell much of the once famous city of Venice, of Milan, Lucerne, and other points subsequently visited; but it is enough that I have given my readers an idea of the use I made of my time during this absence from the scenes and activities that occupied me at home. I assume that they will rejoice that after my life of hardships in slavery and of conflict with race and color prejudice and proscription at home, there was left to me a space in life when I could and did walk the world unquestioned, a man among men.

CHAPTER X

THE CAMPAIGN OF 1888

PREFERENCE FOR JOHN SHERMAN—SPEECH AT THE CONVENTION—
ON THE STUMP.

Returning from Europe in 1887 after a year of sojourn abroad, I found, as is usual when our country is nearing the close of a presidential term, the public mind largely occupied with the question in respect of a successor to the outgoing President. The Democratic party had the advantage of the Republican party in two points: it was already in power, and had its mind fixed upon one candidate, in the person of Grover Cleveland, whose term was then expiring. Although he had not entirely satisfied the Southern section of his party or the civil-service reformers of the North, to whom he owed his election, he had so managed his administration that neither of these factions could afford to oppose his nomination for a second term of the presidency. With the Republican party the case was different. It was not only out of power and deprived of the office-holding influence and machinery to give it unity and force, but its candidates for presidential honors were legion, and there was much doubt as to who would be chosen standard bearer in the impending contest. Among the doubters I was happily not one. From the first my candidate was Senator John Sherman of Ohio. Not only was he the man fitted for the place by his eminent abilities and tried statesmanship in regard to general matters, but more important still, he was the man whose attitude towards the newly enfranchised colored citizens of the South best fitted him for the place. In the convention at Chicago I did what I could to secure his nomination, as long as there was any ground of hope for success. In every convention of the kind there comes a time when the judgment of factions must yield to the judgment of the majority. But my judgment as to either was not the judgment of the convention, so I went, as in duty bound, with the choice of the majority of my party and have never regretted my course.

Although I was not a delegate to this National Republican Convention, but was, as in previous ones, a spectator, I was early honored by a spontaneous call to the platform to address the convention. It was a call not to be disregarded. It came from ten thousand leading Republicans of the land. It offered me an opportunity to give what I thought ought to be the accepted keynote to the opening campaign. After thanking the convention for the honor of its hearty call upon me for a speech I said,

John Sherman, circa 1880.

I hope this convention will make such a record in its proceedings as will entirely put it out of the power of the leaders of the Democratic party and of the leaders of the Mugwump party to say that they see no difference between the position of the Republican party in respect to the class I represent and that of the Democratic party.

I have only one word to say to this convention and it is this: I hope this convention will make such a record in its proceedings as will entirely put it out of the power of the leaders of the Democratic party and of the leaders of the Mugwump party to say that they see no difference between the position of the Republican party in respect to the class I represent and that of the Democratic party. I have a great respect for a certain quality for which the Democratic party is distinguished. That quality is fidelity to its friends, its faithfulness to those whom it has acknowledged as its masters during the last forty years. It was faithful to the slave-holding class during the existence of slavery. It was faithful to them before the war. It gave them all the encouragement that it possibly could without drawing its own neck into the halter. It was also faithful during the period of reconstruction, and it has been faithful ever since. It is to-day faithful to the solid South. I hope and believe that the great Republican party will prove itself equally faithful to its friends, those friends with black faces who during the war were eyes to your blind, shelter to your shelterless, when flying from the lines of the enemy. When your army was melting away before the fire and pestilence of rebellion; when your star-spangled banner trailed in the dust or, heavy with blood, dropped at the mast head, you called upon the negro. Yes, Abraham Lincoln called upon the negro to reach forth with his iron arm and catch with his steel fingers your faltering flag, and he came, he came full two hundred thousand strong. Let us in the platform we are about to promulgate remember the brave black men, and let us remember that these brave black men are now stripped of their constitutional right to vote. Let this remembrance be embodied in the standard bearer whom you will present to the country. Leave these men no longer compelled to wade to the ballot-box through blood, but extend over them the protecting arm of this government, and make their pathway to the ballot-box as straight and as smooth and as safe as that of any other class of citizens. Be not deterred from this duty by the cry of the bloody shirt. Let that shirt be waved as long as there shall be a drop of innocent blood upon it. A government that can give liberty in its constitution ought to have the power in its administration to protect and defend that liberty. I will not further take up your time. I have spoken for millions, and my thought is now before you.

As soon as the presidential campaign was fairly opened and a request was made for speakers to go before the people and support by the living voice the nominations and principles of the Republican party, though somewhat old for such service and never much of a stump speaker, I obeyed the summons. In company with my young friend Charles S. Morris, a man rarely gifted with eloquence, I made speeches in five different States, indoors and out of doors, in skating-rinks and public halls, day and night, at points where it was thought by the National Republican Committee that my presence and speech would do most to promote success.

The Republican party and the nation were pledged to the protection of the constitutional rights of the colored citizens. If it refused to perform its promise it would be false to its highest trust. As with an individual, so too with a nation, there is a time when it may properly be asked, "What doth it profit to gain the whole world and thereby lose one's soul?"

With such views as these I supported the Republican party in this somewhat remarkable campaign. I based myself upon that part of the Republican platform which I supported in my speech before the Republican convention at Chicago. No man who knew me could have expected me to pursue any other course.

This poster for the 1888 Republican convention in Chicago reminds voters of the first successful Republican presidential candidate, Abraham Lincoln, and puts him next to the current candidate, Benjamin Harrison.

CHAPTER XI

ADMINISTRATION OF PRESIDENT HARRISON

Appointed Minister to Haïti—Unfriendly criticism.

My appointment by President Harrison in 1889 to the office of Minister Resident and Consul General to the Republic of Haïti did not pass without adverse comment at the time it was made; nor did I escape criticism at any time during the two years I had the honor to hold that office. In respect to the unfavorable comments upon my appointment, it may be truly said that they had their origin and inspiration from two very natural sources: first, American race and color prejudice, and second, a desire on the part of certain influential merchants in New York to obtain concessions from Haïti upon grounds that I was not likely to favor. When there is made upon a public man an attack by newspapers differing at all other points and united only in this attack, there is some reason to believe that they are inspired by a common influence. Neither my character nor my color was acceptable to the New York press. The fault of my character was that upon it there could be predicated no well grounded hope that I would allow myself to be used, or allow my office to be used, to further selfish schemes of any sort for the benefit of individuals, either at the expense of Haïti or at the expense of the character of the United States. Every occasion was embraced by the New York press to show that my experience in Haïti confirmed their views and predictions. Before I went there they endeavored to show that the captain of the ship designated by the government to take me to my post at Port au Prince had refused to take me on board, and as an excuse for his refusal, had made a false statement concerning the unseaworthiness of his vessel, when the real ground of objection was the color of my skin. When it was known that I had not been fully accredited in due form to the Government of President Hyppolite and that there was a delay of many weeks in my formal recognition by the Haïtian government, the story was trumpeted abroad that I was "snubbed" by Haïti, and in truth was having a hard time down there. After I was formally recognized and had entered upon the duties of my office, I was followed by the same unfriendly spirit, and every effort was made to disparage me in the eyes of both the people of the United States and those of Haïti. Strangely enough, much of this unfriendly influence came from officers of the American navy; men in the pay of the government. The appearance in the harbor of Port au Prince of United States ships of war, instead of being a support to the American Minister, was always followed by a heavy broadside against him in the American papers.

President Benjamin Harrison (1833–1901).

This turn-of-the-century photograph shows a public fountain in Port-au-Prince, Haiti.

CHAPTER XII

MINISTER TO HAÏTI

THE MÔLE ST. NICOLAS—SOCIAL RELATIONS—SYMPATHY FOR HAÏTI—
THE FACTS ABOUT THE MÔLE ST. NICOLAS—CONFERENCE WITH THE
HAÏTIAN GOVERNMENT—NEGOTIATIONS FOR THE MÔLE ST. NICOLAS—
CLOSE OF THE INTERVIEW.

The part I bore in the matter of obtaining at the Môle St. Nicolas a naval station for the United States, and the real cause for the failure of the enterprise, are made evident in the following articles from me, published in the *North American Review* for September and October, 1891.

"I propose to make a plain statement regarding my connection with the late negotiations with the government of Haïti for a United States naval station at the Môle St. Nicolas. Such a statement seems required, not only as a personal vindication from undeserved censure, but as due to the truth of history. . . .

"The charge is, that I have been the means of defeating the acquisition of an important United States naval station at the Môle St. Nicolas. It is said, in general terms, that I wasted the whole of my first year in Haïti in needless parley and delay, and finally reduced the chances of getting the Môle to such a narrow margin as to make it necessary for our government to appoint Rear-Admiral Gherardi as a special commissioner to Haïti to take the whole matter of negotiation for the Môle out of my hands. One of the charitable apologies they are pleased to make for my failure is my color; and the implication is that a white man would

have succeeded where I failed. This color argument is not new. It besieged the White House before I was appointed Minister Resident and Consul-General to Haïti. At once and all along the line, the contention was then raised that no man with African blood in his veins should be sent as minister to the Black Republic. White men professed to speak in the interest of black Haïti; and I could have applauded their alacrity in upholding her dignity if I could have respected their sincerity. They thought it monstrous to compel black Haïti to receive a minister as black as herself. They did not see that it would be shockingly inconsistent for Haïti to object to a black minister while she herself is black.

"Prejudice sets all logic at defiance. It takes no account of reason or consistency. One of the duties of minister in a foreign land is to cultivate good social as well as civil relations with the people and government to which he is sent. Would an American white man, imbued with our national sentiments, be more likely than an American colored man to cultivate such relations? Would his American contempt for the colored race at home fit him to win the respect and good-will of colored people abroad? Or would he play the hypocrite and pretend to love negroes in Haïti when he is known to hate negroes in the United States,—aye, so

Admiral Bancroft Gherardi (1832–1903).

bitterly that he hates to see them occupy even the comparatively humble position of Consul-General to Haïti? Would not the contempt and disgust of Haïti repel such a sham?

"Haïti is no stranger to Americans or to American prejudice. Our white fellow-countrymen have taken little pains to conceal their sentiments. This objection to my color and this demand for a white man to succeed me spring from the very feeling which Haïti herself contradicts and detests. I defy any man to prove, by any word or act of the Haïtian Government, that I was less respected at the capital of Haïti than was any white minister or consul. This clamor for a white minister for Haïti is based upon the idea that a white man is held in higher esteem by her than is a black man, and that he could get more out of her than can one of her own color. It is not so, and the whole free history of Haïti proves it not to be so. . . .

"I am charged with sympathy for Haïti. I am not ashamed of that charge; but no man can say with truth that my sympathy with Haïti stood between me and any honorable duty that I owed to the United States or to any citizen of the United States.

"The attempt has been made to prove me indifferent to the acquisition of a naval station in Haïti, and unable to grasp the importance to American commerce and to American influence of such a station in the Caribbean Sea. The fact is, that when some of these writers were in their petticoats, I had comprehended the value of such an acquisition, both in respect to American commerce and to American influence. The policy of obtaining such a station is not new. I supported Gen. Grant's ideas on this subject against the powerful opposition of my honored and revered friend Charles Sumner, more than twenty years ago, and proclaimed it on a hundred platforms and to thousands of

A letter from Douglass during his time in Haiti in which he mentions Admiral Gherardi as well as Mr. Firmin and President Hyppolite of the Haitian government.

my fellow-citizens. I said then that it was a shame to American statesmanship that, while almost every other great nation in the world had secured a foothold and had power in the Caribbean Sea, where it could anchor in its own bays and moor in its own harbors, we, who stood at the very gate of that sea, had there no anchoring ground anywhere. I was for the acquisition of Samana, and of Santo Domingo herself, if she wished to come to us. While slavery existed, I was opposed to all schemes for the extension of American power and influence. But since its abolition, I have gone with him who goes farthest for such extension.

"But the pivotal and fundamental charge made by my accusers is that I wasted a whole year in fruitless negotiations for a coaling-station at the Môle St. Nicolas, and allowed favorable opportunities for obtaining it to pass unimproved, so that it was necessary at last for the United States Government to take the matter out of my hands, and send a special commissioner to Haïti, in the person of Rear-Admiral Gherardi, to negotiate for the Môle. A statement more false than this never dropped from lip or pen. I here and now declare, without hesitation or qualification or fear of contradiction, that there is not one word of truth in this charge. If I do not in this state the truth, I may be easily contradicted and put to open shame. I therefore affirm that at no time during the first year of my residence in Haïti was I charged with the duty or invested with any authority by the President of the United States, or by the Secretary of State, to negotiate with Haïti for a United States naval station at the Môle St. Nicolas, or anywhere else in that country. Where no duty was imposed, no duty was neglected. It is not for a diplomat to

Overleaf: A turn-of-the-century map of Santo Domingo and Haiti. Môle-St.-Nicolas is located at the northeast corner of the island.

TI POR EL GENERAL CASIMIRO N. DE MOYA.

Nacional Dominicano fecha 18 Mayo de 1905.

A T L Á N T I C O

NOTAS

Para el presente trabajo hemos utilizado todos los hasta el día publicados sobre la topografía de la Isla y muchos que se conservan inéditos, habiendo hecho numerosas rectificaciones sugeridas por nuestros propios prácticos conocimientos y los de otras personas que nos han ayudado con los suyos, y no omitido detalle que contribuir pueda á dar cabal conocimiento del territorio y de su actual población y división política.

Para la posición, delineación y detalles de los puertos y bahías principales nos hemos servido de los más recientes estudios de las MARINAS INGLESA Y AMERICANA, publicados en CARTAS ESPECIALES por los Sres. JAMES IMRAY & SON, Londres, 1886, los de la primera, y por el Hydrographic Office, Navy Department, de los E. E. U. U. de América los de la segunda.

ESCALAS — 1:400,000 — 4 Kilómetros por Centímetro

Signos y Abreviaturas Convencionales.

DISTRITO DE PUERTO PLATA

PROVINCIA DE ESPAILLAT

DISTRITO PACIFICADOR

SANTIAGO

BAHÍA ESCOCESA

BAHÍA DEL SENOR

DISTRITO DE SAMANÁ

BAHÍA DE SAMANÁ

PROVINCIA DE LA VEGA

R E P Ú B L I C A   D O M I N I C A N A

PROVINCIA DE AZUA

PROVINCIA DE SANTO DOMINGO

DISTRITO DE MACORIS

SEIBO

BARAHONA

CANAL DE LA MONA

ISLA SAONA

REFERENCIAS

1. Taller de Fundición
2. Fortaleza
3. Torre del Homenaje (Cárcel)
4. Comandancia de Armas
5. Hospital Militar
6. Academia de Náutica
7. Gobernación y Juzgado de Orden Público
8. Teatro
9. Capilla de los Remedios
10. Administración de Telégrafos Nacionales
11. Palacio del Ejecutivo y del Congreso
12. Gendarmería del Puerto
13. Casino ó Plaza Colón (Ruinas)
14. Aduana y sus dependencias
15. Muelle de la Plaza
16. Planta Eléctrica
17. Iglesia de Santa Bárbara
18. Mercado del Comercio
19. Palacio del Presidente de la República
20. Palacio del Congreso
21. Parque y rotoma de Colón
22. Catedral, Primada de las Indias
23. Instituto Profesional
24. Iglesia y Jardín de Santa Clara
25. Palacio Arzobispal
26. Plaza y ermita del Padre Billini
27. Palacio Municipal
28. Ruinas de San Nicolás
29. Capilla de la Altagracia
30. Manicomio Padre Billini
31. Ruinas de San Francisco
32. Ruinas de San Andrés
33. Club Unión
34. Iglesia de Santo Domingo
35. Seminario Padre Meriño
36. Escuela Normal
37. Iglesia y Jardín de las Mercedes
38. Nuevo Palacio de Justicia
39. Ruinas de La Sabana

CIUDAD Y CONTORNOS DE SANTO DOMINGO

ESCALA 1:10000

EL ESPERILLÓN   VILLA FRANCISCA   GALINDO

GAZCUE   LA GENERAL   SAN CARLOS   ALTAGRACIA

LA AGUEDITA   W. BASS

LA FRANCIA

TABLA

DE LAS DISTANCIAS TERRESTRES, EN KILÓMETROS,
á que respectivamente se encuentran las cabeceras de provincia ó de distrito en ambas Repúblicas.

SANTO DOMINGO

72	SAN PEDRO DE MACORIS								
120	60	SEIBO							
128	124	76	SAMANÁ						
135	194	181	117	SAN FRANCISCO DE MACORIS					
152	216	203	149	35	LA VEGA				
167	231	218	107	48	22	MOCA			
199	258	244	180	64	40	24	SANTIAGO		
245	300	203	229	100	80	96	PUERTO PLATA		
308	380	322	264	204	140	202	236	MONTE CRISTI	
208	290	336	276	244	206	316	305	72	AZUA
									BARAHONA

PORT-AU-PRINCE

			60	MIREBALAIS
				32 LAS CAOBAS
		88	140	SALTROU
		60	120	148 JACMEL
		140	200	220 80 AQUIN
		160	260	284 250 176 LES CAYES
		300	306	790 210 160 40 JÉRÉMIE

Admiral Gherardi's ship the U.S.S. Philadelphia.

run before he is sent, especially in matters involving large consequences like those implied in extending our power into a neighboring country.

"Here, then, let me present the plain facts in the case. They, better than anything else I can say, vindicate my conduct in connection with this question.

"On the 26th of January, 1891, Rear-Admiral Gherardi, having arrived at Port au Prince, sent one of his under-officers on shore to the United States Legation, to invite me on board of his flagship, the *Philadelphia*. I complied with the invitation, although I knew that, in strict politeness, it would have been more appropriate for Admiral Gherardi himself to come to me. I felt disinclined, however, to stand upon ceremony or to endeavor to correct the manners of an American admiral. Having long since decided to my own satisfaction that no expression of American prejudice or slight on account of my color could diminish my self-respect or disturb my equanimity, I went on board as requested, and there for the first time learned that I was to have some connection with negotiations for a United States coaling-station at the Môle St. Nicolas; and this information was imparted to me by Rear-Admiral Gherardi. He told me in his peculiarly emphatic manner that he had been duly appointed a United States special commissioner; that his mission was to obtain a naval station at the Môle St. Nicolas; and that it was the wish of Mr. Blaine and Mr. Tracy, and also of the President of the United States, that I should earnestly co-operate with him in accomplishing this object. He further made me acquainted with the dignity of his position, and I was not slow in recognizing it.

"In reality, some time before the arrival of Admiral Gherardi on this diplomatic scene, I was made acquainted with the fact of his appointment. There was at Port au Prince an individual, of whom we shall hear more elsewhere, acting as agent of a distinguished firm in New York, who appeared to be more fully initiated into the secrets of the State Department at Washington than I was, and who knew, or said he knew, all about the appointment of Admiral Gherardi, whose arrival he diligently heralded in advance, and carefully made public in all the political and business circles to which he had access. He stated that I was discredited at Washington, had, in fact, been suspended and recalled, and that Admiral Gherardi had been duly commissioned to take my place. This news was sudden and far from flattering. It is unnecessary to say that it placed me in an unenviable position, both before the community of Port au Prince and before the government of Haïti. It had, however, the advantage, so far as I was able to believe anything so anomalous, of preparing me for the advent of my successor, and of softening the shock of my fall from my high estate. My connection with this negotiation, as all may see, was very humble, secondary and subordinate. The glory of success or the shame of defeat was to belong to the new minister. I was made subject to the commissioner. This was not quite so bad as the New York agent had prepared me to expect, but it was not what I thought I deserved and what my position as minister called for at the hands of my government. Strangely enough, all my instructions concerning the Môle came to me through my newly constituted superior. He was fresh from the face of our Secretary of State, knew his most secret intentions and the wants and wishes of the government, and I, naturally enough, received the law from his lips.

"The situation suggested the resignation of my office as due to my honor; but reflection soon convinced me that such a course would subject me to a misconstruction more hurtful than any which, in the circumstances, could justly arise from remaining at my post. The government had decided that a special commissioner was needed in Haïti. No charges were brought against me, and it was not for me to set up my wisdom or my resentment as a safer rule of action than that prescribed by the wisdom of my government. Besides, I did not propose to be pushed out of office in this way. I therefore resolved to co-operate with the special commissioner in good faith and in all earnestness, and did so to the best of my ability.

"It was first necessary, in furtherance of the mission of Admiral Gherardi, to obtain for him as early as possible an interview with Mr. Firmin, the Haïtian Minister of Foreign Affairs, and with His Excellency Florvil Hyppolite, the President of Haïti. This, by reason of my position as minister and my good relations with the government of Haïti, I accomplished only two days after the arrival of the admiral. . . . Our first conference with President Hyppolite and his foreign secretary was held at the palace at Port au Prince on the 28th of January, 1891. At this conference, which was, in fact, the real beginning of the negotiations for the Môle St. Nicolas, the wishes of our government were made known to the government of Haïti by Rear-Admiral Gherardi; and I must do him the justice to say that he stated the case with force and ability. If anything was omitted or insisted upon calculated to defeat the object in view, this defect must be looked for in the admiral's address, for he was the principal speaker, as he was also the principal negotiator.

"Admiral Gherardi based our claim for this concession upon the ground of services rendered by the United States to the Hyppolite revolution. He claimed it also on the ground of promises made to our government by Hyppolite and Firmin through their agents while the revolution was in progress, and affirmed that but for the support of our government the revolution would have failed. . . .

"In replying to us, Mr. Firmin demanded to know on which of the two grounds we based our claim for the possession of this naval station. If it were demanded, he said, upon any pledge made by President Hyppolite and himself, he denied the existence of any such promise or pledge, and insisted that, while the offer of certain advantages had been made to our government, the government at Washington had not at the time accepted them. The letter in proof of the different view was, he said, only a copy of the original letter, and the original letter was never accepted by the American Government.

"This position of Mr. Firmin's was resisted by Admiral Gherardi, who contended with much force that, while there was no formal agreement consummated between the two governments, Haïti was nevertheless bound, since the assistance for which she asked had made

Admiral Gherardi aboard the U.S.S. Philadelphia.

Hyppolite President of Haïti. Without intending to break the force of the admiral's contention at this point, I plainly saw the indefensible attitude in which he was placing the government of the United States in representing our government as interfering by its navy with the affairs of a neighboring country, covertly assisting in putting down one government and setting up another; and I therefore adhered to the grounds upon which I based our demand for a coaling-station at the Môle. I spoke in the interest and honor of the United States. It did not strike me that what was claimed by Admiral Gherardi to have been done—though I did not say as much—is the work for which the United States is armed, equipped, manned and supported by the American people. It was alleged that, though our government did not authorize Rear-Admiral Gherardi to overthrow Légitime and to set up Hyppolite as President of Haïti, it gave him the wink, and left him to assume the responsibility. I did not accept this as a foundation upon which I could base my diplomacy. If this was a blunder on my part, it was a blunder of which I am not ashamed, and it was committed in the interest of my country.

"At the close of this conference we were asked by Mr. Firmin to put into writing our request for the Môle, and the terms upon which we asked its concession."

CHAPTER XIII

CONTINUED NEGOTIATIONS FOR THE MÔLE ST. NICOLAS

UNFORTUNATE DELAY—RENEWED AUTHORITY FROM THE UNITED STATES—HAÏTI'S REFUSAL—REASONS FOR THE REFUSAL—FINAL WORDS.

"**A**t a meeting subsequent to the one already described, application for a United States naval station at the Môle St. Nicolas was made in due form to Mr. Firmin, the Haïtian Minister of Foreign Affairs. At his request, as already stated, this application was presented to him in writing. It was prepared on board the *Philadelphia*, the flagship of Rear-Admiral Bancroft Gherardi, and bore his signature alone. I neither signed it nor was asked to sign it, although it met my entire approval. I make this statement not in the way of complaint or grievance, but simply to show what, at the time, was my part, and what was not my part, in this important negotiation, the failure of which has unjustly been laid to my charge. Had the Môle been acquired, in response to this paper, the credit of success, according to the record, would have properly belonged to the gallant admiral in whose name it was demanded; for in it I had neither part nor lot.

"At this point, curiously enough, and unfortunately for the negotiations, the Haïtian Minister, who is an able man and well skilled in the technicalities of diplomacy, asked to see the commission of Admiral Gherardi and to read his letter of instructions. When these were presented to Mr. Firmin, he, after carefully reading them, pronounced them insufficient, and held that by them the government of the United States would not be bound by any convention which Haïti might make with the admiral. This position of Mr. Firmin's was earnestly and stoutly opposed by Admiral Gherardi, who insisted that his instructions were full, complete, and amply sufficient. Unfortunately, however, he did not leave the matter in controversy without intimating that he thought that Mr. Firmin might be insincere in raising such an objection, and that he was urging it simply with a view to cause unnecessary delay. This was more like the blunt admiral than the discreet diplomat. Such an imputation was obviously out of place, and not likely to smooth the way to a successful proceeding; quite the reverse. Mr. Firmin insisted that his ground was well and honestly taken. . . .

"I held that a prompt compliance with the demand of the Haïtian Government for a perfect letter of credence would be not only the easiest way out of the difficulty, but

Douglass, 1893, two years before his death due to a heart attack he suffered after attending a women's rights meeting, where he received a standing ovation for a speech he delivered.

the wisest policy by which to accomplish the end we sought, since such compliance on our part with even what might be fairly considered an unreasonable demand would make refusal by Haïti to grant the Môle all the more difficult.

"I did not understand Admiral Gherardi to combat this opinion of mine, for he at once acted upon it, and caused an officer from his flagship to go with me to my house and prepare a telegram to be sent to Washington for the required letter of credence. To this telegram he, two days thereafter, received answer that such a letter would be immediately sent by a Clyde steamer to Gonaïves, and thither the admiral went to receive his expected letter. But, from some unexplained cause, no such letter came by the Clyde steamer at the time appointed, and two months intervened before the desired credentials arrived. This unexpected delay proved to be very mischievous and unfavorable to

our getting the Môle, since it gave rise among the Haïtian people to much speculation and many disquieting rumors prejudicial to the project. It was said that Admiral Gherardi had left Port au Prince in anger, and had gone to take possession of the Môle without further parley; that the American flag was already floating over our new naval station; that the United States wanted the Môle as an entering wedge to obtaining possession of the whole island; with much else of like inflammatory nature. Although there was no truth in all this, it had the unhappy effect among the masses of stirring up suspicion and angry feelings towards the United States, and of making it more difficult than it might otherwise have been for the government of Haïti to grant the required concession.

"Finally, after this long interval of waiting, during which the flagship of Admiral Gherardi was reported at different points, sometimes at

In World War II, the U.S.S Frederick Douglass *was constructed as part of a Liberty-class fleet of cargo ships. Over 2,700 ships were rushed through production as "emergency" construction to aid the war effort. Seen here is a Liberty ship at sea.*

A lock of Douglass's air.

Gonaïves, sometimes at the Môle, and sometimes at Kingston, Jamaica, the desired letter of credence arrived. The next day I was again summoned on board the *Philadelphia*, and there was shown me a paper, signed by the President of the United States and by the Secretary of State, authorizing myself, as Minister Resident to Haïti, and Rear-Admiral Gherardi, as special commissioner, to negotiate with such persons as Haïti might appoint, for the purpose of concluding a convention by which we should obtain a lease of the Môle St. Nicolas as a United States naval station.

"It may be here remarked that the letter of credence signed by President Harrison and by the Secretary of State differed in two respects from the former and rejected letter under which we had previously acted. First, it charged me, equally with Admiral Gherardi, with the duty of negotiation; and secondly, it was an application for a naval station pure and simple, without limitation and without conditions.

"Before presenting to Haïti this new letter, which had the advantage of being free from the conditions specified in the old one, the question arose between the admiral and myself as to whether or not we should begin our new negotiations, under our new commission, separate and entirely apart from all that had been attempted under the instructions contained in the old letter. On this point I differed from the admiral. I took the position that we should ignore the past altogether, and proceed according to the instructions of the new letter alone, unencumbered by any terms or limitations contained in the old letter. I felt sure that there were features in the conditions of the old letter which would be met by the representatives of Haïti with strong objections. But the admiral and his able lieutenant insisted that the present letter did not exclude the conditions of the old one, but was, in its nature, only supplementary to them, and hence that this

was simply a continuation of what had gone before. It was therefore decided to proceed with the negotiations on the basis of both the old and the new letter. Under the former letter of instructions, our terms were precise and explicit; under the latter we were left largely to our own discretion: we were simply to secure from the government of Haïti a lease of the Môle St. Nicolas for a naval station.

"The result is known. Haïti refused to grant the lease, and alleged that to do so was impossible under the hard terms imposed in the previous letter of instructions. I do not know that our government would have accepted a naval station from Haïti upon any other or less stringent terms or conditions than those exacted in our first letter of instructions; but I do know that the main grounds alleged by Haïti for its refusal were the conditions set forth in this first letter of instructions, one of which is expressed as follows: 'That so long as the United States may be the lessee of the Môle St. Nicolas, the government of Haïti will not lease or otherwise dispose of any port or harbor or other territory in its dominions, or grant any special privileges or rights of use therein, to any other power, state or government.' This was not only a comprehensive limitation of the power of Haïti over her own territory, but a denial to all others of that which we claim for ourselves. . . .

"Is it not strange that our intelligent editors and our nautical newspaper writers could not have found for the American Government and people a more rational cause for the failure of the negotiations for the Môle St. Nicolas than that of my color, indifference, and incompetency to deal with a question of such a magnitude? Were I disposed to exchange the position of accused for that of accuser, I could find ample material to sustain me in that position. Other persons did much to create conditions unfavorable to our success, but I leave to their friends the employment of such personal assaults."

Opposite: Two riveters working on the U.S.S. Frederick Douglass, *1943.*

Douglass's grave in Mount Hope Cemetery, Rochester, New York.

Contemplating my life as a whole, I have to say that, although it has at times been dark and stormy, and I have met with hardships from which other men have been exempted, yet my life has in many respects been remarkably full of sunshine and joy.

I have nearly reached the end of the period of which, in the beginning, I purposed to write, and should I live to see the end of another decade, it is not at all likely that I shall feel disposed to add another word to this volume. I may therefore make this the concluding chapter of this part of my autobiography. Contemplating my life as a whole, I have to say that, although it has at times been dark and stormy, and I have met with hardships from which other men have been exempted, yet my life has in many respects been remarkably full of sunshine and joy. Servitude, persecution, false friends, desertion and depreciation have not robbed my life of happiness or made it a burden. I have been, and still am, especially fortunate, and may well indulge sentiments of warmest gratitude for the allotments of life that have fallen to me. While I cannot boast of having accomplished great things in the world, I cannot on the other hand feel that I have lived in vain. From first to last I have, in large measure, shared the respect and confidence of my fellow-men. I have had the happiness of possessing many precious and long-enduring friendships with good men and women. I have been the recipient of many honors, among which my unsought appointment by President Benjamin Harrison to the office of Minister Resident and Consul-General to represent the United States at the capital of Haïti, and my equally unsought appointment by President Florvil Hyppolite to represent Haïti among all the civilized nations of the globe at the World's Columbian Exposition, are crowning honors to my long career and a fitting and happy close to my whole public life.

NOTE

1 The following is a copy of these curious papers, both of my transfer from Thomas to Hugh Auld and from Hugh to myself:

> Know all men by these presents: That I, Thomas Auld, of Talbot county and State of Maryland, for and in consideration of the sum of one hundred dollars, current money, to me paid by Hugh Auld of the city of Baltimore, in the said State, at and before the sealing and delivery of these presents, the receipt whereof I, the said Thomas Auld, do hereby acknowledge, have granted, bargained, and sold, and by these presents do grant, bargain, and sell unto the said Hugh Auld, his executors, administrators, and assigns, ONE NEGRO MAN, by the name of FREDERICK BAILEY, or DOUGLASS, as he calls himself—he is now about twenty-eight years of age—to have and to hold the said negro man for life. And I, the said Thomas Auld, for myself, my heirs, executors, and administrators, all and singular, the said FREDERICK BAILEY, alias DOUGLASS, unto the said Hugh Auld, his executors and administrators, and against all and every other person or persons whatsoever, shall and will warrant and forever defend by these presents. In witness whereof, I set my hand and seal this thirteenth day of November, eighteen hundred and forty-six (1846).
>
>   THOMAS AULD.
>
> Signed, sealed, and delivered in presence of Wrightson Jones, John C. Lear.

The authenticity of this bill of sale is attested by N. Harrington, a justice of the peace of the State of Maryland and for the county of Talbot, dated same day as above.

> To all whom it may concern: Be it known that I, Hugh Auld of the city of Baltimore, in Baltimore county in the State of Maryland, for divers good causes and considerations me thereunto moving, have released from slavery, liberated, manumitted, and set free, and by these presents do hereby release from slavery, liberate, manumit, and set free, MY NEGRO MAN named FREDERICK BAILEY, otherwise called DOUGLASS, being of the age of twenty-eight years or thereabouts, and able to work and gain a sufficient livelihood and maintenance; and him, the said negro man named FREDERICK DOUGLASS, I do declare to be henceforth free, manumitted, and discharged from all manner of servitude to me, my executors and administrators forever.
>
> In witness thereof, I, the said Hugh Auld, have hereunto set my hand and seal the fifth of December, in the year one thousand eight hundred and forty-six.
>
>   HUGH AULD.
>
> Sealed and delivered in presence of T. Hanson Bell, James N. S. T. Wright.

INDEX

IMAGE CREDITS

Courtesy of Archive.org: xi, 41 Boston Public Library (Rare Books Department) (right); 12 (left); 31 (bottom), 37, 93 (left), 190, 194 University Library, University of North Carolina at Chapel Hill; 38 Library of Congress; 40 Duke University Libraries; 101 (right) University of Illinois Urbana-Champaign

Courtesy of the Art Institute of Chicago, Major Acquisitions Centennial Endowment, 1996.433 by Samuel J. Miller: iii, vi, 88

Courtesy of the Brooklyn Museum, Gift of Gwendolyn O. L. Conkling: 73

Digital © The College of Charleston Libraries: 72

© Dover Publications, Inc.: 54, 84, 130, 163

Flickr: 101 (left) courtesy of the Boston Public Library; 110 © Tim Green; 111 (top right) courtesy of the British Library; 141 © Lisa Cook; 200 Courtesy of the USCapitol; 238–239 (altered) © Tony Fischer

Courtesy of the Gilder Lehrman Institute of American History: 113, image GLOC07484.04

Courtesy of the Library of Congress: x, xii–1, 3, 5, 8, 10, 14–15, 16–17, 18–19, 20, 22, 26, 27, 28, 32, 33, 31 (top), 34–35, 41 (left), 42, 44–45, 46, 47, 48–49, 50 (both), 52, 53, 58–59, 60, 62–63, 64, 66, 67, 68, 71, 75, 76, 79, 82–83, 85, 89 (left), 90–91, 92, 91 (bottom), 93 (right), 94–95, 96–97, 100, 103, 104, 108–109, 111 (bottom left and right), 115, 119, 120 (left), 121, 122–123, 124 (left), 124 (right), 125, 126, 127 (left), 127 (right), 131, 132, 133 (left), 133 (right), 134 (top), 134–135, 136, 138, 139, 140, 142, 144–145, 146, 147, 148, 149, 150–151, 152, 153, 155, 156, 157, 158–159, 160 (both), 163, 164, 166, 167 (both), 168 (both), 170, 171, 172 (both), 176, 179, 180, 181 (all), 184, 185, 186, 188–189, 191, 192, 193, 195, 197, 198, 199, 201, 203 (both), 204, 206, 208, 210 (left), 212, 213, 214 (both), 215, 216, 217, 218, 219 (both), 220–221, 222, 223, 224, 225, 227, 228, 229, 230–231, 232, 233, 235, 236; 71 Geography and Map Division; 207 photographs in the Carol M. Highsmith Archive, Prints and Photographs Division

Courtesy of the Maryland Historical Society, Latrobe Sketchbooks; Museum Department: 24

Courtesy of the Maryland State Archives: 12 (right)

By permission of the Massachusetts Historical Society: 99, 107, 169

Courtesy of the Metropolitan Museum of Art: 4 Morris K. Jesup Fund, 1940; 78 Harris Brisbane Dick Fund, 1933; 129 Gift of Mr. and Mrs. Carl Stoeckel, 1897

Courtesy of the National Archives: 55, 128

Courtesy of the National Gallery of Art, Rosenwald Collection 1943.3.1833: 23

Courtesy of the National Park Service: xiii, 202, 210 (right), 211; 9 Cumberland Island National Seashore; 112 FRDO 3861, 178 FRDO 1670, 209 FRDO 8624, 243 (right) FRDO 4552 Frederick Douglass National Historic Site

Courtesy of the National Portrait Gallery, Smithsonian Institution: 116 (bottom)

Courtesy of the Nebraska State Historical Society: 237, #11940-1-(14)

Courtesy of the Rochester Public Library Local History Division: 116 (top), 117

© The San Diego History Center: 89 (right)

Courtesy of the Sheridan Libraries, Johns Hopkins University: 56

Shutterstock: ii, 6–7, 11, 13, 30, 43, 61, 165 © Everett Historical; 39 © Kris Tan; 51 Richard Peterson; 111 (top left) © Marzolino

Courtesy of the Walters Art Museum: 29

Wikimedia: 57, 65, 70, 77, 80, 161, 120 (right); 25 courtesy of Walker Art Gallery, Liverpool, Presented by Gilbert Winter Moss in 1863; 69 (left)courtesy of Smithsonian American Art Museum, Gift of Mrs. Francis P. Garvan; 69 (right) courtesy of Chiswick Chap; 81 courtesy of Robert Scot, Image by Lost Dutchman Rare Coins; 86–87 courtesy of The Cincinnati Art Museum, Subscription Fund Purchase; 98 © Daniel Case; 105, 177 courtesy of the National Portrait Gallery; 174 © Shopkins91

Courtesy of Yale University Library, Beinecke Rare Book & Manuscript Library: 2, 21, 36, 102, 106 (left and right), 118, 137, 143 (left), 173, 175, 182, 183, 234

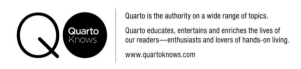

© 2015 Quarto Publishing Group USA Inc. and Warren Street Books

First published in 2015 by Zenith Press, an imprint of Quarto Publishing Group USA Inc., 400 First Avenue North, Suite 400, Minneapolis, MN 55401 USA. Telephone: (612) 344-8100 Fax: (612) 344-8692

quartoknows.com
Visit our blogs at quartoknows.com

Zenith Press titles are also available at discounts in bulk quantity for industrial or sales-promotional use. For details contact the Special Sales Manager at Quarto Publishing Group USA Inc., 400 First Avenue North, Suite 400, Minneapolis, MN 55401 USA.

10 9 8 7 6 5 4 3 2 1

ISBN: 978-0-7603-4850-5

Acquiring Editor: Erik Gilg
Project Manager: Madeleine Vasaly
Art Director: James Kegley

Created by Warren Street Books
Editorial Director: Carlo DeVito
Editor: Katherine Furman
Designer: Ashley Prine

On the front cover and title page: Courtesy of The Art Institute of Chicago, Major Acquisitions Centennial Endowment, 1996.433
On the front case: courtesy of The National Archive, Frank W. Legg Photographic Collection of Portraits of Nineteenth-Century Notables, 1862–1884
On the back case and frontis: © Everett Historical/Shutterstock

Printed in China

Source text transcribed by Apex Data Services, Inc. Images on pages 31 (bottom), 37, 93 (left), 190, and 194 scanned by Lee Fallon and Natalia Smith. Text encoded by Lee Ann Morawski and Natalia Smith. First edition, 2001. ca. 1.5MB. Academic Affairs Library, UNC-CH. University of North Carolina at Chapel Hill, 2001.
pp. x–xi: Henry Louis Gates Jr., from *The Classic Slave Narratives*, edited by Henry Louis Gates Jr., © 1987 by Henry Louis Gates, Jr. Used by permission of New American Library, an imprint of Penguin Publishing Group, a division of Penguin Random House LLC.
pp. 8–9: William S. McFeely from *Frederick Douglass* by William S. McFeely, © 1991 by William S. McFeely. Used by permission of W.W. Norton & Company, Inc.
pp. 100–101: Lerone Bennett, Jr. from *Before the Mayflower* by Lerone Bennett Jr., © 1961, 1969, 1988 Johnson Publishing Company. Used by permission of Johnson Publishing Company.
pp. 154–155: James Oakes from *The Radical and the Republican* by James Oakes, © 2007 by James Oakes. Used by permission of W.W. Norton & Company, Inc.
pp. 196–197: Cornel West from *Cornel West Black Prophetic Fire in Dialogue with and Edited by Christa Buschendorf*, © 2014 by Cornel West and Christa Buschendorf. Used by permission of Beacon Press Books, under the auspices of the Unitarian Universalist Association of Congregations.